Life is Short, Art is Long

SECOND EDITION

Maximizing Estate Planning Strategies for
Collectors of Art, Antiques, and Collectibles

Art & Antiques says this book "guide[s] collectors in long-term thinking about their art."

The *Financial Times* says "Mendelsohn writes clearly and gives sensible advice about some of the rules and complications of art appraisal, trusts, foundations and insurance, and how to navigate the potential minefield of dealers and auctioneers."

BusinessWeek says "Face Facts. Don't delude yourself into thinking your kids will cherish what you spent years accumulating.... Avoid a fire sale. If you don't develop a succession plan, your collection could ultimately be carved up at an auction or disappear into eBay's maw. 'A hastily arranged auction sale can lose up to 70% of the value of the collection' [quoting Mendelsohn]."

The Journal of Accountancy says "Mendelsohn weaves together serious tips and engaging anecdotes about how wooing his wife led to their shared obsession with collecting. Practical estate planning details include instruction about inventorying a collection, having it properly appraised, planning for its disposition and information about how a client can avoid losing 70% of the value of the collection."

The *NY Post* says "Michael Mendelsohn......is on a mission to educate the collecting universe – from celebrities to coffee shop owners – about the pitfalls and benefits of collecting and the implications for their heirs."

TheStreet.com's Malcom Katt says Mendelsohn "estimates that art and collectibles represent 10% to 15% of the $41 trillion in wealth that is expected to change hands over the next 50 years...."

"Mendelsohn's insights are an eye opener for collectors as we sort through the many wonderful and creative options available to us for the disposition of our art."

Richard Rubenstein, President, Rubenstein Public Relations

"I have worked as a financial advisor for over twenty years and own and operate several art galleries. My involvement with charities in both of these capacities has been considerable. With *Life is Short, Art is Long*, Mr. Mendelsohn has filled a very important information void. This book can be of tremendous benefit to collectors, their heirs, charities, financial advisors, and CPA's."

Bill Wesnousky, Senior Vice President, Morgan Stanley

"This kind of resource is very valuable to lawyers, whose knowledge of the art world is limited."

Robert H. Louis, Saul Ewing LLP

"This book is an invaluable and unique resource for every serious collector. Everything a collector and those who advise collectors have to know to intelligently own and work with valuable collections is here in one readable volume. This book is a very welcome addition to every art lover's library."

William Rattner, Lawyers for the Creative Arts

"Michael's new book 'briddges' the divide between the passionate emotions of the art collector and the dispassionate realities of wealth succession planning. As we all know, family dynamics and transfer taxation can raise havoc with even the most carefully planned of dispositions. Michael is uniquely situated to comment on this subject because he is both a collector and a tax professional. Therefore, wealth management professionals—and their clients who collect art and antiques—should have several copies of this well-written and entertaining book on their shelf."

**Scott S. Small, J.D., First Vice President,
Mellon Private Wealth Management**

Life is Short, Art is Long

SECOND EDITION

Maximizing Estate Planning Strategies for
Collectors of Art, Antiques, and Collectibles

Michael Mendelsohn

with Paige Stover Hague, Esq.

www.AcanthusPublishing.com

Published by Acanthus Publishing

Printed in the United States of America
10 9 8 7 6 5 4 3 2 1

Publisher's Cataloging-In-Publication Data
(Prepared by The Donohue Group, Inc.)

Mendelsohn, Michael.
    Life is short, art is long : maximizing estate planning strategies for collectors of art, antiques, and collectibles / Michael Mendelsohn with Paige Stover Hague ; cartoons, Dan Rosandich. -- 2nd ed.

    p. : ill. ; cm.

    Includes bibliographical references and index.
    ISBN: 978-1-933631-31-8

1. Estate planning--United States. 2. Collectors and collecting--United States. 3. Art objects-- Collectors and collecting--United States. 4. Antiques--Collectors and collecting--United States. 5. Liquidation--United States. I. Hague, Paige Stover. II. Rosandich, Dan. III. Title.

KF750 .M36 2007b
332.024/016/0973

ISBN: 978-1-933631-31-8
UPC: 9-781933-631318

To my children, Leslie and her husband Chris, Andy, and Marni, thank you for pretending to understand our passion for collecting.

To my grandchildren, who will be inheriting our "Oh My Gods."

To my wife, Gael, whose inspiration and love instilled the collecting genes in me. May I some day be the person you see in me.

Acknowledgements

As you read this book you will see I have a three-level categorization scheme for looking at your art and antiques assets. I must think in triplets. My acknowledgements seem to also come in threes:

Thank You:

Mike Black, Katy Conlon, Chris Coogan, Shari Feldman, Ned Gusick, Alice Hoffman, Anna Marie Manetta, Frank Maresca, Sarah Martin, Carolyn Holliday McKibbin, Gabe and Sandy Miller, Elizabeth Nollner, Roger Ricco, Natasha Pearl, Richard Schneidman, Scott Small, and Margot Steinberg.

Special Thanks:

Roy Adams, Liz Clement, Allan and Kendra Daniel, Alexandra Duch, Peter Hastings Falk, Fred Giampietro, Joe Jacobs, Robert Louis, Catherine Pappas, William Rattner, Charles Rosoff, Bill and Norma Roth, Richard Rubenstein, Linda Scott, Franklin Silverstone, Joseph Thompson, Bill Wesnousky, Rebecca Woan, Bill Zabel, and Tom Borek for his inspiration.

I Couldn't Have Done It Without You:

Elaine Nethercott, Antoinette Pauly, Steven Friedricks, George Kasparian, and; Bob Katz, for a lifetime of sharing; my editor and sounding-board Paige Stover Hague; and my mother, Betty.

"life is short, art is long"
Hippocrates
(and many others, but it seems to have started with him)

Table of Contents

Foreword

Michael Mendelsohn has spent most of his professional life as a lover and collector of art. He has learned the "business" of collecting art inside and out, and combining this with his background in finance he has come up with an innovative approach to planning for art and antique assets using sophisticated vehicles to monetize a collection or secure appropriate tax deductions.

In this book, *Life is Short, Art is Long – Maximizing Estate Planning Strategies for Collectors of Art, Antiques, and Collectibles,* he shares his wealth of experience in a sympathetic and meaningful way that will prove invaluable to collectors of anything, anywhere. His common sense wisdom in addressing the many challenges of collecting, including acquisitions of items which later prove to be "mistakes," setting and realizing achievable goals for collecting, working with others who collect, seeking proper and insightful professional advice from those who deal with the legal and accounting aspects of art collecting, maintaining the enjoyment of collecting at the highest level, and differentiating between auctioneers and dealers, are among the many topics handled with expertise which would be known only to a collector of his stature.

He is also candid about the upsides and the downsides of collecting. He writes poignantly of collectors' tragedies in disposing of their pieces for much less than their market value, or acquiring pieces which have no market value at all and, actually, turn out to be someone else's property. He walks the reader through the forest of dealers and auctioneers, making note of what trees grow and what trees do not, of where there is help and where there is hindrance. The rules and complications of art appraisal, valuation, insurance, trusts, foundations, private disputes among collectors and their families, and fiduciary duties of those entrusted with art on behalf of others are, if you forgive the term, artfully handled.

As an advisor to many families and individuals who collect art, my hat is off to Michael, and I offer my personal thanks to him for sharing years of invaluable insights and practical advice with all of us. Michael would say, I believe, that to love art is not necessarily to understand it or a guarantee that you will find the proper assistance to accomplish appropriate planning strategies during your lifetime. This book will undoubtedly become an indispensable reference for collectors who are looking to implement a plan for the disposition of their collection that accomplishes their intentions.

As a friend and collector much in need of his advice, I salute Michael not just as an exceptional collector but as an exceptional counselor on the subject. Michael may very well embrace the theme we have all heard, that in your early years, you control your possessions and in later years, they control you. Michael's book is a work of art in itself and frees us at any age to experience the joy of our possessions.

Roy M. Adams
New York, New York
November 13, 2006

Introduction

Collecting has become a billion-dollar passion for Americans. Having found treasures at flea markets, major galleries, or the imposing sales rooms at Christie's, we continue our search for "stuff" that we fall in love with and must buy. If we're lucky, this stuff may even go up in value. Most of us, however, spend little or no time contemplating how our treasures can build a lasting legacy to be shared with our children, sold, or gifted to maximize the value to our favorite charities and our family.

In the early nineties I discovered for myself just how little time people actually spent thinking about where their collection was ultimately going to end up. It was about this time that I realized the collection Gael and I had assembled had become a significant part of our net worth. But, even with my legal, tax, and estate planning background, I wasn't quite sure what steps I should take to plan for these art assets.

I began by doing what every financially-savvy person does before making an investment—I did some research. I went to the members of my advisory team as well as some friends and colleagues at law firms, accounting firms, insurance agencies, and banks and asked what planning strategies they were recommending to their clients who had significant collections of art, antiques, or collectibles. After being met with many blank stares and the response "we usually recommend Sotheby's or Christie's," I realized there was a gap in the system … and I wanted to build a "briddge" to span it.

I have spent the last 20 years researching; talking to experts in the fields of law, tax planning, estate planning, financial planning, and art; and working with dealers, museum curators, and auction houses in order to come up with effective planning approaches for people who collect. The strategies we have identified utilize the same legal and financial planning tools your advisory team works with every day. Traditional planning professionals are just not accustomed to using these tools to plan for art assets. In fact, I discovered to my amazement that most advisors don't even ask about their client's art assets much less plan for them. I wrote this book to change that.

I wrote this book first and foremost to give you, the collector, the information you need to ask the right questions when you are speaking with the members of your advisory team. If they are not asking, the information in this book gives you a sufficient background so that you can proactively inquire about approaches to planning for your art assets so that you can get the result you want from the collection you have put so much time and money into building. Do your children want the art or do they want the cash? Do you want to give your finest piece to the museum on whose Board you sit? Do you need a strategy to create some liquidity from your collection because you have spent all your money buying new pieces? Do you want to sell some of your pieces to free up some cash to fund a scholarship at your alma mater? This book will help you figure out several approaches to accomplish any of these objectives.

Written by a collector for other collectors, *Life is Short, Art is Long* will be your first glimpse into how you and your advisory team can build a "briddge" to address all of the planning issues affecting the ultimate disposition of your art, antique, and collectible assets. We put the second "d" in " briddge" to remind everyone that *denial* is not an effective way to plan for the disposition of your art. Optimizing the value of the pieces in your collection requires some up-front planning on your part. But the trade-off is the wonderful feeling you will have once you have put your plan in place. Knowing you have left a meaningful legacy in the form of your collection for the future generations of your family, who will be able to benefit from and appreciate the exceptional things you accumulated during your lifetime, is the final payoff for all the energy you put into assembling the collection. If you plan well, the legacy of your collection can last forever.

PART I

Addicted to Collecting

This book is divided into two major parts. The first part consists of strategies and tips for assembling a world-class collection or a not-so-world-class one that simply delights you. The rest of the world does not understand the passion, the obsession, the overpowering drive to own and possess things that are beautiful, unique, amusing, or simply quirky that makes those of us who are collectors happy. It's not about the value, usually; it's about the things. Whether it's books, pottery, stamps, earrings, wine, or cars—those of us who collect love acquiring the individual pieces that make up our collection. It's the thrill of the hunt!

In this first part of *Life is Short, Art is Long*, we address the fundamental issues that collectors should understand once their collection starts to come together.

- How to build the right kind of relationship with a dealer.
- How to work with a museum and benefit from the knowledge and contacts of curators to enhance your collecting sophistication and the value of your pieces.
- Where the auction houses fit into the picture and how they operate.
- How to inventory and catalog the collection so that it can be properly insured.
- How to care for the collection to preserve the value of your pieces.
- How to determine the value of your collection for different purposes and how appraisers work with collectors throughout the collecting process.

Falling in Love— First with Gael, Then with Art

"Tell me what you collect, tell me how you collect, and I will tell you who you are."

—Jean Willy Mestach, artist and collector

The Winter Antiques Show 2006 – An Exercise in Values Clarification

Never in my wildest dreams did I ever think I would say "no" to a million dollars cash. But my wife Gael and I have just spent the last six days doing that. We were at the Winter Antiques Show in New York, where the prize of our collection, Morris Hirshfield's painting *American Beauty* (see Photograph 1), was being offered for sale by our trusted art dealer Fred Giampietro for $1.35 million. When a collector offered to buy the painting for a slightly lower price, Fred pulled us aside to tell us it could be the first contemporary folk art piece to hit the seven-figure mark. At the eleventh hour, we decided to decline. As we stood off to one side and watched the crowds of people shuffle by and gaze lovingly at our beautiful piece, the fact that we ever even toyed with the thought of selling something we love so much seems crazy to us now. *American Beauty* has become a part of our family. And though we've received some pretty high offers for the painting, and would really love all that cash, Gael and I are almost 100% sure we're never going to sell the piece. We have a special place for it on the wall, and if we sold it now, we'd be pained by deep and unforgivable regret every time we stepped in our living room and saw that it wasn't there. We'd be haunted forever by that all too familiar collector's curse—Seller's Remorse.

How did a poor kid from Brooklyn fall so madly in love with art that he would say "no" to over a million dollars? It's a long and complicated story, but I think it's a story all collectors share. It's a story about passion; it's a story about love; it's a story about triumph; it's a story about heartache and loss; it's a story about people—the artists we collect, the loved ones we collect with, and the international family of collectors and dealers we meet every time we go to an auction or a show.

And after all is said and done, collectors pass away, but collections have the chance to leave enduring legacies. The collection will continue to tell stories for as long as it exists. These legacies not only keep great works safe to inspire future generations, they also tell the stories of the people who built the collection—those individuals with the foresight and appreciation to go to great, almost heroic, lengths to bring separate works together for a feast of the mind, eye, and soul. One of the great gifts of any collection is the story about personal growth and discovery that is universal to all collectors. And, if properly planned, that immortality can extend to you.

Life is short, art is long.

For Gael and me, collecting has been a process of continuous discovery. Our passion is for contemporary folk art, and the objects gathered in our collection represent our zeal for things that are invested with an extraordinary individuality and vitality, be it an oil painting, a sculpture made of stone, musical instruments from the 19th century, objects made of tin, or figurative dolls—including two lifeguard training figures. The works that we value are those that tell stories about what it means to be alive and those that convey an idiosyncratic expressiveness of vision to the viewer. But, on the most basic, personal level, the objects in our collection represent remarkable experiences that have profoundly changed our lives and the way we look at the world.

The Accidental Collector

Some collectors are born. Other collectors are made. My wife Gael is a perfect example of a "born collector." We like to joke that when she was born, she collected the other babies' ID bracelets in the nursery ward of the hospital. As a child, she collected stuffed animals, charms, stamps, and dolls from around the world. Now as an adult, she even collects dogs.

After buying our first Chinese Hairless Crested, Muffie Potter, Gael decided she absolutely had to have one that was spotted. She spent months looking for her polka-dotted dog and when she finally found her (Minnie) she brought her home only to find that six months later, the polka dots disappeared. While we love Minnie, Gael was determined to get what she wanted. Needless to say, Gael finally found her true polka-dotted hairless, Maggie, and one other, Sushi, —now our collection is complete at four!

Gael not only loves to own things; she loves to own the finest things. Growing up, she liked only the nicest cars—not for what they were worth, but for their style. Gael's artistic eye is astounding, as is her distinct talent for appreciating the cutting edge of the visual arts. In another time and place, she could have been Peggy Guggenheim (who also collected dogs along with her excellent modern paintings), or Helena Rubenstein, the cosmetics tycoon who amassed a fabulous and truly visionary collection of primitive African art.

I, on the other hand, had no artistic eye. Before I met Gael, I thought Picasso was a soccer player and that Monet played for the Montreal Canadiens hockey team. I fell into collecting basically because

I fell in love with Gael. I am what you would call an "accidental collector."

Well, actually, I did collect one thing: during the two years I was single after my first marriage and before I met Gael, I built one of the great Fila tennis clothing collections in the world. I had as many tennis shirts and shorts as Bjørn Borg: the green ones, the red ones, the cream ones—with matching wristbands, socks, and sweaters. If it was Fila, I had it. I was also the typical bachelor at the time. Everything I made I blew on electronics and fancy speakers. My apartment was all chrome and mirror. Clap once, my lights came on. Clap twice, my stereo. But I didn't think of myself as a collector, and I certainly never thought about collecting anything else—until I went on my second date with Gael.

We met on a blind date. She was an art teacher whose trend-setting taste extended to wearing wigs and long, flowing skirts to class years before the rest of the world caught up. She was—then and now—a remarkably beautiful and unique woman. What I quickly realized was that she was also a remarkably determined woman. It was the middle of summer in New York, easily over 100 degrees and oppressively humid; nevertheless, Gael had decided that the perfect way to spend the day was in the middle of an asphalt-paved flea market. At one table, she zeroed in on about a half dozen plastic salt and pepper shakers, carefully scrutinizing them, holding them up to the light to check for scratches and other imperfections. She studied them the way a jeweler scrutinizes diamonds for imperfections trying to decide which to purchase. She studied these shakers as if she were oblivious to the sweltering heat—in New York in the summer, that's determination. After what

---

Lessons to Live By: Know Your Options

Oh what I wouldn't give for those doll houses and miniatures now. When we needed to make room for our growing folk art collection, we didn't know that options other than selling them for pennies existed at the time. What we could have done was to gift them to a children's hospital or children's museum, creating smiles for the children and better tax benefits for ourselves.

seemed like an hour of deliberation, I was tired, hungry, hot, and cranky. So I asked the dealer how much they were. Each was $2.50. Ten dollars and some haggling later, I bought all of them for her. Gael was thrilled. So much so that, a week later, she proposed. Three months later, I was married to this thoroughly amazing woman.

Once married, collecting quickly became a way of life for me, and I spent many an hour at a flea market "in search of ..." Our new home was soon filled with all sorts of quaint objects such as doll houses and miniatures, so much so that Gael was actually featured in the doll house magazine, *Nutshell News.* We had rooms and walls to fill and so our interests were chiefly decorative, as my bachelor pad furnishings had been consigned to the scrap heap. (I'm sure there is many a collector out there today who would love to have my chrome furniture, which would now be classified as "retro," once again proving the cliché that one man's junk is another's treasure.)

The Love Affair Heats Up

There comes a moment in every serious collector's life that's something of a watershed where his or her collecting activities take on a new meaning and significance. Now, collecting isn't just a hobby. It is a passionate, hot, and heavy love affair. And like every love affair, it's expensive, and it takes a full-time commitment.

One day Gael was walking down Madison Avenue when she chanced upon the Jay Johnson Gallery. Something drew her through the door. Once inside she found something that would change the course of both our lives. It was an art form she had never seen before. It was bright and colorful and it had an immediacy and vibrancy that felt revelatory. When Gael asked Jay Johnson what this art form was, he replied simply, "folk art." Gael was immediately determined to collect it. She called me only minutes later and said, "There's something I really want us to collect, and it's called folk art." Of course, when Gael asks for something, I want to make her happy, so I said, "Yes, let's collect folk art ... what is it?" She explained what it was and told me to come down to Jay Johnson's and see it myself. I did, and I was equally impressed. Gael and I both wanted to buy the store! Sensing he had just reeled in two new big fish, Jay invited us over for dinner that night.

13

Later that evening Gael and I raced over the Tappan Zee Bridge to the artist community where Jay lived. Jay's house was truly fabulous. I was used to living with stereos and mirrors, but Jay lived with his folk art. He had fish decoys and musical instruments covering his walls, and a lot of fine examples of "decorative folk art." I was blown away. It never dawned on me that you could "live with your art." I learned you could use the pieces you collect much like an artist to tell a story about your life or about the artists you collect. Fortunately, Jay made the tragic mistake of kidding that everything in his house was for sale. Gael and I bought his living room, his bedroom, and his kitchen and, after months of payments, his "stuff" became ours, and it stayed that way for many years.

Pretty soon Gael and I were attending every folk art show, museum exhibition, flea market, and auction we could find. I remember the first serious piece we bought and how I almost choked when I saw the price tag. It was a $16,500 antique bureau. Now, this may not seem like a lot for a fine antique today, but in 1968 I paid $17,500 for the first home that I purchased in East Northport, New York. Here I was about to buy a bureau for a mere thousand less. It seemed like sheer insanity. But once I crossed this psychological (not to mention financial) barrier, there was no turning back. It's like buying your first Armani suit for $2,000. Once you buy one and get over the "sticker shock," buying the second is much easier.

Why folk art? For us, it was a combination of many factors. First and foremost, we loved looking at it, finding it endlessly stimulating. In those days, very few people were collecting this type of art, and so we became pioneers of sorts. Because so many works of outsider art and contemporary folk art are anony-mous or beyond the accepted canons of taste, collectors of this material constantly have to face up to their insecurities. But though many of the pieces in our collection were of unknown artists (and therefore lacking paperwork), the appeal of the objects themselves and the stories and secrets that they held overrode any anxieties we had. Even more appealing to us was the fact that these pieces didn't originate as a commercial venture.

These objects were by and large made to satisfy their creators' most private and passionate urges and to give meaning to their inner lives. (In other words, they weren't created for the wine-and-cheese gallery opening crowd in Chelsea, where an artist's career can be made or broken by a review in the

New York Times.) And each one of these objects was either one-of-a-kind or scarce, which felt like a tonic to our increasingly mass produced, homogenous era. For example, the Possum Trot dolls in our collection are child-size dolls carved from redwood and sugar pine that were made by Calvin and Ruby Black some time between 1953 and 1972 in order to attract customers to their rock and crystal shop in the Mojave Desert. Fewer than 60 dolls were ever made, so we were honored to have owned six of them at one point. We still own three, having gifted the rest to the Newark Museum.

Quoting from the press release that was issued announcing the gift: "Briddge Art Strategies, Ltd. announced a structured gift … to the Newark Museum on behalf of the Gael and Michael Mendelsohn Collection of Contemporary Folk Art. The total Possum Trot environment consists of 57 female wooden dolls carved … by Cal Black and dressed by Ruby Black. A majority of the dolls are now housed in museums throughout the country. The environment represents one of the most important in the outsider art tradition."

The bottom line for our passion is this: folk art challenges us. It broadens our horizons and asks us to think beyond the limits of the conventional. Knowing that Gael was keen to learn more about folk art, Jay Johnson steered her to Dr. Robert Bishop, Director of the Folk Art Museum and a highly-regarded professor at NYU. Gael returned to school and got her master's degree in Folk Art. Her passion was all-consuming and, as her expertise grew, she even curated a well-received show at the South Street Seaport Museum titled "The Outsider and the Sea."

And that is one of the powers collecting holds over you: you want to learn everything there is to know about it. Not only because you love it, but because you'll never know when a hidden treasure will come to auction unannounced, and your research will give you the upper hand. Friends of mine always say, "Serious collectors must have great art libraries."

"You never pay too much for a great piece, you just buy it too soon!"
–Gael Mendelsohn

Falling In and Out of Love with Art (and Dealers)

As you become more immersed in collecting, you will want to create your own rating system to indicate the desirability of a piece you are contemplating. Gael and I have devised a three-tiered rating system—the "Ohs," "Oh Mys," and the "Oh My Gods." Artwork that caught our eye fell into one of three categories. The "Ohs" are nice pieces that we look at but probably do not buy. The "Oh Mys" are intriguing pieces that we give very serious thought to buying, and often do (and these are the core of the collection). And the "Oh My Gods" are the pieces that we couldn't spend another moment on earth without and are willing to travel through any and all the circles of Hell in order to ensure that these pieces are ours and ours alone.

Whether spotted at a gallery or at auction, you will occasionally come across an item that you believe is a once-in-a-lifetime acquisition opportunity. You are willing to pay almost any price for this "Oh My God" piece. You are not thinking about the financial as-

pects of the transaction at the time of the purchase—
you have fallen in LOVE. These are the pieces that
have a special place in the heart and in the home of
the collector. These pieces become an extension of
the collector's personal identity.

Lessons to Live By:
Money Matters -
Or Does It?

The collector is, in a way, like an artist assembling pieces that tell the story about his life, who
he is, and how he views the world. If you collect with someone you love, as I do with my wife
Gael, a collection tells the story of your love affair. Do financial considerations come into play?
Certainly, but really only when it comes to buying, not selling. Most collectors, unless they're
super rich, have to consider how they're going
to pay for their new piece—how they're going to
finance it. Will they have to sell a less important
item to have the cash to buy the new one? But
even in this situation the money is secondary.
Gael and I have set the all-time record for maximum price paid for pieces bought at auction. We
wanted them so badly—had to have them—that
we didn't care how we were going to afford them or how much it was going to
put us in debt. But as Gael always
says, "You never pay too much
for a great piece, you only
buy it too soon!"

Knowing When to Let a Piece Go ... to Make Room for Better Pieces

The interesting thing about our collection is that there are many pieces that were "Oh My Gods" when we purchased them that aren't even in our collection anymore. At the time they were right for us. During the lifespan of a collection, it's entirely possible (and even likely) that a collector's tastes will change and the emotional connection he or she has with a piece will lessen in intensity and the piece may become an "Oh." That's because collecting has stages, kind of like falling in and out of love. For example, we purchased an important Howard Finster painting, *The Story Map*, which hung for years in our dining room. As our tastes gravitated towards three-dimensional objects, the painting somehow stopped being an "Oh My God" for us. So we sold it, and now it is someone else's "Oh My God."

As your collection grows, so does your need to plan accordingly for the pieces in the collection. There are several reasons for doing this:

The first reason is practical. Unless you can afford to buy a bigger house or rent a loft just for your collection, it's impractical to think that you can just keep purchasing without ever having to weed the collection. A discriminating eye will allow you the time to leave that place over the mantel empty to find something you truly love, so that when you do buy it, you have a place for it. Collectors will do almost anything to make more room for their beloved objects. Walls are knocked down, windows removed, and fireplaces filled in. One couple, who already owned a beautiful 15,000 square foot home with two galleries that encompassed more than half of the house, decided to purchase a second house bordering on their property for their art. Rumor has it that they are now scouting a third house. On the other end of the spectrum, there are people like the 40-something collector in Los Angeles who has managed to accumulate over 700 cutting-edge works by contemporary artists by stacking them strategically in his one-bedroom apartment!

Some collectors, "the packrats," have found a way around this problem by putting most of their collection in storage. Often they never even open up the boxes or the crates (just knowing they own the object is enough for them). But since Gael and I prefer to live with our art, this was never a thought for us. We're not interested in storing it—when we lend objects for a show, we even go so far as to hang the photograph in the place of our missing piece, so we can still enjoy it. We've literally rearranged everything in our house to accommodate our collection. In fact, our house is our collection, or as we like to call it, a "houseum." We've closed windows, filled in sliding doors, blown out walls, and expanded rooms to showcase our prized objects. In fact, at one point when we were trying to find a place to put a particularly large Thornton Dial painting, I asked Gael if we really needed to have a front door! What was the big deal about just entering through the garage? Well, reason (and the front door) won out, and we managed to find another place for the Dial. Overall, finding the perfect spot can be a daunting process of trial and error, requiring patience and persistence. Not to mention hiring professional picture hangers, whom Gael always drives crazy.

19

The second reason why plans are so essential is more personal, based on recognition and good old-fashioned ego. Art is a reflection of who the collector is and what he stands for. In the small world of art, people judge a collector, good or bad, by the type of pieces he collects. When a collector passes away, he will still be judged, because his name, if his collection remains intact, will forever be attached to what he owned.

A few years ago, Gael and I met a Top 100 collector couple from the South at the Outsider Art Fair in New York. We introduced ourselves, and within seconds he was bragging about his great collection. He asked if we were going to the Newark Museum to see the exhibition of folk art, *A World of Their Own: 20th Century American Folk Art.* We said, "We've just seen it. It was great, you'll enjoy it."

At the time, we had thirteen of our pieces in the exhibition, but just as Gael was about to mention this, I nudged her to be quiet, and simply told them we'd see them Sunday when they got back. That Sunday we were sitting having a cup of coffee when the bus from the museum came back. The collector and his wife saw us and ran over as fast as they could, harried, excited, and out of breath: "We didn't know you collected. Your pieces are magnificent! Why didn't you tell us?" This is the true payoff for you the collector: the recognition in the other's person eye when he or she knows you have the best.

Third, the more time you spend in the art world as a discriminating buyer—the more time you spend talking with knowledgeable dealers and making friends with other knowledgeable collectors—the more personally invested you are in not only your collection, but also in the entire form. You start to build a rapport with the museum community. You spend time researching and reading about what you collect. All of this develops your taste and your eye. I compare it to wine: when you're 18, any kind of wine tastes good, just as long as it gets you drunk. But as you get older and sophisticated, as your pallet matures, you start to notice the subtle differences between the box wine on the shelf and a bottle of Lafitte-Rothschild.

And, finally, having a discriminating eye serves a tactical purpose. The more you collect, and the more money you have tied up in "Oh" or "Oh My" pieces, the less cash you have to buy the rare "Oh My God" when it hits the market. That is unless you're like the New York Yankees and have an unlimited payroll. But the majority of collectors, including Gael and myself, have to be very crafty when it comes to financing collections. You have to make sure you're buying a piece that's really worth the money, and you have to be careful not to let your emotions take control and force you into bidding for something you really can't afford to buy—but more about this in Chapter 6.

As your tastes change, you must be ready to allow your collection to change with you. And if that means replacing a piece that's no longer an "Oh My God" with a current "Oh My God," then careful planning will help you achieve your goal. Rather than feeling like you are getting rid of an important and meaningful part of your collection, you can choose to honor the older piece by creating a transfer plan that will allow you to develop the capital you need to really grow your collection.

Just as you fall out of love with certain pieces or types of art, you can outgrow your dealers as well.

Gradually, over time, you may begin to notice that the dealer you have been buying through has been bringing you fewer "Oh My Gods" and is offering you "Oh Mys" and mostly just "Ohs." This happened to us once. It wasn't really the dealer's fault; it was simply that our tastes had changed. This dealer sold decorative folk art pieces—these were pieces that looked great in your living room, but really had no long-term value. This approach was no longer good enough for Gael and me. A fire was raging in both of us to own the best, which also meant we would have to be smarter financially in terms of how we bought, sold, and gifted our pieces. Fortunately, we were about to meet the people who could show us how to do both.

Becoming a Top 100 Collector

While many art dealers have, fairly or unfairly, poor reputations, dealers have always been important taste makers—from the legendary Joseph Duveen, who supplied Rembrandts and Raphaels to the likes of John D. Rockefeller and William Randolph Hearst, to Leo Castelli, who first brought Abstract Expressionism and the works of artists such as Johns, Stella, and Rauschenberg to the public consciousness in the 1950s.

We first met dealers Roger Ricco and Frank Maresca at an antique show when a red violin case with a profile of its maker drew us to their booth as if by magnetic force. Gael told them, "We'll let you know tomorrow." Without Gael knowing, I bought the piece before the end of the show. The next day when Gael called to purchase the piece, Roger and Frank told her, under my instructions, that they had sold it the previous day. Gael, distraught and in tears, rushed up the stairs to our bedroom to tell me the horrible news. Realizing how upset my poor wife was, I realized that my little joke needed to come to an immediate end. Imagine her shock and elation when I opened up the closet door to present her with the coveted violin case! To this day, that piece still brings a smile to our faces. Over the years, Roger and Frank have helped push the envelope of our taste and imagination, opening doors and challenging our aesthetics with their own sophisticated ways of looking at objects. Nowadays when we acquire a piece, we still measure it by their stamp of approval.

But of all the dealers we have known and worked with over the years, it was really meeting Fred Giampietro that proved most fortuitous for Gael and me as evolving collectors. It was Fred who became instrumental in our acquisition of several major works (including that Hirshfield!). And it was Fred who taught us the most basic lesson that any collector must learn: quality is more important than quantity.

We first crossed paths with Fred at the Philadelphia Antique Show. At the time, we were already thinking of having someone oversee our collection. It seemed logical at that point for us to enlist an expert to help us make the most intelligent purchases and, equally important, to show us how to strengthen our overall collection by reallocating our art portfolio.

It was also getting to the point that if we were to make a mistake in acquiring a piece, it would be a costly mistake indeed. There were factors such as provenance, authenticity, and period that we increasingly needed to take into account when purchasing a piece. Fred's attitude was if a piece had any sign of weakness—for example, if one portion might be

Lessons to Live By: Keep the Best and Sell the Rest

One of the worst-kept secrets of building a great collection, like the one Gael and I are aiming for, is to follow this simple rule: keep the best and sell—or gift—the rest. I get asked "Why?" all the time. As collectors, it's easy for us to lose sight of the fact that collecting is about more than just amassing stuff. It's about gathering the crème de la crème of whatever it is that we're collecting. And, by collecting nothing but the best and selling the rest, you'll create a great collection while building a nice nest egg that will give you the funds to buy those really great pieces when they (infrequently) come up for sale.

out of sync with the rest—that was reason alone to pass. Integrity and spontaneity were what he considered the best indicators of a truly great piece. But perhaps the best way to describe Fred's influence is to say that he gave us a strong sense of the responsibilities that come with serious collecting, of the myriad obligations a collector has—to the art, the artists, to our community, and the public at large—which we treat with the utmost seriousness.

When we first began to work with Fred as a dealer and advisor, he came to our home to see our collection. It was a little unnerving, like parading around naked for all your friends and neighbors to see. But after examining the entirety of our collection, he made some undeniably salient points. In fact, Fred's insights are ones that are applicable to any collector, no matter what they collect.

First of all, Fred pointed out that we had collected too many pieces by the same artist. His philosophy was that if you are going to own five paintings by the same artist, they should be the best five she or he created. If you can't have these, then you simply pass on owning the artist. His second piece of advice was even more to the point; up until then, we had never started out with any grand ambitions for our collection, other than to buy art that we loved. In other words, we were the classic collectors who didn't realize how serious we actually were about our collecting. Fred suggested that we aim higher. He told us that with his help, "we could build one of the world's greatest folk art collections." I remember his words echoing in my head all night.

Fred's proposition of creating such an important collection really hit home with me. It could be our own little slice of immortality, and a way to truly honor the aesthetic and objects we had decided to share our lives with. Fred told us that it would hurt. I remember Gael saying, "I don't want it to hurt." It meant giving up things that we loved—difficult for any collector under any circumstances. We said some bittersweet good-byes, and more or less renounced some of the purely decorative folk art that we had acquired over the years.

I like to call these works our "blue paintings"—paintings that we bought to match the blue couch in our living room, which also matched up perfectly with the blue lamp we also were decorating with. Every collector has these blue paintings in their collection, usually relegated to some little-used room in the house, if not gathering dust in the attic (or mold in the basement). But, since our interests in collecting were never geared towards having an encyclopedic collection, we took the leap. We developed a strategy to gift parts of the collection and sell part at Sotheby's. The sale was, well, less than successful—in fact, to call it woeful would be kind—because many insiders in our world of art knew we were selling the bottom parts of our collection, which depressed our sales. But the lessons learned were important and I'm keen for other collectors to learn from these mistakes. I offer some effective strategies that I subsequently developed for successfully dealing with

25

Lessons to Live By: Money Matters

One of the great methods used by collectors to have the cash to buy those "Oh My God" pieces is to create an Art Fund; the trick to this is selling or gifting the "Oh" and the "Oh My" pieces to bring in the capital. Read more about this in Part II of the book.

auction houses in Chapter 6.

Thus, our collection began its journey away from traditional folk art and closer to contemporary folk art. We started to acquire more three-dimensional objects, which had been a weakness of the previous assembling of our collection. Fred showed us art ahead of other people, and also tipped us off when he had something at a show that he thought would be good for us. Within six or seven years, Fred had vaulted us from hobby collectors to being named one of the "Top 100 Collectors in America" by *Art & Antiques* magazine. As word got out, we were profiled on the A&E Networks series "The Incurable Collector," and parts of our collection were prominently featured in national publications such as the *New York Times*, *New York Magazine*, and *Metropolitan Home*, among others. In January of 2000, our collection was the subject of an exhibit at the Ricco Maresca Gallery in New York, and we are so glad we followed their guidance to create a beautiful book, *The Intuitive Eye*, which was published in conjunction with their show. It was truly thrilling for us.

Our collection now spans all different media—paintings, sculptures, photographs, drawings, furniture, etc. If you were to come to our house, which, fittingly, in keeping with our interest in history and preservation, is located on the oldest private golf course in America, you'd see it now holds a variety of different collections that Gael and I have assembled over the years: musical instruments from the turn of the century (banjos, concertinas, violins, saxophones, and tambourines), anniversary tin, PEZ® containers, and lunchboxes. Then there are Gael's collections of Bakelite and costume jewelry, cookie jars, beaded fruit, and vintage handbags from the 1920s to 1940s, including animal-shaped wicker pocketbooks. Gael even devoted an entire room of our home to kitsch, an installation that celebrates (and dignifies) all sorts of bizarrely wonderful stuff—everything from velvet Elvises to lamps with dangling dinosaurs and glittery plastic flowers (see Photograph 2). With so many wonderful objects in our collection, people might wonder what still drives us. The answer is simple: we're looking for the one thing we can't spend another moment on earth without, even though we don't know what exactly it may be or where it could come from.

So now you know my story, a story that is still evolving as our collection grows and shifts. It's my sincere wish that through this book I can help other collectors—aspiring collectors, serious collectors, acquirers of "stuff," and those who don't even realize how serious their collection has become—think about and plan their collections in such a way that all their hard work and care won't end up as part of some dreary estate settlement or an obituary they won't be around to read. I encourage collectors to have fun and enjoy their collections while they are around, and I hope that you will be inspired to use some of your art to help further or develop your own philanthropic interests while addressing some of your personal financial concerns.

Before we get into all of that, however, I must say that for all of the fabulous art I have seen over the years, when people ask me what my greatest "Oh My God" moment was, I have a quick answer for them. It was meeting Gael.

2

When One is Not Enough– Understanding the Passion of Collecting

"A collector, first of all, has to be a collector with a capital 'C.' The collector with a capital 'C' is a very rare and special species. They're people who have a quasi-religious enthusiasm for art. They look at art, and think about art, and devote all their waking lives to the pursuit of art."

–Leo Castelli, art dealer

What Makes a Collector?

I never thought I'd have anything in common with William Randolph Hearst, Imelda Marcos, or the Queen of England. It's not that I have a gigantic estate overlooking the ocean on the California coast, a thousand pairs of shoes lined up as far as the eye can see, or that I'm opening a session of Parliament anytime soon. I'm just a dad who loves golf and my wife (not in that order), and lives in a nice part of Westchester County, New York. But there's something that binds me to those people and overrides time and place and circumstances. Imelda has her shoes, Hearst his Old Masters paintings, and the Queen, her jewels, horses, and stamps. Underneath it all, we're a part of the same type of species: you see, we're all collectors, or as I like to say, accumulators of "stuff."

Collectors and their stuff come in a variety of flavors. Over the centuries, collectors have amassed collections that most anyone wishes he or she could have, such as Impressionist masterworks, vintage cars, wines—but also stuff that you've never heard of or would ever want in your home. Some collectors' stuff is so extraordinarily valuable and important that museums all over the world would love to add it to their collection. Others' collections are purely sentimental in their value. But for most serious collectors, there is a genuine thrill possessing something that no one else has. And, as different as the collections, the reasons why we collect are varied. Some of us, like Gael and I, collect for the sheer love of art; for others it is about status, money, and power. These are not the wrong reasons to collect, just different reasons. In fact, America's treasure trove of priceless artworks is inextricably tied to tycoons such as

J.P. Morgan, the Mellon family, and J. Paul Getty, who amassed collections to compete with their fellow titans of industry.

But despite the differences in taste, interests, and motivations, a true collector knows that collecting is a quasi-religion: a way of life that infuses the essence of one's being. For the collector, art and its appreciation becomes a way of life. It is part concept, part process, and part belief; it is alternately emotional and intellectual, and sometimes both at once. Passionate collectors, like ourselves, derive stimulation not only from their desired objects, but also from their spirited, sometimes quixotic quests for their own personal Holy Grails—and there are all too many fellow collectors who secretly fear the thought of completing their collection, so wedded are we to the thrill of pursuit. True collectors relish the challenge of the hunt, increasing and refining their area of knowledge, and owning beautiful objects that retain and even increase in value.

By their very nature, collectors have to be fixated with multiples—because for the real accumulators of "stuff," one is simply not enough. Collecting is filled with incalculable joys, not to mention the occasional heartbreak when a coveted piece slips away. Building a collection requires diligence, time, enthusiasm, astuteness, fortunate timing, and sometimes just sheer dumb luck. Of course, having deep pockets never hurts either. Over the course of a collection's lifetime, it assumes its own character, finds its own shape, and develops a pulse of its own to the point where the collector is no longer the master of his or her collection but merely a curator or a temporary custodian of a small slice of human history.

Our Passion for Folk Art

Our enjoyment of contemporary folk art stems from the fact that each work of art possesses its own distinctive and genuinely wonderful story that tells not only about the object but about the artist as well. These narratives offer not only a window into the psyche of its creator but into the culture of its times. It was the work of the artist William Edmonson that drove this home for us. Edmonson was one of the most important stone carvers in American history. The son of freed slaves, Edmonson carved memorials and tombstones out of limestone. In 1937, Edmonson's work was the subject of the first individual show to be given to a black artist at the Museum of Modern Art. Apart from Edmonson's historical importance, the dignity of his carvings and their liveliness and animation moved us, particularly one of his now better-known pieces, the *Mermaid* (see Photograph 3), carved circa 1935 to 1940. When we first encountered it, Gael and I both thought it was one of the most beautiful things we had ever seen! Unfortunately, so did the Philadelphia Museum of Art, who was in the process of buying the piece. Then—call it fate, sheer dumb luck, or fortuitous timing—the museum decided not to complete its purchase, and we were lucky enough to be able to add it to our collection. This piece, more than any other, forced us to grow up as collectors in a hurry. Not only did it take us a full year to pay for it, but we also took on the responsibility of telling the story about a breathtaking work of art that is nothing less than part of this country's heritage.

But perhaps no story is quite as intriguing or astonishing as that of Henry Darger. In 1911, at the age of 19, Darger began to write and illustrate a saga that eventually spanned 15,000 pages! These illustrated volumes, discovered by his landlord when he was cleaning out Darger's room after his death, are entitled: *The Story of the Vivian Girls in what is known as the Realms of the Unreal, of the Glandeco-Angelinian War Storm, caused by the Child Slave Rebellion.* Today a portion of this work hangs in our bedroom. When we visited the room in Chicago where he lived and worked, maintained just as it was when he was alive, we had the sense he had just stepped out and would be back any moment. Darger is the subject of a highly-acclaimed 2003 documentary by Oscar-winning director Jessica Yu, and we found it is gratifying to see Darger's work move into the public eye, beyond connoisseurs of "outsider" art.

Sometimes the enthusiasm we have about a particular piece comes from having met the artist in person, such as Thornton Dial. Dial's paintings are large, vivid, provocative, fable-like works (see Photograph 10). When Dial came to New York for the first major exhibition of his work, we threw a cocktail party for him at our home in Westchester so that he could see how his work looked in a modern setting.

Some time later, Gael and I were staying in high style at a Ritz–Carlton in Georgia, enjoying the amenities at this beautiful, plush hotel. But Dial's home in Alabama was just a three-hour drive away, so Gael convinced me that since Dial had visited us, we should drive there, just for a brief visit that afternoon. Somehow we wound up staying overnight at Dial's small rural house with about thirteen of his family members! And for breakfast, Mrs. Dial, a marvelous cook, made southern fried food that we'd never had before. We have wonderful memories of this visit.

Collecting for Passion, Not Profit

I recently sat on a round-table sponsored by *Avenue Magazine* discussing "art as an investment." I shared the podium with some notable collectors, appraisers, and art experts, including Michael Moses, who was developing a very interesting model to track the internal rate of return of art as an investment. I usually like to sit at the end of the table in a panel discussion so I can listen to what everyone else has to say before adding my two cents. Initially, the panel was talking about what a great investment art is and how the internal rate of return on art is the same as buying stock, and how they bought this piece and now it's worth this much. Then it was my turn to speak. "When you go to a dealer's booth and see a piece, how many of you buy it because of how much you think it will be worth thirty to forty years from now?" No one raised a hand. "That's because art is a love affair, not an investment. I've yet to find a collector who looks at a piece of art at a show or auction and figures out in his mind he can make 10%

"Beautiful . . . but will I get a 10% return annually, if I buy it?"

a year on that painting. It doesn't happen." By the time I stopped speaking, everyone on the panel and in the audience was nodding his or her head in agreement.

Art is not an investment; it is a love affair. I think most collectors feel this way. If art is any kind of investment, it's an investment in passion—the passion of collecting the pieces, the passion of showing them off, and the greatest passion, knowing you own them. Though some collectors may like to say in public that it's a financial investment, I believe they don't really mean it. They're justifying their irrational passion for collecting things many people don't want or understand. The truth is we collect because we love it and because the collection is an extension of who we are, both now and into the future.

35

Art is an investment in passion—the passion of collecting the pieces, the passion of showing them off, and the greatest passion, knowing you own them.

In fact, I believe collectors who purchase art for financial reasons alone and not for passion are setting themselves up for disaster. The market is an unstable place. Artists come and go every year and many artists who were set to become the next Picasso vaporize and fall off the map. In fact, I compare people who buy art for investments to those speculators who found themselves trapped in the NASDAQ® in the late 1990s—the artist du jour whom everybody swears is the best investment ever is no less a potential market bubble than a dot-com. I highly encourage you to buy for passion. For Gael and me, it makes more sense to buy pieces with the intention of owning and collecting the best things that stir your passions. I bet you could almost guarantee a higher return on that strategy every time, rather than just buying what was hot at the moment, because what takes your breath away will probably do the same for a lot of other people. And, once you become an investor, you lose all that passion and tend to make mistakes.

Several years ago there was a London transfer pension that tried to become the first art-based mutual fund. Their final return on investment was 8%, but that return came from only a few selected items. Everything else was a failure. The way I see it, the art world is full of dealers, appraisers, and collectors who are a lot smarter than I am when it comes to picking the next big trend in the art world. I find it's better to go with passion. I may not make a million dollars, but at least it's something that looks good in our living room and makes us happy.

Diversifying your asset portfolio by including art, antiques, and other valuable "stuff" can be a gamble that may save you from some pretty bad investments. In 1987, I was heavily invested in the stock market, which was flying high at the time. One day that summer Gael got a call from a dealer telling her about a quilt that was going to be sold at the Winter Antiques Show in New York. It was created by a woman named Cecil White and was the most-documented 20th century folk art quilt at that time. The dealer told Gael that she would give her the opportunity to buy it first if she was the first person at her booth when the show opened.

I had never seen Gael so passionate about a single piece of art. Prior to the opening, Gael convinced me to shift the money we had in the market to our art fund. I thought she was crazy because the market was exploding upwards. She was so excited that she changed my mind. "You know, I'm a little nervous about how much money I have in the market anyway," I said to her. "Maybe I can pull some out." I called my broker and told him to sell some of my holdings and send me a check. Gael made me swear many times not to touch the money until it was time to buy the quilt.

Everybody knows what happened that autumn: Black Monday. On October 19, 1987, the market dropped 508 points after margin calls. What I had left in the market got wiped out—but I had very little left. Setting my money into the art fund for that quilt became the best investment gamble I ever made. But I never would have made the call if it wasn't for Gael's passion.

And what happened with the quilt? On the day of the show, Gael arrived six hours early at the 69th Street Armory and was told she couldn't stay there that long before the show opened. More than a dozen of the show's personnel guaranteed that she could have the first position in line when she came back at 5 p.m., an hour before the show opened. When she arrived, there were over 100 people in line. I can't tell you the war that broke out when all the other collectors watched Gael go to the front of the line. She did indeed get the first place in line. When the show opened, she made like Marion Jones and sprinted to the dealer's booth, where she quickly evaluated the piece and uttered the magic words: "I'll take it!"

When Passions Go Bad

As is true with any love affair, it's possible to be blinded by passion and love, so much so that you overlook things that to any rational mind would seem obvious. That's what happened to a friend several years ago.

Gael and I met this friend through one of my other passions, collecting eyeglasses. I own over 110 pairs in myriad shapes and styles and colors that match every outfit I own. When I wear a blue shirt, I wear blue glasses. I even got into pink before pink became fashionable. When I play golf, which is six days a week in good weather, my glasses match my golf shorts. My friends call me "Elton."

One day Gael was at the Triple Pier Show in New York when she saw a heavy-set gentleman wearing a great pair of glasses. She bee-lined straight towards him. "My husband would love those glasses, where did you get them?" The man told her where he got them, and noticed that Gael was wearing some costume bracelets. "Oh, you collect bracelets too?"

It turned out the man was the "king" of collectors of Bakelite and costume jewelry, among other things. This man was so well-known that when he walked into a show, dealers pushed everyone out of their booths to get to him. He and Gael hit it off that day, and he really became her mentor, helping her put together a small but fabulous collection of Bakelite and costume jewelry—bags, necklaces, and pins. One day, this friend invited Gael and me over to his apartment to see his collection, the finest of its kind.

Though I never got to see the collection personally (I had to run downstairs to stop my car from being towed) Gael told me it was amazing. "You wouldn't believe it! He has Judith Lieber bags still in the sales boxes, and every Barbie™ ever made, including the first one, still in its box!"

At the time, our friend lived in a really bad section of town—a real den of druggies and thieves. For the life of me, I couldn't understand why someone who could afford to own some of the finest, most expensive pieces in the area in which he collected couldn't afford to live somewhere a little bit nicer, or at least safer! When I asked our friend why he didn't move somewhere else, he just brushed me off, "Well, I've always lived here. I like it."

A few months later, Gael and I returned from an art expedition (some people call it a vacation) to more than a dozen voicemails on our machine. "Did you hear about so and so (our friend)?" At first, I thought he died—he weighed at least 350 pounds at the time. But he hadn't died. Worse, he had been indicted. He worked in the accounting department of a major law firm and, as it turned out, he would make up employees and cash their checks—just to feed his passion for collecting.

Knowing the trouble he was in, he called me with one concern at the forefront of his mind. "Michael," he said, "most likely I'm going to jail and they're going to take all the stuff out of my apartment. Can you call the law firm and manage the sale so that the pieces are sold as collections? I'd like to see these things stay together." Here was this man facing three to nine years in prison, but his mind was on his Barbie™ dolls and Judith Lieber bags, and keeping them

39

together! His collection ended up selling at auction, where many of the buyers got fabulous bargains.

This is just one extreme example of a collector who went a little too overboard with his passion. But we've all done crazy things to get a piece—yes, even me. Several years ago, as I was preparing to leave for a very important business meeting in Florida, I received a call from our dealer, Fred Giampietro, about an auction in Manchester, New Hampshire that weekend. He said there was a five-foot Statute of Liberty lamp sculpture estimated to sell between $2,000 and $3,000. But, if he had it in his gallery, he'd offer it at the next Winter Antiques Show for $100,000. "It's out of place at this New Hampshire auction," he said, "and unless another collector or dealer knows about it, it's yours."

I knew the auction he was talking about: a year ago, at that same auction, Gael and I bought a piece for only $1,000 that was worth over $20,000! I immediately cancelled my business meeting, regardless of the consequences, and called Gael right away. We threw together some clothes, packed up Muffie Potter, and rushed up to New Hampshire just in time for the auction. The hotel has posted a "no vacancy" sign, but miraculously, someone cancelled and a room opened up. It seemed the stars were aligned and everything was going our way.

The next day we went down to the show around 9 a.m. to preview the pieces on display. The Statue of Liberty lamp was there. We fell in love immediately, but no one else even seemed to notice it. In fact, people were resting their drinks on it, talking like it didn't exist! This was a good sign, but Gael and I kept our emotions at bay. Fred had warned us not to show that we were interested. In fact, he hired a couple to do the bidding for us just so our enthusiasm wouldn't be seen by other collectors—talk about having a good dealer that knows you.

When the piece came up for bidding around 3:30 that afternoon, the auctioneer laughed. "I don't know what this is … will anyone give me a $100?" Immediately, the phone rings (those damn phones) and somebody on the other end bid the $100. The couple bidding for us bid $200. We had agreed not to bid beyond $35,000 for the piece, but honestly I never thought it would even come close to that amount. However, as the bidding went on, our couple bid as high as $50,000, but the phone bid was $55,000. We lost the piece.

On the four-and-a-half-hour drive back to New York, with an empty trunk, we felt deflated. Here we had cancelled all our plans—at a great potential cost— and now we were driving home without what we had hoped would be our newest acquisition. In January of the following year, at the Winter Antique Show, there was the piece, looking great, with a price tag in excess of $100,000. When the dealer saw our interest in the piece, he started giving me the dealer "speak." I turned to him and said, "Who do you think was the under-bidder in New Hampshire?" Win some, lose some. It was sold to another collector.

One Collector's View:
William D. Roth, Esq.

A fellow Top 100 Collector and good friend, Bill Roth is probably best known for the collection he and his wife have assembled of contemporary African art, with a focus on textiles and head-dresses. He's also one of the more passionate collectors that I know. With that in mind, I've asked him to write a few words about collecting, some of his personal experiences, and some of his theories on timing and education. So, without further ado:

When Michael asked me to contribute some of my experiences as a collector to this book, I immediately called him to tell him that Norma, my wife, should be the one to write the section—not me. Michael replied with a chuckle that everyone who knew either one of us knew that it was through our wives that we had been introduced to the world of collecting and that although we both considered ourselves collectors now, it was our wives (Gael and Norma) who were the real stars. With this caveat, I shall proceed.

Initially, let me state my strong feeling about the important role art collectors play in the art world. Individual collectors have been responsible, and still are, for the finest collections in American institutions. There would be neither the great nor the small museums in this country without the patronage and philanthropy of collectors. As we travel, Norma and I always visit any museum that is available to us. Since our collecting interests are diverse, all museums have always been fair game.

Being a lawyer, looking at the objects was never enough. My training led to an obsession with reading the fine print on many of those tiny labels that most visitors ignore. Over time, I discovered that every institution was fortunate in patronage, sometimes by large donors, sometimes by small ones. The same names seemed to reappear often. The pattern was obvious. Museums are the beneficiaries of collectors who have, through their patronage, helped to build significant collections. In major museums, the collectors' names are well-known. Names like Rockefeller, Morgan, Frick, Hirshhorn, Guggenheim, and Mellon lead the long line of superstars. However, equally significant for the smaller institutions are all those other donors whose names are not as famous, but whose gifts make it possible for the public to visit the museums and enjoy the treasures these people collected over their lifetimes.

One of my favorite theories is the "Fifteen-Minute Theory" of collecting. This theory has to do with marketing and the fact that so much art today is hyped by dealers, auction houses, and critics. Once something becomes "fashionable" and "popular," everyone wants it. Prices will skyrocket, and it will no longer be a matter of the intrinsic value of the object but rather the value in a "fashionable" marketplace. At that point, prices will soar and the premier objects of great quality will become so expensive that real collectors (unless extremely wealthy) will be driven from the field. Therefore, Norma and I like to collect in the "fifteen minutes" prior to the discovery by the marketplace of the next great artist, period, or genre. Or, to put it in the words of John Walker, the former director of the National Gallery in Washington, it is to "collect the right thing at the wrong time."

In all situations, there are limiting circumstances—for collectors, it often has to do with funds. Choices always have to be made, and I frequently recall the day when we made the wrong one. In the early days of our collecting, Norma and I set out to visit Sonnabend's Gallery in the famous 420 Building on West Broadway in the days when Soho was a place taxi drivers had a difficult time locating. On this cold morning, we were admiring a painting by a young artist that Michael Sonnabend represented. While we were waffling back and forth, Michael said he had something special to show us. He brought from the stacks a magnificent Jasper Johns silver encaustic target painting. Norma nearly fell over. The light reflected off the painting in a way that I'd never seen before and that I'll never forget. All the texture came to life. It was amazing.

Michael Sonnabend said simply, "It's $160,000 firm." We just stared. Norma glanced at me and saw the look in my eyes (it said, "Never in this lifetime!"). She gave Michael a smirk and then winked, "I don't think it matches the sofa." Michael roared with laughter. Later, at our hotel room, when we ran all the numbers, the conclusion was that after cashing everything, including the pension plan and selling her Porsche, we could only raise half the sum we needed. We returned to Sonnabend Gallery the following day and bought the painting by the young artist and said good-bye to the Johns. Years later when one of Jasper Johns' paintings sold at auction for $17,000,000 we agreed that the target painting we passed on was far better. Oh, I still feel the pain of passing on such a masterpiece! And the other painting we did buy? I can't even tell you where it is—somewhere in storage.

Perhaps one of the greatest benefits of collecting art is the opportunity one has to meet such interesting people. Dealers, artists, curators, scholars, writers, other collectors—there is a world of wonderful and truly amazing people out there that I would not have met had I not become involved in collecting. A day does not pass without some contact with a friend who has involvement in the arts and whose friendship I would not have, had my life not become involved in this crazy world of collecting.

Early on, in the late 1970s, Norma and I would go to New York and look up artists' names in the phone book and just telephone them directly. We generally had seen these artists' works only through a picture in a catalog or magazine, and we did not know any other way of contacting them. Occasionally, we would meet these new artists in a gallery, if they had representation, but if not, then they would invite us to their studio. Those were exhilarating experiences! To this day, some of the artists that we met through effrontery remain among our closest friends. Their works are also some of the jewels of our art collection. That is how we first met Miriam Scha-piro, Joyce Kozloff, and Robert Zakanitch, all of them founders of the P&D (Pattern and Decoration) Movement, which we collected in depth. It is particularly gratifying for me how, almost thirty years later, we are now getting calls from curators who are anxious to borrow works from this part of our collection as they discover this pivotal movement of 20th century art and realize the importance of these artists whose works we collected so long ago.

Our collecting interests are what people would refer to now as "eclectic." We had our first real significant direction as contemporary art collectors under the inspiration of the P&D Movement in the 1970s. Our collection found other avenues of exploration as the actual roots and sources of the art that influenced and inspired the artists we were collecting became evident to us. It appeared that the artists we were collecting were a new breed who were exploring sources outside the Western mainstream and were basing their art on fresh non-Western sources. Norma and I were immediately fascinated by their inspirations and intriguing sources and began studying, reading, visiting museums, and expanding our own horizons in order to better grasp the complexity of this new movement.

It was an amazing new world: from Chinese textiles, to Japanese kimonos, to Moroccan tiles, to Byzantine mosaics, to manuscript illuminations, to Indian miniatures, to American quilts, to Celtic scroll work, and pre-Columbian weaving. It was exciting and enticing beyond words! Suddenly we wanted to collect in some of these new, more exotic areas.

Books made everything possible. Not having the background to be informed collectors in non-traditional areas, we educated ourselves by arming ourselves with many volumes covering these new fields of interest. Over the years, we've amassed a library of thousands of books and catalogs. It is impossible to collect intelligently without reference material. I am the "librarian" in our partnership. Each time a new catalog arrives, I check to see if anything new has been published in our fields of interest. As a result, a month does not pass without at least one box of new books arriving. There are hazards in my enthusiasm, as I am sometimes fooled by a changed dust cover into duplicating a book we already owned. I am convinced publishers switch covers to fool people on the chance they'll go by the image rather than read the information, as I sometimes have, and thus purchase a second copy. Fortunately, it does not happen too often.

Books can serve as introductions to objects, to museums, to ideas, and to individuals. Years ago, we were in the museum shop at the Met in New York, a favorite place to browse for books. Norma came across a new publication, *The Power of Headdresses*.[1] It was a gorgeous book covering headdresses from all over the world. Since Norma has become seriously interested in headdresses, finding the book was a stroke of good fortune. She read it from cover to cover. It became a bible in our pursuit of headdresses.

To our surprise, the book's author, Dr. Daniel Biebuyck, was heralded as the first Golding Chair of African Art at the University of South Florida in Tampa (only 50 miles away from us). Norma was ecstatic. She managed to worm her way into one of his highly-coveted graduate classes by going directly to Dr. Biebuyck and begging to audit the class by promising to sit quietly in the back and not disturb anyone. He refused to admit her under those circumstances, as he demanded full participation from every student. Norma promised to write papers and do everything required of all the students, including oral reports, in order to get into the class.

Needless to say, she proved a worthy student. She never told him she collected African art or headdresses. That same year, we were first named among Art & Antiques magazine's "Top 100 Collectors in America." It happened that Dr. Biebuyck saw the article soon after Norma completed the course. He asked her, "Why didn't you tell me you collected African art and headdresses?" Her reply was simply, "You never asked." After that, Daniel Biebuyck and his lovely wife became very special friends who shared many wonderful stories of their years in Africa. Daniel's many books have a special place in our library because they are both brilliant fieldwork on African art/ethnography and because they are colored by the fact we've had the privilege to share his friendship.

The reason it is so very important to know one's chosen field well is that regardless of one's so-called "good eye," each area of expertise is going to have pitfalls that only scholarship and experience can avoid for the collector. When Norma and I first collected in the area of African art, we were fortunate to have excellent dealers provide guidance. We were in this way introduced to top quality material from the start. After a while we became more confident and started exploring on our own. This led to an experience we'll always remember.

An antique dealer in the Sarasota area who had always been a terrific source for decorative items appeared at a show with a couple of African pieces. We expressed interest. He had a long story about a man he had met in Africa and how his son was attending a university in America. The son would annually supply him with some fine items to sell as a way of paying the tuition. The story sounded good. The item that had caught our eyes was a carved Chokwe chair that was priced at $2,000. It was a case where the "greed factor" took over the "good sense factor." Since the story sounded plausible and the dealer was someone we knew, we bought the chair. After all, a carved "Chokwe Chair" had to be worth at least $7,000! What a great deal! The chair took its place in our living room among other prized possessions.

A month later, we were paid a visit by a highly respected Belgian dealer who was a specialist in African art. Being a man of perfect breeding and impeccable manners, it was with obvious discomfort that he leaned toward me at the conclusion of his visit and he said, motioning toward the chair, "Why would you want this, when you have so many wonderful things?" Norma and I quickly begged him to explain why he said that. He flipped the chair to show how it had been artificially aged with ash—our eyes were opened. All the obvious clues of a fake were so apparent. We had not looked. When we tried to return the chair to the antique dealer, he refused to give us a credit. He was rude and refused to discuss the issue. Ultimately, it was his loss because we never dealt with him again. To this day, we have kept the chair as a reminder of the experience and a mistake that we'll hopefully not make again.

We now laugh about stories like the fake Chokwe chair and the missed Jasper Johns painting, but ultimately what has made collecting such an enrichment to my life is that we have been able to assemble a collection of objects that is both important and unique in more ways that I can possibly list, while at the same time it is something we have been able to share with others. Collecting has also brought many talented and brilliant people into my life whom I would not otherwise have known, and that would have been for me a truly tragic loss.

The Advisor's FYI: What Are Your Clients Collecting?

One out of three people in America is an accumulator or collector of something. That means right now many of your current clients are probably passionate collectors in need of services you can provide. How do you uncover this passion? You have to get into a dialogue. When you go to a client's house or office and you see art, antiques, or a collection of something, ask the client about the objects. The passionate collector will talk to you for hours about the things that he or she adores.

At the very least, you can help clients to name an art trustee in their will who will look after the collection, find the right auction house, set a reserve, and know when to sell it—someone other than children, who are often greedy (no offense).

Besides the wonderful additional planning opportunities this will create, you're upholding your fiduciary and ethical responsibilities. Think about it. If a client passed away and you sold his or her real estate for 20 cents on the dollar instead of getting the maximum price, you could be open to a lawsuit by the children for malpractice. But you may be doing the same thing when you allow a client's art collection to get sold at auction without doing your homework. And finally, it helps you to get to know the client better—to establish the trust that will secure your relationship and lead to many other planning opportunities down the road.

The Expert's Perspective:
Peter Hastings Falk—
Fueled by Passion,
Balanced by Expertise: Art as an
Asset Diversification Strategy

When you look at the world's most important art collections formed by private collectors, the single most consistent underlying theme for their success has been passion. Financial sense is a critical part of the strategic overview, but it's passion—coupled with the expertise of an insider—that brings success.

Here's why. Passion is a natural cultural instinct that has proven to be the underlying driver of the market ... and it will continue to serve as its perpetual driver. We must always consider that the art market is one of the world's oldest markets, dating back to the 14th century. During Rembrandt's era, regular public auctions were conducted in Amsterdam, Paris, and London. By the mid-1700s, auction catalogs began to be published, bringing more prestige to these events. Yet, despite hundreds of years of robust activity, the art market has remained a truly unregulated market. Owing to the inaccessibility of market data, the press could not provide any meaningful analysis. Even today, journalists delight in headlining sensational new auction records for paintings by history's most famous artists. Consequently, the public has long perceived of the art market as a "prestige domain" reserved only for the wealthy or connoisseurs. And along with that prestige has come the continuous competition and passion for collecting fine art.

So why, during the past few years, has so much been written about fine art as an attractive asset class? Why has the financial press been buzzing about the viability of art as an "asset diversification play" for a portion of an integrated capital investment portfolio? What has changed to cause financial managers to take a closer look at art and consider that it may play some role in the greater scheme of their fiduciary responsibilities? It's not just the headlines in the press touting record-setting multimillion-dollar prices.

What has really caught the attention of financial managers is the ability of econometricians to finally be able to make sense of large amounts of transaction data. The new availability of art price information in both electronic and printed forms has provided a new dimension of access to a larger audience. For the first time, the art market is becoming transparent. Record prices are rarely accidental, especially when demand is increasing and supply is dwindling. In this regard, the art market has attained the underpinning of increasingly commodity-like behavior, which has become the source of its consistency and security. This is the reason why wild price fluctuations in the art market are very rare.

The databases of auction price results that were started three decades ago have now reached a critical mass large enough to attract the attention of economists. More than four million sales results have been complied over the past few decades—of course, this is dwarfed by the daily transactions recorded in the equities markets. But finally, economists do feel encouraged that they have at least enough data points in art sales to seriously analyze the marketplace and make some valid observations.

Over the past few decades, I have been a pioneer in documenting and publishing this data, so it is gratifying to see economists like Mike Moses at NYU, Will Goetzmann at Yale, and others digging into the data, applying various analytical approaches—such as repeat sales analysis and hedonic regression analysis—and arriving at the same favorable conclusions about art as a viable investment vehicle.

Important among these economists' findings are the twin facts that the broad art market beats the traditional equities markets and that it bears a very low correlation to those markets. The conclusion is that an investment in art can represent a smart diversification move.

Gradually, the old art market practices—which thrived on opacity—will dissipate as collectors become aware of the benefits of arming themselves with comprehensive market data. Sure, dealers' profit margins will shrink. But the new accessibility to the art market will create security and cause the market to expand. Therefore, if you are considering forming an art collection, you are at a critical historic juncture fueled by a new, much larger wave of buyers who have not yet fully discovered the huge potential value of putting information sources to work for them. You are in a transitional period that may represent the most favorable buying environment the marketplace has ever seen and the likes of which may never be equaled.

From the outset it is important for each investor to clearly identify the type of reward he or she is seeking from the investment. Now, this may seem simplistic, but the fact is that some people focus strictly on financial reward. Others focus strictly on improving their personal lives and their social standing by surrounding themselves with beautiful objects. After all, the effect of social bootstrapping that can come from having a great art collection can be a powerful impetus by itself. Both objectives can be satisfied.

Financial advisors want statistics to support any significant investment in art. They like the idea that you can see the correlations with traditional benchmarked portfolios. At the same time, they are dealing with clients who may be passionate about a particular style of painting, historical period, or group of artists. The point is that, together, the analytics and the passion make a perfect marriage.

That means collectors and the advisory community need the nitty-gritty figures not just on the market segments, but on individual artists, showing a return on investment for each. You want to look at both auction records and dealer prices. And you want to integrate these figures in order to show a correlation between risk and return.

You want to know about costs. How long will it take for the painting to work off the dealer's built-in profit or the auction house's premium added? And, when it comes time to liquidate, what are those costs? And what about other fractional costs, such as appraisals, cataloging, and insurance? And, if your collection grows to the point where it warrants museum exhibition treatment, what about publishing and other promotional costs?

Let's assume the collector is passionate about some type of art. Instinctively, he or she wants to build, or continue to build, an art collection of major stature, of museum quality. The financial advisor has told him or her that asset diversification is a huge issue. The advisor has also suggested that, financially, it appears that art has great risk/return characteristics for buying and selling that can be favorable so long as certain conditions are met. Everyone's objective is to increase the odds for profit and avoid the pitfalls.

I believe the proper approach is to find a balance between the passion that drives the building of a great art collection and a careful analytical approach. The only way to do this is through acquiring true expertise. The essential ingredient is expert selection, tempered by econometric analysis and catalyzed by active asset management. Remember, for centuries, the art market has thrived on a seller's expertise versus a buyer's ignorance. So, make sure you validate that expert's qualifications. This strategy will always greatly outperform the conservative returns of passive accumulation. And that's just the financial return on investment.

The other, and more complex, measure of return is the "psychic dividend." By the way, we're not talking about art collections that are purely decorative in nature, with absolutely no concern for investment. These can still yield a "psychic dividend." People can simply enjoy living with them with no reasonable expectation for a financial return. Basically, this is what you get when you hire an interior decorator as your art buyer. We're talking about a different level of quality and historical importance. A level where the more educated a collector becomes about his or her collection, the more the passion increases. The collector is personally enriched and, as a happy consequence, is also financially and socially enriched.

Let's consider the ideal investment condition: "absolute certainty." Anyone can walk into a wine shop and blindly pay $75 for bottle of cabernet sauvignon, and chances are very high that it's going to be good. You don't have to be an oenophile to be near-certain that you will be buying a very high quality bottle of wine. But what if that wine has to be drunk within a year in order for you to realize your maximum pleasure and the return on your investment? And what about those $25 bottles that are just as good now, and have a very long rack life. In five to ten years will they have appreciated in value by a significant multiple?

There are two points here: First, if you're looking for "absolute certainty" in your acquisition choices, then art could be too expensive. The Picasso that sold at Sotheby's recently for $104 million is a perfect example. It's at the very tip of the art market pyramid, high in the stratosphere. The number of potential buyers for that piece could be counted on one hand. This would represent the highest risk and the lowest liquidity. That same $104 million could have been put to work building a significant art collection that, ultimately, would yield returns far greater than that single Picasso.

A qualified art advisor who thinks strategically will not be focused on buying artists who are at the peak of their price point, like that Picasso. Rather, he will be looking for the best buying opportunities in undervalued market segments that also match the collector's passion. The highly qualified art advisor puts "idiosyncratic risk" to work for his clients because he has the experience and the judgment to back up his recommendations. "Idiosyncratic risk" is the "wild card" that either makes or breaks the investment potential of your art collection. It can't be charted or graphed no matter how many data points you place in consideration. Selecting the right art advisor who has this special ability to identify "idiosyncratic risk" greatly reinforces the probability of higher returns on your art investments.

In the art world, what do I mean by "idiosyncratic risks?" Envision two paintings by the same artist. Both are the same size, same medium, similar subject matter, even painted around the same date. If we go strictly by the data, these two similar paintings should reasonably have about the same value. But no: one is worth "x" and the other is worth "4x." Why? Because, even though art really does possess many commodity-like characteristics, it also has certain embedded characteristics that will always throw a wrench in any economist's graph. The most potent is aesthetic quality. But there are others, such as historical importance, provenance, and physical condition. These idiosyncratic characteristics simply cannot be quantified.

Take this example, which would be completely lost to a statistical graph. Thomas Hill (1829-1908) was one of the most prominent landscape painters in late 19th century America. He was widely admired for his views of New Hampshire's White Mountains. But his views of the Yosemite Valley are the most sought-after of his paintings. In November of 2000, Sotheby's was fortunate to be able to offer two large and masterful landscapes by Hill. The compositions were very similar: immediate foreground with trees framing a glimpse toward an unspoiled valley in the middle ground, and then majestic peaks rising in the distance. Technically, both were superbly painted and in fine condition. Both were large, three by five feet. Both were painted in the same year: 1869. It's not often you find two paintings matching that closely.

The only major difference between these two paintings was the place depicted. But what a difference to the marketplace. One was a view of Yosemite Valley. The other was a view of Mount Washington in New Hampshire. First to come to the auction block that morning was the Yosemite painting. Sotheby's estimated that it would sell for between $125,000–$175,000. It brought a record price for Hill that still stands today:

$346,750. Applause broke out in the saleroom. And it was in this heated atmosphere, that the second Hill—the scene of Mount Washington—came up next on the block. Sotheby's was aware that this sister painting from the East should bear estimates that were a bit more modest, so they said it should fetch between $70,000–$90,000.

Based on the comparable quality of both paintings, it certainly would seem logical that the Mount Washington painting could also double its estimates as its sister just had and fetch $180,000. Remember, a record-setting price had just been achieved for Hill only moments earlier. The saleroom should have been heated, but the sister painting fell flat on its face. It failed to get a bid. Not even a bid at 15% of the final price for the Yosemite painting.

These two landscapes by Thomas Hill are representative of the way the art market really works. Because art has as many idiosyncratic characteristics as it does commodity-like characteristics, you can now see why true scholarship—true expertise—plays such a critical role.

Collectors want their private collection to be managed in the same way as any other assets in their investment portfolio; that is, to the most rigorous fiduciary standards of financial management so that the family can efficiently invest in fine art with the objective of a higher probability of better returns.

So, how does this "management" work with fine art? What about just hanging the paintings in our home and resting comfortably in the knowledge that we hired an insider, a smart picker? And what about being confident that, just as we appreciate those paintings as they hang on our wall, they are also appreciating in value?

Where does active "management" come in? Fine art, like any significant asset of value, can be managed in an optimized manner. Let's say the family is committed to building a very special art collection, and they are passionate about a particular style or subject matter within art history. Here, the objective is long-term. And while the works in this collection can certainly be hung and enjoyed on an exclusively private basis, it is important to point out that their return on investment can also benefit from a "value-enhancement program."

The essential foundation of this strategy is scholarship. Not hype, but real scholarship. Scholarship that results in a book on the collection, published concurrently with museum exhibitions to reinforce historical value and awareness. In this way, the collection can be branded and promoted in a sophisticated way whereby its unique nature and quality are emphasized. This is proactive value-enhancement.

Down the road, when the family decides to dispose of the collection, they will not only have improved the liquidity of their art, but greatly improved their chances for much higher returns. First, they can sell outright through gallery owners, private art dealers, or even other private collectors. Or, their collection will have achieved such stature that it may very well warrant being marketed via an auction house, accompanied by its own catalog. Or, the family will certainly want to weigh the benefits of making a charitable contribution of all or part of the collection to an art museum. In this way, the capital gains on the sale can be offset by the tax benefits gained from making the charitable contribution.

The first management step is to identify artwork that can be acquired at a reasonable price, possibly underpriced, but which has a very good prognosis for appreciation—much like buying value stocks. Finding these bargains depends upon research to validate quality and historical relevance. It also depends upon market research. The art advisor acting on your behalf must be an opportunistic buyer and seller so that he or she is leveraging both ends of the deal. And that's where the short-term objective comes into play. During the process of building the primary collection, we want to buy and sell art works opportunistically in order to maximize return, especially with regard to "trading up." For example, let's say the family is concentrating on building a collection of 19th to early 20th century American floral still-life paintings. And, in the process of research and buying, the collection manager uncovers a small but important private collection of 19th century marine paintings. The owner is eager to sell the group at a price so deeply discounted that the manager sees a quick turnover opportunity. This process of active buying and selling for the short term means that family is, de facto, conducting its business very much like that of an art dealer.

Whether you are planning on expanding an art collection or building a new one, I want to give you the resources, the framework, and the rules of the game that will allow you to approach the venture—and communicate with your art advisor—like a smart insider in the art world.

1. First, define your passion. Specialize. It is the soul of your collection. Build a thematic collection or even several smaller collections. And don't feel you have to be trendy. As Will Goetzmann once pointed out, "The single largest source of risk for the art investor is taste—the possibility that a work of art will fall from fashion and undergo devaluation."[2] Make sure your passion has a scholarly underpinning.

2. Get expertise. Self-educate. To fully implement your plan, contract with an art advisor who will serve as the active manager of your collection as well as your curator and consultant. He or she must have a balance of solid scholarly credentials and be very market-savvy. On one side, he must speak the language of the pure academics, because he turns to this network when needed for authenticating a work and assessing its importance. Academics are not asked to weigh in on value—that's the other side of the coin. It's your advisor's responsibility to secure authentication and a fair market value appraisal, which are two very different parts of the picture. Appraisers can't authenticate. And authenticators can't appraise. So, your advisor must think like a detective. He must apply solid art historical research as well as analytic research to improve the decision-making process, thereby stacking the deck in your favor.

3. Consider all selection criteria. Your acquisition process must be thorough in its consideration of all quantitative and qualitative factors for each work of art, including but not limited to: physical condition, rarity, signature and other marks of authenticity, historical and aesthetic relativism, subject matter, past and current market response as measured by auction records and gallery records, importance of the artist, future market projections as to longevity and permanence of the artist, provenance, and market conditions and the economy.

4. Conduct research and reconnaissance. For American art, if you are interested in doing your own homework, AskART.com can be a great resource and starting point. It is also useful in providing advance information. Most auction catalogs are received several weeks in advance of the sales, and are entered immediately. A proprietary search program automatically alerts you to when the specific artists on your "buy" list are about to be offered for sale. This is another step that puts you on an equal footing with art dealers.

5. Balance quality and price. Research and identify the sellers. Make the suppliers—key dealers, private collectors, and even artists' estates—aware of your desires. Be a stealth buyer. Identify potential purchases as quietly as possible. Quality is certainly an important consideration, but price is the guideline. And quality at half price is even better. Remember that great bottle of wine that cost only $25? Make sure your advisor always keeps an eye on those paintings that, even though of quality, failed to sell at auction. The price will often be discounted about 35%. And, while on the subject of buying, your advisor will make certain that every purchase agreement includes a guarantee of authenticity, provenance, and good title. I've been involved as an expert in some contentious cases involving good title on Nazi-looted art. My testimony has centered on the value of stolen paintings by masters such as Picasso, Monet, and Malevich. Believe me, this is a headache you want to avoid.

5. Think arbitrage. Take full advantage of "geographic buying"—buying at lower prices in a region where the item is not in great demand, and selling in the region where it is in the highest demand. For example, because many American artists studied and lived in Europe during the 19th and early 20th centuries, their works appear at European auctions, particularly in France and England. Quiet monitoring of these auctions often yields very favorable buying opportunities well below value. Even within the United States, part of your strategy should be to ferret out works by certain American artists in regions where they are less recognized.

6. Care and presentation. Once you buy the art, make sure it is cataloged and insured. Make sure paintings are in the most appropriate frames, because proper presentation enhances value. Your advisor will also make sure that, if needed, the work is cleaned or restored by a professional conservator.

7. Implement a value-enhancement program. Because I have assumed your goal is to build a collection of real importance, I keep pounding away at two points. The first is that every move you make should have a solid foundation of scholarship. The second is that you should think long term. And long term means that during the course of your "holding period" your collection will be pro-actively managed. Certainly, you can sit on your investment and profit. But the strongest disposition strategy will already have considered the importance of actively pre-marketing the collection. And, one of your key tools for value-enhancement will be a scholarly publication, a well-written and a well-illustrated book. And, hopefully, that book is published concurrently with a museum exhibition, one that may even travel to other museums.

8. The end game. Be flexible. Since you have carefully developed recognition and respect for your collection, you will have several viable options for disposition. Perhaps you have created a private foundation. Perhaps the collection will be donated to a museum. Or, perhaps you will have a single-owner auction. These are issues you will discuss with the members of your advisory team.

The Dance of the Collector—Strategies for Intelligent Collecting

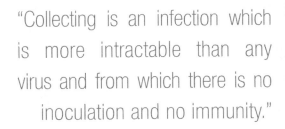

"Collecting is an infection which is more intractable than any virus and from which there is no inoculation and no immunity."

—Arthur Sackler

Putting together a collection can be an exciting and intoxicating task, and because it's such an emotional endeavor, even the most experienced collectors fall into traps or make dumb mistakes. And though many collectors have imaginative taste in art and objects, their strategies for collecting are sometimes too conventional for their own good. Most collectors use tried-and-true approaches such as poring over auction catalogs and attending shows around the globe, from ArtChicago to Artforum Berlin, from Art Basel in Miami to Artissima in Turin, Italy. They know which galleries are reputable and the importance of provenance and authenticity. But too few of them know how to do what Gael and I call "The Dance of the Collector."

The Dance of the Collector is the ultimate in poker face strategies. It means being studiously unenthusiastic while viewing a work of art you are dying to buy, so the dealer and other collectors don't know you want it—if they did, it would hurt your negotiations with the dealer or alert another collector to your find. It means hiding your growing sense of desperation so the dealer doesn't cut off the negotiation before you can get the price where you want it. Believe me, this skill takes a lot of practice to perfect, but once mastered, it will serve you well. But, more than this, The Dance of the Collector is a whole way of approaching—one might even call it carefully choreographing—the method by which you give your collection life.

In this chapter I have included the twenty most effective steps to this dance, some artful strategies for intelligent collecting that have been culled from years of talking and working with collectors, analyzing how they operate at shows and auctions, and, of course, many steps learned by trial and error while collecting with Gael. They say in life that there's no substitute for timing and luck. We agree, but we also believe collectors can and must make their own luck simply by cultivating the right approach to collecting. If you utilize your resources effectively, you are more likely to put yourself in the position of being in the right place at the right time. Good luck!

Step One: Don't Follow, Be the First!

There's nothing like it in the world. You're standing there, waiting for the doors to open up, when it hits you: the rush of adrenaline, that tight little knot in your stomach. The feeling you get just before you run into the show. You look around at your fellow collectors, and everyone seems to be dealing with the pressure in his or her own special way. Some people are effervescent, some are sullen, and some won't even look you in the eye or say a word. When I describe it to friends of mine who don't collect, I often compare it to how the gladiators must have felt before entering the ring to do battle with some ferocious lion, or worse, with each other. I know that everyone around me in this line is a lion or a gladiator and that only a few of us are going to walk out as winners. Once the doors open and you actually get into the show, you forget all common sense. Things get even more intense. No one walks leisurely. Everyone knows exactly where they're going, and good luck to the little old lady who gets in the way.

Shows are prime battlefields for collectors. They're places where alliances are formed, turf is defended, and conquests are made. When a bunch of equally motivated, like-minded collectors converge with their checkbooks, nothing short of trench warfare is possi-

Lessons to Live By: Shows Wait for No One – Not Even Oprah

Regardless of why it's better to be first, regardless of who you may have to push out of your way, one thing is certain: if you're not first in the line, you will miss out. The world of collecting doesn't wait for anyone, even if you're a celebrity. Case in point: several years ago Oprah casually walked into the Winter Antique Show a few minutes before 8 p.m. on opening night and was surprised that nothing was left. If you're not there on the stroke of 5 p.m., or at the very least don't have a rep there, my advice is to stick to auctions.

ble! To survive, if you want that priceless Napoleon figurine, then you need to have a well-thought-out battle plan to get to it first or this will end up being your Waterloo.

This may sound silly. For many of us, our early education probably included some fable or moral that ended with a line about the first becoming last and the last becoming first. A quaint sentiment, but one that every collector knows is dangerous. Often, as collectors establish rapport with a dealer, they can get the scoop on a particular piece that would be perfect for their collection but the dealer isn't authorized or is unable to display or sell until the show. When that happens it's important for the collector to know what his or her options are. Most importantly, that involves making a deal with the dealer to have first crack at the piece by being the first person at his or her booth. Remember Gael's quilt?

Also, another advantage of being first in line is that you have an opportunity to meet other interesting collectors, kindred spirits who may just have a hot tip for you; you just never know.

Step Two: Remember the Java.

You might think I'm crazy when I say coffee and snacks are the collector's ultimate secret weapon, but they are. It's not because all that coffee and sugar gives you the energy to exhaustively canvass the floor of the show. They actually do the opposite: the snacks serve to pull you away from a piece that you love! When you fall head over heels for something, ask the dealer to put a hold on the piece for twenty minutes. This may be hard to do with a piece you've just fallen in love with, but it's always best to take a break and collect yourself at the coffee area, which you have strategically located in advance.

Grabbing a latte and a brownie can help you regain your bearings and once again shift back into a more rational mind-set. You can talk over the impending transaction with your spouse or advisor. You can cool off and quell those impulsive emotional responses you're having, and return to the dealer's booth with a renewed sense of self-control. You'll be able to assess the piece with greater detachment and, if you do decide to take the plunge, to negotiate from a more confident standpoint. Whether or not you decide to purchase the piece, you'll sleep better that night knowing you made a careful, thoughtful decision—about the art, not your diet!

71

Step Three: Learn to Sit on Your Paddle.

Of course, keeping your emotions at bay at auction is a lot more difficult. There's no time for the coffee break, so you have to be extra cautious of letting emotion take control of your paddle and lead you into a bidding war you can't handle.

This is an easy thing to tell someone to be aware of, but until you're sitting in that auction room with a burning paddle, you can have no idea how easy it is to get carried away. Even I, an experienced collector, found myself susceptible to emotion at an auction at

Sotheby's. You have to understand that I'm an avid golfer. I live on Saint Andrew's Golf Club, the oldest golf club in North America. Several years ago, when I first heard JFK's golf clubs would be part of Jackie O's sale at Sotheby's, I told Gael I would really like to buy them and gift them to our club to be added to the wall of historic golf memorabilia. Over the six months prior to the sale, those golf clubs were featured on every major magazine cover and in many television shows. I watched my hopes turn into a pipe dream. When the clubs went to auction, Gael and I used some contacts to get seats in the very front row. Within ten seconds of bidding, the clubs were already up to $50,000. At $75,000, I raised my hand just for kicks. By the time I put my hand down, the bid on the clubs was up to $200,000. My hand was never raised again. As I put my hand down and sat back, the red-hot bidder behind me got into a bidding war against a phone bidder. The clubs eventually sold for $800,000. Gael and I laughed at the thought of who would be so carried away to bid such a high price for a "got to have" object. Later, we learned the successful phone bidder was Arnold Schwarzenegger. So far, even with the risky "for kicks" bid, no harm was done.

The next item in the sale was four of JFK's golf head covers—it's always the little things that get me in trouble. The covers were never publicized, they weren't in the catalog, and they weren't on television. If you weren't in the room, you wouldn't have known they existed. I *was* in the room and suddenly, I was bidding $3,000, $4,000 … When the bid shot up $15,000, Gael turned to me, panic-stricken, and said, "Are you crazy? What do you think you're doing?" "I have to have to these covers," I said. "They're only $15,000. The clubs went for $800,000."

Soon, the bidding shot up to $25,000. The rush was incredible. Even though I knew it was too much for a set of golf covers, even for JFK's, I couldn't let my paddle lay still! At this point, Gael was flailing and grabbing my hand trying to stop me from bidding. I don't know what came over me. Maybe it was the thrill of the competition, or maybe it was the knowledge that I'd forever be a hero at my country club if I could bring these JFK head covers home. Whatever was driving me that day, it wasn't rational. After a round of bidding with the same guy in the back of the room, I made my final bid for $32,500. It was two thousand short. The club covers sold for $35,000, which when you add the then 15% auction fee and taxes, was more like $43,000.

Of course, part of me was disappointed to have come so close to owning a rare piece of history. But the other part of me (and all of Gael) was much relieved. Though the golf club covers would have looked great at our golf club, they were supposed to be a fun, inexpensive purchase. In hindsight, I've realized that I let my emotions take me to a dangerous level of bidding that could have cost, not just myself, but both Gael and I, the ability to make competitive bids on items that were vital to our collection at auctions or shows down the road. And for what? A momentary whim, that was all. Today, I am much more conscious of keeping my emotions under wraps. If for any reason I don't think I can stick to my game plan, I'll tell Fred my max price and let him do the bidding for me. This way, he can bid but without being driven by the same passion that would consume me.

One Collector's View: Richard Schneidman's Tiffany Bowl

"About 15 years ago there was a Tiffany bowl with a martele rim up for auction at Christie's. The pre-sale estimate was $2,000 to $3,000. I decided to bid up to $5,000. But, the piece sold to a well-known antiques dealer for $10,000! The next day, the piece was displayed in his shop window with a $20,000 price tag. Needless to say, I was quite upset for not getting it. I walked by that store every day and saw the bowl displayed in the window. The days turned into months, months turned into years. The piece sat in the store window for three years!

Finally, I approached the dealer and said, 'I know how much you paid for the piece and I would like to offer $12,000 for it.' He smiled, and the deal was done. I walked home that evening with a smile knowing the bowl was finally getting a real home—a home with me."

Step Four: Letting the Gladiators Duke It Out.

No matter how excited I am about a piece, I never bid early at auction. Instead, I usually let two people go at it until one bidder knocks the other bidder out.

Playing your hand this way gives you the psychological edge. It lets the person think he or she won the fight and own the piece, only to see a new contender come in. Think of it as bringing in a fresh all-pro lineman in the final quarter of a hard-fought football game. Suddenly, your competitor thinks, "Oh my god, I just blocked this other guy, now I have to block this guy too?" You can really wear a person down to the point where he or she will say, "I've had enough. I don't know who this person is or what they're up too. I'm bowing out." This approach works so well for Gael and me that, unless we're competing against another collector who never puts the paddle down and has unlimited funds, like an Arnold Schwarzenegger, we'll win the piece we want every time.

Step Five: See Two? Love Two? Buy Two.

This is a collecting truism: collectors never regret what they do buy, but they are forever haunted by the things they didn't. There are many instances where we passed on purchasing an object, only to kick ourselves afterwards.

Every collector gets burned by not following this adage at some point during his or her acquisition years. My most memorable regret was several years ago. I had just finished paying a substantial amount for an important acquisition when Gael and I went to the American Antique Show. We promised ourselves that we wouldn't buy an expensive item, but we knew that we had to have something from the show. As fate would have it, we discovered a wonderful sculpture, which we would have certainly purchased if we hadn't vowed to stick to a strict budget. So to compensate, we bought another, less expensive sculpture, which, even though we loved it at the time, was of lesser quality.

Big mistake. Now every time we look at the piece we bought, all it does is remind us of the one we passed up. We've never forgiven ourselves for that one. In retrospect, each time we bought a piece but passed up something truly great, we should have found a way to make both purchases by finding more creative ways to finance it. Collectors should be aware that many dealers will allow you to pay in installments. And if installments aren't a possibility, there are several other ways to generate the liquidity needed to purchase the pieces. (More about this in Chapter 12.)

Step Six: Always Establish an "Art Fund."

It's impossible to predict when a significant piece will suddenly be up for grabs, so I encourage all serious collectors to develop and maintain a degree of financial flexibility, which will enable them to make that major, albeit spontaneous, purchase when the time comes. Setting up an art fund as soon as possible allows a collector the flexibility to bid at auction or buy at a show the pieces that could end up defining his or her collection. I would even call an art fund a best-practice method that ensures a collector has the opportunity to maximize his or her collecting resources.

There are several innovative options that one can explore in setting up this fund, beyond tucking money under the mattress. At several points during Gael's and my collecting careers, it would have been impractical for us to set aside tens of thousands of dollars for potential purchases and nothing else. The alternative, which we discovered worked wonderfully, was to establish a credit line against pieces already in our collection. Several major banks (Citibank, Mellon, and UBS to name a few) and several firms (Fine Art Capital) understand the art world and have set up ways that enable collectors to borrow against the value of their collections for many different purposes. By having access to an art line of credit, we discovered we had the cushion necessary to gain that essential leverage in negotiating for a piece. The credit line also puts us in a position to act on an unexpected opportunity when we stumble upon those long-lost paintings and sculptures that are a must-have for our collection.

Another reason why the art fund is essential is because it allows you to move quickly to purchase something, preventing the guy behind you from scooping it out from under you. That ability, along with the ability to promptly pay the dealer in full, is an effective way to do business over the long term. It ensures good relationships with the dealers and auction houses who may be in the position to find that long-lost German Expressionist painting you have always coveted. Gael and I knew of a now well-known collector of relatively modest means who took to establishing credit lines to buy the "Oh My God" paintings that he needed to have for his collection. Decades later, his collection of Picassos was worth hundreds of millions of dollars!

To find out which method of establishing an art fund would work best for you, I recommend that you consult your financial advisor—he or she has an intimate understanding of your particular financial situation and will be best able to find the most appropriate method of creating the fund.

Step Seven: Collectors Should Be Seen, Not Heard.

In their excitement about their latest discovery, many collectors simply talk too much! They say where they saw the piece, how much it's worth, how much it's selling for, and how great it is. And what the collectors don't realize is that they are hurting their chances of getting the piece at the price that they want for it.

In the marketing world, there's a kind of marketing called "WOM," which stands for "Word Of Mouth." WOM marketing relies on consumers to talk up their product—this kind of buzz is often more effective at selling a product than having a big bucks television ad. When collectors talk up their future purchases, they are effectively doing the same thing. They are creating a buzz that will drive up interest in, and potentially the price of, that piece. Collectors oftentimes

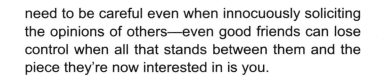

need to be careful even when innocuously soliciting the opinions of others—even good friends can lose control when all that stands between them and the piece they're now interested in is you.

Lessons to Live By: With Friends Like These ...

Not just once, but twice, Gael and I have been burned by talking about something that we wanted. It can be irresistible—who doesn't want to share dreams and hopes with people that they like? But the results can not only strain a friendship, they can also be expensive. The first time this happened was when we made the mistake of telling a friend of ours about a piece we were planning to bid on at auction. When the piece came up for bidding, we suddenly realized that we were bidding against none other than our friend, who had decided if it was desirable for our collection then it was good enough for him. He kept bidding up the price, and while we won the auction, we nevertheless wound up paying almost double than if we had just kept our emotions to ourselves and our mouths shut.

The second incident happened to Gael while she was at the Triple Pier Show in New York with three other friends, all of whom are collectors. Gael found two vintage bracelets that caught her eye. She bought one but hesitated over the second. As she tried to make up her mind, Gael offhandedly asked one of her friends if she liked the bracelet and then took a few minutes to walk away and consider her purchase—remember step two? Fifteen minutes later, she decided that she did indeed want the second bracelet. When she went back to purchase it, the bracelet was gone—sold to Gael's friend who scooped it up the moment Gael moved on.

Yes, these people are still our friends, but we've learned to play our cards even closer to the vest. Unless you want to be disappointed, never, ever tell a fellow collector about a piece before you've paid for it and own it. Better yet, wait until it's in your home and on display.

Step Eight: Don't Be Fazed by the Presence of Green Dots.

Often at a show, collectors will stumble upon an "Oh My God," only to have their heart sink when they see the dreaded green dot next to the object. Personally, it drives me nuts when I see one of these. A green dot indicates that an object has been placed "on hold." But is it really on hold? In my experience, it makes sense for the collector to try for the piece anyway. Now, I'm not advocating that you encourage the dealer to do something unethical, like selling you a piece that is legitimately on hold. What I'm suggesting is that you approach the dealer and tell him or her that you are interested, and that you'd like to put the object on second hold—this means that if the first buyer decides not to take the piece, then you have second dibs. Don't hover around that dealer's booth after placing the second hold; rather, disappear for an hour or so. When you return to the booth, it's possible that the first buyer will have miraculously changed his or her mind or disappeared altogether, and the piece is suddenly available for you to purchase. And, of course, if there was no first buyer and the dealer just wanted to drive up interest—after all, we always want what we can't have—you'll be first on the list for the piece.

Regardless of whether the green dot has been used as "psychological bait" to pique a buyer's interest, it's important to not let it dissuade you from making a play for the piece. It is equally important, however, to recognize that you shouldn't change your opinion and make a play for something simply because you think someone else wants it.

One year at Art Basel in Miami, Gael and I saw a marvelous contemporary painting that we simply had to have. We ran to the dealer's booth only to see the dreaded green dot. We were told it was on hold for a museum for purchase. Knowing how complicated it is for institutions to purchase objects (agreement among curators, trustees, acquisition committees, etc.), we made an offer that was good for the next hour only, if the museum passed on it. Fifty-four minutes later, the piece was ours. Remember this story when you see your next green dot.

Step Nine: More Is Less. Less Is Great.

This is a simple step: always buy the single best thing you can buy. For example, if you have the opportunity to buy four nice paintings each costing $25,000, or a single masterpiece worth $100,000, always choose the one great piece. A collector should choose quality over quantity every single time, as it is said, "great things are rare and rarely lose their value." It's just that simple.

Step Ten: Learn How to Trade with Other Collectors.

Trading with other collectors is one of the most creative, and tax-friendly, ways of enhancing an existing collection. And it's probably one of the least utilized methods, since most collectors don't realize that they can take advantage of the "Like-Kind Exchange" rule in section 1031 of the Internal Revenue code. (For more about this technique, see Chapter 13.) This code provision allows for two collectors to trade artworks of a similar kind without incurring the 28% federal capital gains tax. For example, when Gael and I decided to concentrate more on three dimensional pieces, another collector of folk art had a piece we were interested in. Since we in turn had a sculpture this other person was interested in, we decided to swap pieces of like-kind. It was a tax-friendly win-win situation for both of us.

The key to doing an exchange successfully is to utilize an impartial third party, such as a professional appraiser, a dealer, or even a fellow collector, to document the value of the exchanged pieces. The third party can assess the value of each artwork or object to ensure that both collectors are receiving a work of equal value. Just remember: whoever this person is, it's crucial that he or she has no financial stake in the deal.

81

Step Eleven: Join the Acquisitions Committee of a Museum.

Some savvy collectors of contemporary and emerging artists have found a clever way to zero in on which artists they want to collect by joining a museum's acquisitions committee. The beauty of this approach is that the museum gains access to the collector's expertise and contacts and the collector becomes privy to the inner workings of the museum, gaining inside information about what the museum is planning to purchase. This information will allow the collector to buy the works of a relatively unknown artist at a good price before receiving the museum's imprimatur. Because, once word gets out, the artist's prices will inevitably rise.

Step Twelve: Never Be Third with a Dealer.

Courting a dealer is an extremely important step in the dance of the collector. A good working relationship with a few of the top dealers in your area of interest should be the backbone of your collecting strategy. But, for serious collectors, it's not good enough just to be on the dealer's radar screen—they need to be button one on the dealer's speed dial. Being first gives the collector the chance to be offered interesting things ahead of everyone else. It also means the dealer will be willing to go that extra step in helping a collector locate the strongest examples of an artist's work. But to get the benefits, I repeat, a collector needs to be the first person that dealer thinks of, or at the very least the second, when the dealer has an important piece. It can take a lot of effort to get into this position—not only does a collector have to actually pull out his checkbook and make purchases from time to time, but often a dealer must be pursued with the same persistence and sensitivity that it would take to land a coveted 7:30 p.m. reservation at the hottest restaurant in Manhattan or to ask the prettiest girl in school to the dance.

> ## Lessons to Live By: Refer Business
>
> If you use the tactic of referring other collectors to dealers' galleries, which will really help you score points, just remember to refer entry-level collectors —you don't want to create competition for yourself!

It also takes the human touch to achieve this position. Years ago, a collector I know became interested in an artist who was a special favorite of Jacqueline Kennedy Onassis. Ms. Onassis had taken this particular artist under her wing and her friends were snapping up the artist's work like hotcakes. The collector, who was not in this rarefied social circle, went to the artist's dealer and asked to be put on the list for any upcoming works. "Impossible," he was told. But the collector returned to that gallery week after week, unyielding in his determination to own one of the paintings. The dealer was equally unyielding in his insistence that future works were unavailable. Finally, during one of his visits to the gallery, the collector and gallery owner realized that they were from the same small community in Pennsylvania. All of a sudden, a piece of the artist's work was magically available. Talk about the power of small talk. The collector excitedly went to view the piece, but wasn't taken with it and passed. The next week the dealer called again: suddenly another painting was available. This time the collector loved it and bought it on the spot.

You must keep in mind the impossible is always possible; persistence pays off. And there are a variety of other clever ways to schmooze your way into being

83

in the top one or two collectors on a dealer's list. Invite the dealer to your home to look at your art or collectibles. Let him or her get a feel for what you already have in your collection, for the spatial possibilities and constraints of your home. Listen closely to the advice offered. Let the dealer take you under his or her wing. Go to the dealer's openings. Gael will show up religiously at certain dealers' openings, which they greatly appreciate. She also further endears herself to the dealers by making referrals to the gallery.

Step Thirteen: Don't Do It for the Money.

Anyone who tells you that your artwork or collectible is sure to fetch double its price in a few years is more likely a salesperson and not someone genuinely interested in your collection. Consider these numbers: first, turning around and selling something at a gallery triggers a 10 to 30% commission; second, selling at auction creates both buyer's and seller's commissions, which can reduce the ultimate value of the piece. No sound investment vehicle comes with a double-its-price guarantee and that many fees. And even if the piece is appraised at a high value, collectors often forget that an appraisal is a *hypothetical* price. Collectors should always take appraisal prices with a grain of salt. An appraisal is defined by the IRS very simply as the price a willing buyer and a willing seller will accept, both having knowledge of the artwork and both not under the compulsion to buy or sell. (More on appraisals in Chapter 8.) For example, if a collector were to buy a piece for $50,000, even if it is appraised as $100,000, it's not a given that a collector could turn around and sell it for the appraised price. Especially since the dealer has probably paid only about $30,000 for the object; the balance of your purchase is his or her profit.

A few years ago, a journalist was doing a story on *Antiques Roadshow®* on PBS. In his story, he described how a woman who brought an antique cup and saucer had her piece appraised on-air by the expert who worked for Sotheby's. The cup was extremely rare because it had a mustache strainer, which in the old days literally allowed men to dry their mustache off after sipping tea. The expert went on and on for three or four minutes about how great the piece was, how much history it had, how it was in top condition, and how it was the most unique cup of its kind he had ever seen. The estimate of value: $45,000. The camera shot straight to the cup's owner, and she screamed, "Oh My God"—which, in my opinion, ought to be the name of the show, rather than *Antiques Roadshow®*, because that's what the owners always scream. The expert thanked her for bringing the piece, and off the cameras went on to the next vignette.

What the television viewers didn't see, and what the journalist then went on to write about, was what happened off camera. The woman just found out something she owns is worth $45,000. Naturally, she wants to sell it right then and there to the expert who stated the value. So off camera she taps the expert on the shoulder and offers to sell it to him for $20,000. He curtly says no and walks away. Now the journalist is curious. "I don't understand," he says to the woman. "An expert on national TV said the cup and saucer are worth $45,000, and yet he won't buy it from you for half that amount?" "I don't understand either," the woman said, "I've been trying to sell it for $9,000 for years, and I haven't had one offer." It just goes to show that appraisals are useful in certain contexts, but not necessarily an indication of the price you can get for the piece in the open marketplace.

Step Fourteen: Be Skeptical If an Object or Artwork Is Called "Museum Quality."

It certainly sounds great when a dealer tells you that the piece you have your eye on is "Museum Quality." But how often does the potential buyer take into account how few pieces in a museum's collection get displayed? My educated guess is that about 97% of a museum's collection is usually kept in storage! Moreover, many museums own works of decidedly inferior quality. This axiom is nothing but a time-tested sales technique—ask yourself, if the artwork or object in question truly belongs in a museum, then why isn't a museum buying it?

Gael and I should have asked ourselves this once when we were in Nantucket for an art show and saw dealers there we had bought from before. They took us to the back of the booth and showed us this chest they hadn't put out because it was of much better quality than the majority of the items in the show. They said it was "Museum Quality" and that it would be going to a museum if a private collector didn't buy it. It was a beautiful chest and Gael and I decided to buy it. We put the deposit down and agreed to pay the balance when the chest was delivered. Gael took some pictures of the chest and during the rest of the show we talked about the chest to everyone. We were both very happy that day on our trip back to Westchester.

Not a day later we got a call from a very good friend. He said these people had a habit of taking new chests and making them old to the point that you could smell the lacquer. The show was still going so we asked our friend if he would go look at the piece and verify this for us. He called us back and said it was very new stuff. When the dealers came to deliver the piece at our house a few days later, we told them we weren't interested and wanted our deposit back. At first they refused, but we put another dealer on the phone who said he would verify it was a fake. It was our mistake, but luckily we had a team of fellow collectors and dealers to bail us out.

Step Fifteen: Staff Your Collection – Appoint an Art Advisor.

I like to say that a special collection is like a special needs child, and as such needs the same level of care and attention. Put it this way: if something happened to one of your children, as a responsible and devoted parent, you would most likely devise an entire program to ensure that your child received the best care possible and the most opportunities for his or her growth and development. This would most likely include making provisions for your child to have a legal guardian should you become incapacitated. The same type of thinking should hold true for your collection. You should appoint someone, be it your children, advisors, an art consultant, or a dealer, to be the trustee of your collection in case of unforeseen circumstances. The bottom line: discuss your collection with your children and advisors now—not during the reading of your will!

Discuss your collection with your children and advisors now—not during the reading of your will!

Beyond having a trustee, you should also consider hiring an art advisor. Many collectors would be well served to employ an art advisor to assist them with buying and selling art. As a collection becomes increasingly important, it's valuable to have a second (or third) pair of eyes to offer an evaluation of an object's merits and overall place in the collection. This can help stave off many expensive mistakes by tempering a collector's enthusiasm for a piece.

88

The role of an art advisor can change on a case-by-case basis. For instance, when purchasing a piece of furniture, a restorer might serve as an art advisor to make sure a piece is right and has not been restored (and isn't a fake). Art advisors can work on a fee basis or on a commission basis, and collectors should factor the cost of this fee into the overall purchase price of the object. They can serve as an independent voice for the collector, becoming almost a personal curator for the collection. They can negotiate for you in order to save time, and even go to shows in order to preview exhibitions for you. And, unlike a dealer who has taken you under his or her wing, the advisor isn't trying to sell you any of his or her wares; rather, you're paying the advisor to protect your interests.

Step Sixteen: Broaden Your Horizons.

For many Americans, the art scene means one place: New York City. But to Gael and me, that's narrow thinking. We've found some amazing pieces in untraditional venues. And we know of some collectors and dealers that are now routinely tracking graduate students at certain prestigious art schools, such as Yale and CalArts. There are new artists that come onto the marketplace all the time. Imagine if you had found Basquiat or Andy Warhol at the outset of their careers! Not only would you own a fantastic painting, but it would be worth millions of dollars.

If you think there is no fertile new terrain in the art market left to be mined, think again. At the time we first began collecting contemporary folk art, very few people were collecting in this area. If we hadn't had an open mind, we would never have been able to assemble the kind of collection that we have. Several years later, the market for this type of art exploded, expanding tremendously with major shows popping up and many seasoned collectors entering the field. Areas of new collectibles that are particularly well-positioned to climb in value are as diverse as photography from the 1970s, Whitefriars glass, Modernist patio furniture, and Italian plastics of the 1960s and 1970s. And these pieces aren't just to be found in New York. They're hidden away with painters living on small homesteads in Alabama and five-foot models of the Statue of Liberty being sold at New Hampshire auctions.

So don't be afraid to march to your own tune, and don't worry too much about so-called "conventional wisdom" that exists in the art market. Because even if an object doesn't appreciate in value, if you love it, it won't matter.

Step Seventeen: Not All Great Pieces Cost a Lot.

Everyone knows the story of someone finding an authentic copy of the Declaration of Independence at the garage sale. While the odds of repeating this find are slim (to say the least!), a smart collector can profit from the inexperience, mistakes, and just plain sloppiness of others. For example, in July of 2004, the *New York Times* reported on a painting that was being sold by Skinner, a Boston-based auction house.[3] The painting was a portrait of the great Irish tenor John McCormack, painted by a contemporary of John Singer Sargent's named Emil Fuchs. The pre-sale estimate was a few hundred dollars.

As it turned out, the painting was being sold by the Brooklyn Museum, who had not bothered to properly identify it or appraise it. (Surprised that a major museum would actually sell off one of its artworks? Museums frequently deaccession their collections. More on this in Chapter 5.) Poorly placed at an auction, this painting was flying completely under the radar. The astute (and lucky) buyer got it for $360; the piece is worth substantially more, and a better auction could have guaranteed exponentially more. In this case, the price and the quality of the art had nothing to do with each other. However, it's important to point out that the inverse is *also* true; you can pay a lot of money for an inferior piece of art, one that is made with reconstituted parts, or is even a fake. Even the most experienced of collectors can fall prey to this.

Step Eighteen: If You Can, Try Living with the Art at Home First.

Taking an object home is a huge step in the process of assembling a collection. Sometimes you have to see what an object looks like in the context of your other pieces, to live with it and experience it. Gael and I like to make sure a piece of art passes the "house test." On more than one occasion, the object didn't fit in the way we expected, and we returned it.

A work of art demands a level of physical engage-ment—it needs to be scrutinized from several angles, and from various distances. By moving objects from room to room, juxtaposing them against the works of other artists in other media, and viewing them in different lights at varying times of the day, you can discover whether or not a piece is truly for you or not. It's not always possible to do this, but if you've built up a relationship with a particular dealer, he or she may be pleased to accommodate you and al-low you to "try a piece on for size." Of course, this step is dealer-specific. Auction houses have found that it interrupts the bidding flow when they break to let somebody place the piece in her home to see how it looks.

One of the most eccentric pieces in our collection is a large green desk made in 1878 in Sussex, New Jersey by G.P. Alliers (see Photograph 5). For Alli-ers, the desk was an ever-evolving piece, and he worked on it up until his death. It is in the Adirondack style and features such bizarre elements as a built-in kaleidoscope and carved bugs visible under glass. It was so extreme that we were worried that it would overwhelm the rest of our collection. We were able

91

to purchase the piece with a 24-hour return privilege. So, with some apprehension, we had it delivered to our home—only to find that it blended seamlessly with our other objects. Today it is the cornerstone of our collection.

Step Nineteen: Make Sure the Artist Is Passionate About His or Her Work.

This only applies to collectors who are collecting art by contemporary artists or artisans. It's worth taking some time to get to know the artist, perhaps by even visiting his or her studio, so that you can get a sense of the artist's attitude and approach. You're much better off buying an artist who is likely to be around in several years and who won't disappear into artistic oblivion.

The only living artist we collect now is Thornton Dial. Several years ago, we hosted a party honoring Mr. Dial at our home. He and his wife were sitting in our living room admiring one of his paintings. He had never seen his work before in a modern setting — only in galleries, and he was really impressed. The next day, he visited MoMA, and sat fixated in front of Monet's *Water Lilies* for several hours. Upon returning to his home in Alabama, he painted one of his most unusual paintings, *Flowers of the Blue Things* (see Photograph 6). He liked how his other paintings looked in our house and told his dealer, William Arnett, that "the Mendelsohns absolutely have to have it." We bought it and it's now one of our most cherished possessions. Gael and I affectionately refer to it as "our Monet."

Step Twenty: Share Your Treasures and Success with Others.

We believe that art should be seen and that collectors have a responsibility to their art, the artists, and the general public. When a collection reaches that point of greatness it's the collectors responsibility to let it be seen by the public. Many of America's greatest museums, from the Guggenheim to the Norton Simon, owe their genesis to their founder's philanthropic interests. What a great legacy to be part of!

Beyond the contribution to humanity, loaning your prized objects to a museum for a show has several other benefits. Lending a great piece moves you up in the art world's food chain. You'll be invited to a special lender's dinner where you'll meet other fascinating collectors who may share your passions and with whom you may never have another opportunity to rub shoulders. Moreover, having your piece included in a museum show also enhances the artwork's provenance and value.

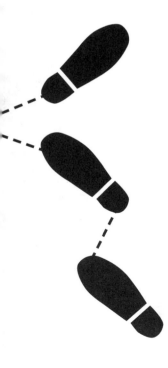

One Collector's View:
Kendra Cliver Daniel—
The Fantasy Became the Reality

Collecting always seemed to me to be broadening. I know that it expanded my life and introduced me to places, people, and experiences that would not have touched me otherwise. It's also goal-oriented. As a seeker, one is positively occupied. Ultimately, the sharing of a collection is enormously satisfying, but when you get down to basics, the real reason for collecting is love. And it is a passionate love, a love of what is perceived as beautiful or comforting or unsettling, an attraction to the familiar or the unfamiliar. It is also a possessive love; therefore, we accumulate. With a sincere collector, the possession is not connected with status or monetary value; it is a matter of not being able to imagine life without the beloved object.

With my fellow treasure hunter and the love of my life, Allan Daniel, I have visually soaked up the beautiful, the edgy, and the intriguing. As to our collections, we have focused on three or four main categories, including 19th century American folk art, original art by illustrators for children, antique toys, and vintage couture jewelry by Yves Saint Laurent. The first trip we took together was to London to attend an auction of original vintage illustration art. After astounding Allan with my ability to keep my bidding paddle in the air, we toured the London galleries. In an old established and elegantly stodgy bookstore, we saw a watercolor of a rabbit surrounded by fairies by the 19th century British artist, John Anster Fitzgerald. It was love at first sight on my part, but Allan was not ready to let go of the hold that classical 19th century American folk art had on him. From folk to fantasy is not an easy switch.

A number of years went by and I saw the image of the rabbit painting in books and calendars. Occasionally I would run into the dealer who had offered it for sale in his gallery and he would assure me that it was sold to collectors who would never part with it and that I should just face the fact that it would never be mine. But the rabbit burned in my brain. Then, the Frick Museum in New York had an exhibition of mid-19th century British fairy art in conjunction with the Royal Academy in London and won a coterie of new enthusiasts, Allan among them. By mutual decision we started to look for art in this category and were able to acquire a very special John Anster Fitzgerald painting of a squirrel among the fairies. But the rabbit remained elusive.

To the month, fifteen years after we first viewed it, I opened an email one day displaying the image of the rabbit watercolor (see Photograph 7). There he was, the longed for rabbit, hidden in a bower, surrounded by fairies who were tending his wound and protecting him from the hunters seen riding off in the distance. It was for sale! And the owners, a couple we knew who lived 3,000 miles away, were giving us first refusal! It is now hanging in our living room; the only piece of 19th century fairy art to hang in a room dedicated to American folk art.

The Dealer—
The Collector's
Right Hand

"Nobody needs a painting the way you need clothing, shelter, food. What happens when you pass a gallery is that you see a picture and you suddenly want it. Buying art comes from the 'hello' experience the picture speaks to you."

—Andre Emmerich,
ARTnews, September 1999

You know by now that I believe in developing a trusted advisor relationship with a dealer who specializes in the area in which you collect. In the early days of collecting, some collectors think that buying in galleries or from private dealers is expensive and not worth the extra that they might pay to acquire a special piece. With today's buyer's premium at auction increased to 20% of the first $200,000, and in view of the emotional tug of war you may experience with another frenzied collector, working with a gallery or private dealer these days will most likely save you money when acquiring a piece. When you look at the added value, in my opinion, there's no contest —working with a private dealer may be your best option. I have found the tradeoff to be worth every penny of commission my dealers have earned.

Here's the added value dealers bring to the table:

• **They have in-depth knowledge and subject-matter expertise.** I have found dealers to be a bottomless pit of expertise. An enormous part of a dealer's job is to be an authority. They spend their days talking with other dealers, collectors, and experts; going to museums and shows; visiting other galleries; monitoring auction sales and market trends; researching artists; and reading magazines, written materials, and exhibit catalogs. Dealers know who the other experts are in the field, both in the museum and the gallery world.

• **They can identify and assess emerging artists or new discoveries worthy of investment.** They know which artists are becoming increasingly collectible and which are not holding their value. Dealers have an informed perspective on the marketplace and are uniquely positioned to offer advice when new items appear.

• **They follow the art market locally, nationally, and internationally.** In addition to being subject-matter experts in their area of specialization, dealers also have their finger on the pulse of what is happening in the market: who is buying and selling what, how much they are paying, which markets are more favorable venues for certain types of items, and what's hot and what's not. As collectors, who presumably have day jobs or participate in other time-occupying activities that feed and fuel our art habit, we cannot possibly stay on top of everything we need to know to be making good decisions in the marketplace. The dealer brings this information to the table, enabling us to buy low and sell high and prevent us from making major mistakes.

• **Dealers provide direction and vision for the collection.** They help develop an overall strategy and focus for an evolving collection. Collectors are often too close to their own pieces and not in tune enough with what is going on in the rest of the art world to have adequate judgment about where the collection should be going as it grows. A dealer who has an intimate knowledge of what you already own and who has developed a sense of your taste and preferences can be an invaluable objective third party when new acquisitions are under consideration.

• **Dealers offer access to works that are never offered on the open market.** Dealers know who owns what, who wants to own what, and where the desired pieces are, regardless of whether or not they are for sale. When a desirable object comes into the market, it may not be offered publicly, because dealers approach appropriate prospective buyers and deals are made privately. Getting yourself into the private circle of the dealer world will open doors to opportunities that otherwise would never come your way. For example, a client of Fred Giampietro's was looking at *The Intuitive Eye*—the book on our collection—and saw a piece he "had to have." He offered us a substantial amount of money for it. Although we had never thought about selling the piece, it was no longer an "Oh My God" for us, so we agreed to sell the piece. Because Fred shared our book with another collector, we were able to obtain additional funds to go out and find our next "Oh My God."

• **Dealers can guarantee authenticity and provide a money-back guarantee in case there are issues down the road.** Because dealers literally trade on their reputations, their expertise, and their connoisseurship, many of them will offer purchasers some kind of trade-in, trade-up, or return and refund policy. The terms and conditions of these arrangements vary from dealer to dealer, and transaction to transaction, but collectors should inquire about and obtain in writing the specifics of these types of arrangements when working with a dealer. These provisions can provide an incentive to buy through a dealer versus purchasing at auction, where you are buying in "as is" condition and virtually without recourse after the hammer falls.

• **Many dealers offer condition reports and will help you identify parts that require repair.** If the art is damaged or has been repaired in the past, reputable dealers will disclose the history and condition of the piece so that you are making an informed buying decision. Dealers will also help you locate an appropriate conservator when the work requires repair or restoration.

• **Dealers can spot a forgery, a falsely attributed piece, or something that has been "reworked."** Because they are looking at pieces all the time and have a great depth of experience with individual artist's works, dealers can tell when something isn't right. They can save you thousands, or even millions, of dollars by spotting a piece that is not what it appears to be or is overtly misrepresented by an unscrupulous seller or consignor.

• **Some dealers will allow you to take art home and give it a "test drive" in your home or office setting.** If you have a good relationship with a dealer, he or she will sometimes allow you to bring a piece into your home or office and try it on for size. This allows you to view the piece in context and allows you to determine if it is the right piece for your collection before fully committing to a purchase.

101

• **Dealers know what should be sold and how to sell it.** Dealers are the arbiters of a network of other collectors who are interested in buying the works that you are interested in divesting. Just as pieces may be offered to you out of the public eye, pieces that you are no longer interested in owning can be liquidated, freeing up cash to make other purchases. Dealers not only advise on acquisitions; they also offer insight into which pieces are no longer a good fit in your collection and can present an outside, informed opinion on what should be sold.

• **Dealers offer privacy.** If I put a piece in an auction and it fails to sell, the whole world knows in a nanosecond, thanks to the Internet and the speed at which gossip travels in the art world. This obviously affects the value of the piece and my ability to sell it at the price I want. Selling through a dealer provides me

Lessons to Live By: Protecting Your Interest in Consigned Goods

Another potential risk a seller takes in consigning an item is the possible failure of the business you have consigned your art to—if they fold, your artwork can become the property of their creditors. There are things that a consignor can do to prevent this. First, he or she should file a UCC-I financing statement with the secretary of state in the state where the consignment shop (gallery) is located within twenty days of delivering the property.[4] And second, the consignor will be protected if he or she can prove that it was "generally known" by the store's creditors that the store engaged in selling other people's goods.[5] While this means the consignor may be able to protect his or her ownership rights, this is unfortunately quite often impossible to prove because of its vague nature.

total privacy and protects the value of pieces in my collection that did not move on a particular day, but which are nonetheless worthy pieces.

• **Dealers offer a consignment sale option.** Many dealers will accept art and antiques for sale on consignment as opposed to purchasing from you outright. This provides a third option, in addition to auction selling and the outright dealer sale, for the liquidation of a piece that could be financially meaningful for you. Because the dealer is not spending her own cash to acquire the piece, she will often charge you a reduced commission on the transaction if the piece sells from her gallery. If the dealer is buying the piece from you outright, she will have to buy it at a price that allows a sufficient mark-up to make a reasonable profit when it is sold to another collector. This inevitably results in the seller realizing less than the retail value of the piece. The advantages to you of a consignment sale are that the piece is displayed in a suitable venue that draws an appropriate clientele of prospective purchasers. The disadvantage is that the dealer does not have the same incentive to move the piece (freeing up her own cash), but this can mean that you will realize a better sales price. Consignment sales tend to work best when you have a really good piece that you know will be sought after, and you can be flexible with the timing.

• **Dealers can provide someone to bid on your behalf at auction.** There are several reasons why you sometimes want someone else to bid on your behalf at an auction. As your collection matures, you will gain notoriety in the art world and acquire a reputation in the community of collectors, dealers, auctioneers, and other hangers-on. It sometimes can work against you to bid publicly for an item, because your very interest in the piece can drive the price up. Dealers can arrange to have an unfamiliar person, who has been thoroughly prepared ahead of time and is fully informed on the upper limit of your bidding, stand in for you to conduct the bidding. The other scenario in which you might want someone to bid on your behalf is if you are subject to "auction frenzy" and can get carried away in the thrill of the moment, overspending on the purchase. The shill will have a much cooler head and will withdraw from the bidding when the ceiling has been hit.

• **Dealers provide connoisseurship.** Dealers, as a result of having looked at thousands of items of art and antiques, have developed that fine eye for quality that is commonly defined as connoisseurship. It is a hard to define skill, or perhaps art, that comes only with vast experience of looking at and absorbing every detail of very fine things. It is a combination of subject-matter expertise, having the innate "feel" for quality, and intuition. But it is the magical differentiating factor that informs good judgment in knowing what to buy and what to pass on. When you have developed a trusted advisor relationship with a dealer, you acquire, along with all the other perks, the benefit of his connoisseurship. I think of connoisseurship as the X-factor—it's that special something you can't quite put your arms around that can transform a mediocre collection into a world-class one.

The Expert's Perspective:
Fred Giampietro

There are two unforgettable events in the life of every art collector: First, the moment we find a piece that grips us on the most intimate and visceral level. Then later, the daunting realization that we need an exit strategy for the collection we have amassed. Our initial finding often sparks an insatiable desire to see and learn as much as possible, ushering both art and culture into our daily lives.

I remember my first experience vividly. It was my freshman year at a small college in central Florida, and I had only recently met Kathryn Nichols, the woman whom I would eventually marry. As the daughter of a painter, Kathy had experienced a childhood immersed in the arts. It was a foreign world to my family and to me, but one day Kathy coaxed me into visiting an antiques shop on the edge of campus. The feeling that came over me next was nearly indescribable: a fire erupted within, and it demanded constant fuel.

From that day forward I thought only of the hunt, longed for that perfect object, and anticipated the deal. These same impulses to learn, build, and upgrade drive both dealer and collector. For this very reason, the best dealers view their clients' collections and their own as one—and these parallel impulses allow dealers and collectors to rely on one another in many ways.

Most beginning collectors follow a simple precept: Buy as much as possible, as cheaply as possible. Although it sounds reckless, this mentality represents an important stage for the fledgling buyer. Here, in the flea markets and junk shops scrounging for a better buy, lies a host of personalities who will become a support structure in the collector's life for years to come. We learn very quickly how to distinguish the honest and knowledgeable dealers from the less scrupulous—and more importantly, who has the best material.

At this point, the collector must choose between two very different buying strategies: One involves staying the old course, buying cheaply, trusting no one, and waging a one-on-one battle for every piece. But some will choose a wiser path, forming a long-term alliance with a reputable dealer—an individual to trust with evaluating and authenticating works, advising on price points and creating a personalized, well-rounded collection with investment potential in mind.

The best dealers are not only immersed in their markets, but know every facet of these markets at all times. Furthermore, veteran dealers have access to the finest pieces, which are typically sold privately and are seldom seen at shows or auction houses. Dealers have a responsibility to offer their most faithful clients the first buying opportunity. It would be a fantastic feat for the typical collector, tending to an unrelated career, to maintain up-to-date knowledge of the markets. Entrusting a dealer with a collection insures consistency throughout the collecting process and a crucial resource when planning an exit strategy.

The collector, however, must remember one tenet: loyalty. A dealer in a long-term alliance becomes a confidant—an individual who navigates every aspect of the collecting process. The best dealers will reciprocate the loyalty of their clients. When dealers and clients clash, it is typically the result of a client having played one dealer against another. It is best to find a trustworthy advisor and stay with him or her.

Dealers usually require compensation in the form of a small percentage of anything bought or sold. Compensation typically ranges from 5 to 20% depending on the value of the transaction. Still, some dealers will work for an annual retainer. Whatever the fee, it will be money well spent. Tackling the art market without a dealer can be likened to playing the stock market without financial advice.

A good dealer will have a multi-faceted strategy for building a collection. The first task is to identify the client's areas of interest and to discern the types of items that will form the nucleus of his or her collection. Setting goals for the collector is easily and often overlooked. A collection can serve many purposes, ranging from the client's sheer enjoyment to investing opportunities to the possibility of donating a collection to an institution. The next task is to decide upon a fixed annual budget.

This budget is best spent according to a set of guidelines. I recommend that my clients divide their annual budget into three parts (subject to modification): the first third should be spent on one item, the second third on two to five items, and the last third on ten to fifteen items. The goal is to accumulate a broad range of items, covering as much of the value spectrum as possible within their field of collection. I often build subsidiary collections within a collection. For example, while working in the broader field of American folk art, a client might build a collection of miniature portraits. This practice helps to personalize and strengthen the collection. It also lends a depth to the collection that becomes important if the client decides to dismantle the collection. The key to this method lies in buying the strongest pieces in each of the three price tiers, a process both fun and challenging.

When it comes to choosing a dealer, the client should conduct a great deal of research. Don't be afraid to seek interviews and ask direct questions. Ask dealers for references; speak to their previous clients as well as their bankers. The Internet is a powerful tool for doing broad research on prospective dealers. Ultimately instincts and comfort level will guide the client toward choosing the right dealer. Nonetheless, it is a good idea to have agreements written and signed.

Collectors often invest a substantial percentage of their net worth in their collections. It is important that they protect their investments with fine arts insurance and life insurance. The former protects a collection against fire, theft, and damage. Most insurance companies can quote a fine arts policy that insures for the collection's replacement value. The chosen dealer can provide a written appraisal for a small fee. I recommend AXA or Chubb insurance companies. Furthermore, a good life insurance policy provides a financial cushion that allows time for the proper dispersal of a collection, while simultaneously protecting against possible federal and state estate taxes. By my estimate, having ample time to sell a collection can improve the results by up to one-third.

Lastly, we must discuss auctions. Dealers both love and hate auction houses, a battleground where they compete for both material and clients. Collectors must realize that auction houses do not make guarantees, and pieces are often misrepresented on the block. For this reason, dealers often sell unwanted or problematic inventory at auctions. A collector must have dealer representation at auction. The dealer will inspect the piece for authenticity, note its condition, and recommend a bidding range.

Selling at auction presents a second set of risks. We frequently hear sellers' tales of auction success, especially in trade publications that focus on record-breaking items. In truth, for each record broken there are thousands of items unsold or sold to dealers at wholesale prices.

When it comes to selling there are only two choices: auction or dealer. The auction house lets the buyer decide what to pay, whereas the dealer dictates what the buyer will pay. Auction houses disguise their commissions in the form of a "buyer's premium." This is a fee that the buyer pays, which can rise as high as 20% of the selling price. While this practice seems to spread the fees between buyer and seller, it really comes out of the net sale result to the seller. When all is said and done, the seller can lose as much as 50% in commissions and fees at a typical, large auction house. A controlled sale through a dealer will produce the best results and can reduce expenses by more than half.

With the proper expertise at hand, collecting art can be an enjoyable, challenging, and ultimately lucrative process. And perhaps more importantly, it offers us the opportunity to live with masterful works of art that bring a sense of history and culture into our homes. History chiefly remembers civilizations through their art, and there is much to learn by living with it. By collecting we become part of a great tradition of appreciation and knowledge.

The Museum and the Collector

"I collect these objects to learn from them. In some moment these things are going to teach me something. For me, this is like a library. These are my books."

—Jose Bedia,
ARTnews, Summer 2000

We all have our own personal motives for collecting art, but underneath it all lies a passion universal to all collectors. It's this passion that drives us to bring together in one place a snapshot of humanity that we have captured and embodied in our collection. When collectors are thinking about the ultimate disposition of their collection, they often want to keep the best parts of it together so that it can be enjoyed and appreciated by others. They want to leave a legacy in the form of the special items that they love so much and share a little bit of themselves and their personal values as these are reflected in the collection. One of the first ideas that will spring to a collector's mind is donating the collection to a museum.

Museums are increasingly dependent on the gifts of collectors to bring new works into their permanent collections. The price of fine works of art is increasing, and the acquisition budgets at most institutions cannot compete with the private collector in buying these works of art. The museum community spends much of its time courting significant collectors in hopes of obtaining gifts of major works. Collectors need to be aware that museums do not accept every work of art that is offered to them, and when accepted the work does not always remain on display or even a part of the permanent collection. Museums have donation policies that should be scrutinized carefully by anyone considering a museum gift. Curators and museum staff are very willing to discuss these policies in an effort to be completely clear about the terms of acceptance of a gift.

The quality of the artwork offered generally has a bearing on whether or not the gift will be accepted. The more highly regarded the artist and the particular piece, the more likely it will be accepted. Sometimes a museum will want to accept selected items offered but will not and should not accept the complete collection. The curator may select the finest pieces and decline the rest. In this situation the collector has a dilemma—does she allow the collection to be broken up, or should she talk to other museums in an effort to find one that will accept the entire collection? Some museums will refuse gifts simply because they do not collect in the area of the item being offered. In this situation the collector will need to identify museums that have an interest in the area or period of the item being donated.

It is also imperative that the museum community work with their donors to create better gifts in the form of significant pieces from the collection and implement methods to turn the value of the other pieces in the collection into endowment or curatorial funds to care for the art while it is in the permanent collection. Working with the curator and the museum's planned giving director, the advisory team will be able to create a significant, meaningful, and financially responsible gift of art and money.

An art advisory team (consisting of an art succession planner, the family attorney, an accounting firm, and a money manager) can provide tremendous assistance when a collector is looking to donate all or part of a collection to a museum. The first decision to be made is which items should be offered to which museum. Qualified art advisors are generally

Lessons to Live By: Talk and Get It in Writing

While the collector can't ensure the fate of his or her piece in perpetuity, he can make sure that his wishes will be granted at least during his lifetime. It's important for the collector, with his advisory team, to engage the museum in a dialogue and contractual process that will spell out and protect the collector's interests as much as possible. Don't hesitate to talk to other families who have donated to the museum you are considering and to talk to the museum about its deaccession policies and how they might affect your gift.

113

very knowledgeable about which museums include the type of art being considered for donation to their permanent collection. Secondly, the art advisor can act as a liaison between the curator and the family, expediting the negotiations and taking care of the details. The advisor can also manage the production of a video where the collector discusses the pieces donated—how and where they were acquired, what the collector knows about the history of the pieces, and any special stories that add to the uniqueness or provenance of the donation. Finally, the advisor knows how to ask for concessions from the museum that will contribute to the legacy factor of the gift, such as the preparation of a catalog, the wording on the donation plaque, assistance with building the endowment or curatorial fund, and, perhaps most importantly, how the gift is announced and how the accompanying celebration is handled. The party is often the most fun in giving the gift.

114

For Collectors Only: A Collector Keeps His Collection Together and Enjoys the Party

In the early 1990s, a Philadelphia accounting firm introduced me to one of its clients, a brilliant collector who, although he had a very comprehensive estate plan, had not included his collection in that planning—a situation which I find is unfortunately true for many collectors. This collector had many significant pieces of beautiful pottery that he hoped to give to a museum, which would display it all together as a collection.

We contacted the major New York museum to which he wanted to make the gift. The curator expressed interest in several of the finer pieces, but then asked, "What's going to accompany the gift?" The collector was incensed that the museum cared more about money than the collection and asked us to explore other options. The Chicago Art Institute expressed interest, but the collector, understandably, wanted to see the collection end up somewhere closer to him so that he could occasionally visit it. Then fate intervened. At the time, I was working with a curator at the Philadelphia Museum of Art to make a gift from our own collection. I mentioned the pottery collection to this curator, and he lit up. Not only was he thrilled the collection might come to Philadelphia, but he had a perfect place in the museum in which to display it.

We worked with the museum to structure the gift, and the process went smoothly. The party celebrating the event was well-attended by the collector's extended family, including children and grandchildren, his friends, and the Philadelphia art community. It turned out to be one of the most wonderful nights of the collector's life. He walked through the gallery, resplendent in his tuxedo, and talked about each item—its special characteristics, and how and where it was acquired and shared special stories about his collecting life. Accompanying the opening of his exhibition was a fabulous coffee table book about the collection, with beautiful color photographs of each piece. Best of all, the collector had realized his vision for his collection and created the family legacy he had always hoped might happen.

The Expert's Perspective:
Joe Jacobs

Around 1988, when Gael and I began wrestling with donation questions for ourselves and our collection, we had the pleasure of meeting the renowned scholar and curator Joe Jacobs. Like Fred, Joe gave us some profound advice that we have continued to use throughout our collecting career. Here are some of his insights on museum donations.

In my experience, collectors often see themselves as promoting not so much their collection as the art itself, which they often passionately believe in and support. These collectors see themselves as having created a cultural legacy, a reflection and expression of an era that embodies the thoughts, feelings, spirit, and goals of a particular moment in time. And when approached from this perspective, collectors stop seeing themselves as the owners of their treasures and begin to see themselves as the temporary custodians of this powerful bit of history until it passes into the public domain. Ideally, but not necessarily, this happens when the collection or some pieces from it enter into a museum's permanent collection.

The issue for many collectors, however, is how to develop a meaningful relationship with a museum and how to decide when to transfer title of individual works or an entire collection to a public institution. Equally at issue is whether museum donation is indeed the best route to go, both for the art and for the collector. To answer these questions, we first must look at how museums function and what happens when they receive a gift.

Today's Museums – Unstable and in Perpetual Flux

The public tends to view museums as bastions of authority. "If the work is being shown in a museum, it has to be good," most people think. A favorite term with collectors, dealers, and scholars is "museum quality," a term implying a work is good enough to be acquired by or presented in a museum. But who makes this qualitative determination and who decides what gets collected and shown? Who decides how art is displayed in the gallery—to its advantage or poorly lit and hidden in a corner? Generally, these decisions are made by museum curators and directors. Directors, until recently, were former curators and trained art historians who got promoted into administrative positions.

The museum profession, like the art history field, is one that defies absolute standards on the intellectual or creative side. There are guidelines for storing, cataloging, conserving, and handling works of art. But there are no guidelines for what to acquire and how to interpret and present it. Not only are these aspects of museum stewardship not scientific, their success is not measurable the way a corporation's success can be measured by its bottom line.

Many museums today analyze success by attendance and profit, often sacrificing intellectual or artistic integrity for the sake of "gate receipts." This unfortunately means that many museums are moving away from the goal of educating and broadening the public's artistic awareness by introducing them to new artists, styles, movements, and ideas. Instead, many museums are responding to financial pressures by offering heavily commercialized exhibitions featuring familiar artists that prove to be a big draw, but which do not expand the understanding of art or broaden the public's exposure to less familiar forms. Equally disturbing is the quest to bring new audiences into museums by targeting ethnic, racial, religious, and other special interest groups. Shows have also been designed for teenagers that showcase hip-hop culture, skateboarding, or surfboard design. Some museums have targeted families—a Sesame Street exhibition proved to be a huge success, with audiences lined up around the block at many big city museums. While such exhibitions can attract large numbers of people who don't normally come to museums, these visitors rarely become members and don't usually return until the museum again presents an exhibition targeted to their interests. What is critical is that museums present work that is good, powerful, and strong and develop within its visitors an appreciation for and an understanding of all types of art.

Budget restraints also affect the quality of the works displayed in museums, because financially burdened curators cannot acquire or show the old masters and other major artists who have risen to the art Pantheon. Instead curators working under financial limitations are restricted to a second, third, and even fourth tier of quality, the quality of which is increasingly debatable the further you get from the upper echelon.

The human factor also raises difficulties when trying to understand how quality is defined. Curators and directors often disagree as to which artists, movements, styles, and specific works are important, and their individual preferences can put a personal spin on the works exhibited in institutions. Since art history is not a science, there is no right way to develop a museum, build a collection, or organize exhibition and educational programs. As a result, the museum often reflects the personal interests as well as the experience and education of the professional staff. The broader the interests of and the better educated, sophisticated, and intelligent the curator, the better the museum will likely be. Museums with a larger staff, which allows for diverse views, experiences, and voices, generally are better, more highly regarded institutions.

Because individuals and personalities drive museums as much as any mission statement or published goals and objectives, all museums are susceptible to change, and sometimes this change can be dramatic. Curators are a nomadic lot, generally staying at an institution for less than five years. The strong personality driving the direction of a permanent collection can cause a sudden shift in the acquisition activity triggered by the departure of this person and the consequent shift in the professional staff. Occasionally, the curatorial staff and the director are governed by the decision-making of a power-

119

ful board of trustees, who can dramatically affect an institution's educational programming, exhibitions, and acquisitions, putting a highly individual spin on what should be a more open-minded process based on extensive study and professional experience.

This all boils down to a cautionary tale for collectors and advisors: There is no guarantee any museum is going to honor your intention for how it will use your gift. Even the biggest, such as the Metropolitan Museum of Art in New York, can change course, although the likelihood that a titanic-sized museum, like the Met, will change quickly and radically is quite unlikely.

The Met, the Museum of Modern Art, the Solomon R. Guggenheim Museum, and other major museums all periodically sell works in their collections, generally deemed duplicates or inferior examples of other holdings they have. Nonetheless, the sales are often controversial, with many outspoken critics predicting the sold works will be sorely missed in the distant future and greatly regretted in coming generations. The art historians can always reevaluate deaccessioned works, elevating them from a secondary to major status.

Learn from the Past: How the Vision Evolved at the Guggenheim

In 1939, Solomon R. Guggenheim, who had amassed an extraordinary collection of abstract art, established a Museum of Non-Objective Art, which opened in a former automobile showroom on 54th Street in Manhattan. Here, the public could see the extraordinary abstract paintings by such twentieth-century masters as Vassily Kandinsky, Paul Klee, and Piet Mondrian that Guggenheim had collected during his lifetime. In 1959, the museum moved to a new building on Fifth Avenue at 89th Street that had been designed by Frank Lloyd Wright, whom Guggenheim had hired before his death ten years earlier.

The museum was directed by Hilla Rebay, who had been with Guggenheim since the 1930s, and she had helped him form the collection. After her death in 1967, a succession of directors has been at the helm of the museum but none as controversial as Thomas Krens, who took over in 1988. Under Krens, the museum became increasingly international in scope. The museum expanded to Venice in 1979 when it took over the palazzo and collection of Guggenheim's recently deceased niece, Peggy. Krens' vision pushed its boundaries even further to include locations in Bilbao, Las Vegas, and Berlin, and a partnership with the Hermitage in St. Petersburg, Russia. Kerns also expanded the exhibition and collection programs to include not only twentieth century non-objective art, but Latin American colonial and Russian art dating back centuries, an exhibition of motorcycles (of which Krens is an aficionado), and Giorgio Armani couture.

In the 1990s the museum sold a number of its Kandinskys in order to acquire a major collection of minimal art belonging to an Italian collector. This action generated considerable public outcry, especially from those scholars who felt that it was invaluable for study purposes to see as

121

many Kandinskys as possible in one location as well as to keep Solomon Guggenheim's original vision intact.

However, it is an understatement to say that Guggenheim's original vision has evolved with each curator over the years to the point that it is long gone. This is not to say that the succeeding generation of directors is either right or wrong. Krens' changes are bold and adventurous, and in the future may be perceived as farsighted and brilliant. But the point to be made is museums are constantly changing and being redefined, with earlier visions being dashed, dismissed, or dramatically restated. What is the core of a collection today could in the future be an aside in storage, or a prime prospect for deaccessioning.

Learn from the Past: Even Professionals Make Mistakes

A classic blunder was made by the Museum of Art at the Rhode Island School of Design (RISD) in Providence. In the 1940s, it sold Pablo Picasso's *La Vie,* considered his masterpiece from the Blue Period. Today, *La Vie* is probably worth over $100 million and is prominently installed at the Cleveland Museum of Art. Picasso, of course, was a famous artist when the RISD museum's director sold the painting. The decision to deaccess the painting was based on the director's personal dislike for the artist—he apparently bought into the position held by many uninformed members of the public that the artist was a hoax. The real irony here is that RISD used the proceeds of the sale of the Picasso to buy a fake Raphael, which they later sold only to buy another old master forgery.

A second example is presented by the case of Albert Bierstadt, who, along with Thomas Cole, John Kensett, and Frederic Church, is considered one of the great Hudson River School painters. Nonetheless, Bierstadt fell into art historical oblivion shortly after his death in 1902, not to be resurrected until the late 1950s and early 1960s. Meanwhile, The Newark Museum in Newark, New Jersey, which has one of the nation's great collections of American art, deaccessioned for a pittance almost all of the more than ten Bierstadts it had received as gifts in the 1920s. The collection had only one or two insignificant works by the artist when William Gerdts, today recognized as one of the great scholars of American art, was hired as curator in 1954. Realizing Bierstadt's importance, Gerdts searched for a major landscape by him, ultimately spending much more money for his great find, a great Rocky Mountain picture, than the museum received for all of the deaccessioned works put together.

How, When, and Where to Make Your Gift

Collectors who cherish the works they have accumulated and see themselves as temporary caretakers of a "cultural legacy" will want to carefully and thoughtfully chaperone their transition into a public institution for everyone to enjoy and appreciate.

The criteria for selecting an institution to which to make a gift are relatively broad. Most important-ly, the work must be appropriate for the receiv-ing institution. If the collector cares about how the object will be used, this is an especially high concern. If the collector values the gift and wants it seen and appreciated by the public, then it will need to go to an institution that will immediately put it into the galleries and keep it on display for long periods of time.

Some pieces are so important that they belong in the National Gallery, the Met, or another ma-jor museum outside your community. If you have a Monet and your local museum specializes in American art or Contemporary art, then obviously your gift is inappropriate for the local museum.

Plan Your Museum Gifts with Care

Sometimes your gift can change the direction of a museum, encouraging it to collect in a new area. Your local museum may not be interest-ed in quilts, for example, but if you have a nice collection, your gift could motivate the museum to expand into this field, building upon this gift, which would be the core of the collection. But the size of the gift in these cases is important. For instance, if your local museum that has an excellent American art collection but no quilting, then a gift of one quilt may prove to be inappro-priate—they may not have the supporting infra-structure needed to both display and preserve the piece and one quilt probably wouldn't be worth the investment. But, an entire quilt collection, one that tells an entire story of American art, may be the encouragement the museum needs to create that infrastructure. Also, particularly if there is a supporting endowment, they now have the incentive to hire a curator with expertise in that area.

If it is a work on paper that, because of its fragility, cannot be subjected to light and exhibited for lengthy periods, then it needs to be donated to a museum that is known for its holdings in this area, publishes its collection, and readily makes it available for scholars and public alike to view privately. Collectors who want to see their gifts used should consider donating to museums that periodically publish their collections, and even make their holdings available online.

Once you decide to make a gift, ideally you will make it with no restrictions. Museums generally will not let you stipulate that the work has to be perpetually or even periodically hung in the galleries or that it cannot be sold. Most of the better museums will not permit any restrictions accompanying gifts—they will simply refuse the gift. Restricted gifts are refused for good reason—the future is entirely unpredictable. For example, you may want to donate a wonderful Picasso Blue Period painting, the pride of your collection, and while both you and museum staff cannot imagine ever wanting to deaccession it, there could be good reason for doing so down the road. The museum may acquire a very similar but even better example than your Picasso, making it an inferior duplicate that is ideal for selling to generate acquisition funds. There is a

125

flip side, however: while many museums do not allow gifts that come with restrictions, many will agree to exhibit a gift when given and, if given an entire collection, to publish a catalog that accompanies the initial exhibition. Also, you can stipulate in the gift document that when pieces from the gift are sold, the family needs to receive credit for the new purchase.

Some major donors feel so passionately about their collection and their own legacy that they want to stipulate that their gift will always be on view as a collection in the galleries. Some collectors donate a body of work, requiring that it always be shown together, in effect, functioning as homage to the collector rather than an educational experience for the museum visitor. This restriction severely limits the context in which the work can be shown and ties the curator's hands.

One of the most famous examples of this type of restriction is the Robert Lehman Collection at the Met. This extensive and diverse collection spans a wide variety of media, from textiles to paintings, and is perhaps best known for its Renaissance, Impressionist, and Post-Impressionist paintings. It is housed in its own building within the museum, in effect becoming a museum within a museum. Lehman's great Monets, Renoirs, and Gauguins are separated from the museum's permanent collection of Impressionism and Post-Impressionism, which are gloriously installed in the nineteenth-century galleries. Instead of being seen within the context of other works by these artists and the development of Realism and Impressionism in France, they are isolated as revered fine art objects, virtually devoid of the original meaning and content the pictures held for the artists themselves and contemporaneous collectors and viewers, as well as for scholars and curators today.

Often regional collectors give work to such prestigious museums in New York and Washington as the Met, the Museum of Modern Art, and the National Gallery, forsaking local museums for the social cache that they feel comes by giving to world-renowned institutions. At these larger institutions, the galleries are filled to capacity, displaying only a mere 3% of their permanent collection, with the remaining 97% in storage areas that are bursting at the seams. The collector's gift becomes yet one more gem in an enormous treasure chest, appreciated by staff yet rarely making an appearance in the galleries, and often earmarked for deaccessioning in the distant future. Meanwhile, the regional museum is clamoring for high-quality work to put into its galleries, which all too often are filled with a hodgepodge of pieces and generally do not contain enough high-quality pieces to tell a consistent, interesting story about art.

Some collectors like to give locally, in effect supporting and developing the museums in the community in which they live. And ideally, the local museum is good and will care properly for the gift and use it effectively. In some situations, however, the collector will want to question whether the local museum has the ability to properly care for the art. These museums sometimes do not have full-time professional art handlers and often no conservator. In contrast, larger institutions have a professional staff that does nothing but move and install art and conservators caring for the collection. And while the smaller museum may have an outstanding curator, causing the collector to feel confident about the handling and care of the art, there is no guarantee that his or her successor will have the same qualifications. Large prestigious museums tend to attract the most experienced and qualified curators, conservators, and registrars, while smaller institutions often have a younger, less experienced professional staff, frequently just starting in their careers.

Despite our cautionary words about smaller, regional institutions, generally they should be considered as your first option when evaluating where to make a gift of a piece from your collection. After all, there are no guarantees about the future of your gift even at the world's great museums, which may relegate your work to storage and never even publish it. Giving to a local museum brings the added long-term benefit of giving back to your community. It also helps build the museum, which, if it periodically receives significant gifts, will gradually develop into a major museum, although this may take a while. As the collection grows and becomes more important, it will attract more qualified people to oversee and manage it.

If you collect and think you may be interested in donating to a museum, you should consider becoming involved with the institution. Becoming a member, ideally at an upper level, will give you more immediate access to staff. Join any support groups, especially for specific departments if the museum is large enough to have different departments and support groups, such as a Friends of American Art, or of Prints, or Photographs, for example. Try to meet the curator who is interested in your area and gauge his or her interest in and opinion of your collection. This will also allow you to learn about the curator's interests and goals and help you determine whether or not the museum would be a good fit for your gift. But always keep in mind that museums are very personality-driven—the present curator may not share your goals and interests, but the next one may, and your gift may attract a new curator more attuned to your personality or influence.

Is Donating to a Museum Your Best Financial Route?

Many collectors who see themselves as custodians of a public trust prefer to donate to museums —this seems to be the default option. But it is not the only option. Collectors need to also look at universities and, in the case of minor works, they should consider donating to other non-profits, such as hospitals and nursing homes. While these institutions must have a use related to the gift, this is a technical hurdle easily surmounted. With proper tax advice and estate planning, a collector may find that any of the options or a blend of options may make the most sense financially, as well as philosophically.

Tragically, however, too many collectors who intended to donate their collection to a museum fail to make the proper arrangements in their wills, and fail to do the proper financial planning that goes with it as well. The collection falls to disinterested children or relatives, who, following the advice of an accountant or lawyer, ship the work off to an auction house or a dealer for dispersal. The results rarely maximize the financial potential of the collection—to the contrary, they generally fall far short.

Besides the estate tax on the sales, there are the commissions from either the auction house or the dealer. Since these commissions are based on selling the work, the vendors want to liquidate it as quickly and efficiency as possible, often sacrificing price for expediency. Expediency is often a pre-requisite of the heirs as well, who are anxious for cash to pay the estate taxes. As a result, many heirs prefer to go to auction, which on the surface seems to promise the collection will be liquidated immediately and all at once. This can be an especially dangerous course to take.

If the work is of extremely high quality that virtually guarantees there will be two eager bidders driving up the price of the work, then auction can be an especially effective course to take. However, all too often, there are not enough bidders to realize a good sale, and consequently an inordinate percentage of all lots at an auction are "bought in," meaning the work does not sell. 20 to 30% of the lots at most auctions fail to sell.[6] Keep in mind that dealers often stock their inventory from auction sales. This means they sell their auction purchases for significantly more than they paid at the sale, often 50% to 100%.

Clearly, this means auction prices are not the highest market prices. Because auction houses and dealers are often desperate to get work on consignment, they will say most anything within reason to obtain it, often giving pie-in-the-sky estimates.

Another important thing to keep in mind is that, unlike a dealer with whom you have a personal relationship, or a museum that cares about a collection, auction houses are not in the industry to help you or your collection. They are here to liquidate—and that means getting the consignments and then getting the sales. Auctions houses are notorious for offering pre-sale estimates that look wondrously good to clients, only to call these same clients the day before a sale to strongly suggest dramatically lowing the reserve on their lots (the reserve is the minimum price at which the work can sell). Lowering the reserve will allow the auction house to make a sale and get its commissions from both buyer and seller, while selling your work for significantly less than you anticipated, an anticipation based on their estimate. In other words, you were told your work would sell for, say, $40,000 to $60,000 with a reserve of $40,000, only to find out that $30,000 was the most anyone would bid on it, and the price it sold for after you agreed to lower your reserve. Deduct auction house commissions and capital gains tax, and suddenly you do not have much of your already disappointing $30,000 left.

This brings us back to the financial predictability and social responsibility of donating to a museum: with proper estimates for your art, and the most advanced and sophisticated estate planning methods like PowerGifting™ discussed in this book, you can realize a much better financial return on your collection by exploring donation options while helping to develop your community or the nation's cultural legacy. While museums are inherently changing for better and worse, they tend to gradually progress, despite periodic setbacks, reversals, and digressions. For collectors passionate about art and viewing themselves as caretakers of a cultural legacy, museums are by the far the best route to go. Even if the museum goes in a direction that renders your gift obsolete, the museum is still most likely the best steward for its future.

The Auction House and the Collector— The Power of the Paddle and Other Cautionary Tales

With Contributions From
Elizabeth Clement, AM

"God help us if we ever take the theater out of the auction business or anything else. It would be an awfully boring world."

–A. Alfred Taubman

The Headlines Speak for Themselves:

"The auction business is all about how the rich transfer their things. Take away the trappings of uniformed doormen, flags, and high-toned locations, and what you have left is a high-end tag sale. Sotheby's and Christie's were founded in an age when non-noble people started to amass possessions, and their function remains the disposition of goods following the dislocations of distress, divorce, disaster, and death. The first order to business every day at an auction house is to study the obituary column and work out who is in the best position to write the letter of condolence."

Robert Lacey, "A Grand Old Rivalry"
Vanity Fair, January 1996

Many people, outside the art world, think that auctions are the primary way art is bought and almost the only way it is sold. When they stumble into the art world, usually through a problematic inheritance caused by poorly executed estate planning, auctions are the first thing they think of. The advisory community is particularly guilty of this type of mono-focus and failing to explore alternative ways to liquidate art assets. This isn't to say that auctioning fine art and antiques is a bad idea. There are circumstances when buying or selling at auction is a good solution, and the well-planned auction sale can be a strong disposition tool in the right circumstances. People inside and outside the art world need to be aware, however, that the auction house is simply one alternative among your acquisition/liquidation choices—

not the only option. Our goal in this chapter is to give you enough information so that you can make an informed decision when you are buying or selling and that you have a basic understanding of how the game is played.

Auctions have been a way to buy and sell goods for centuries. They are a particularly effective way to sell art, antiques, and collectibles because of the uniqueness and condition factors, and they have proven to be a mainstay of the secondary art market. An auction house generally provides a level playing field for buyers: pretty much anyone can get in, and, if you have a major credit card, you can get a number or a paddle so that you can bid. You can even make arrangements ahead of time so that you can bid over the phone, and mailed bids are also accepted.

The Headlines Speak for Themselves:

"Times could not have been worse for Sotheby's, for Christie's, and for Phillips, dePury & Luxembourg …What collector would want to sell in a shaky economy with war in the air? To make matters worse, no superrich collectors died this winter, so there were no big estates that an auction house could use as bait to lure other property."

Carol Vogel, *New York Times*, April 30, 2003

135

Auctions are attended by people at all levels of expertise in the art world. Most assuredly, the top collectors in the world buy and sell art at auction. They are the ones you are reading about in the sensational newspaper headlines. Dealers buy and sell art at auction. Museums buy and sell art at auction. And people who don't know what they are doing also buy and sell art at auction. Auctions inherently involve risk. Understanding and managing this risk will make you a far more effective auction participant.

The risks for buyers generally involve not knowing exactly what you are bidding on and the risks for sellers involve unrealistic monetary expectations and the failure to sell.

But before you run out and get the latest Sotheby's catalog, understand that buying and selling art at auction is not for the faint of heart or the inexperienced. You need to know the rules of the game (and there are many) before you get in too deep. While the newspapers are full of headlines about incredible sales prices of major works of art and rare antiques, journalists don't write about all the pieces that no one bids on, that do not meet the reserve, or that simply sell for less than the seller expected. Much of the energy at an auction sale is driven by the collector or dealer hoping to find a "sleeper"—a desirable item that has been overlooked by others which will not attract a lot of bidding activity and sell for a low hammer price. Sometimes auction bidders get genuinely great buys. But, for every ecstatic collector who finds a bargain, there is a seller who receives less than the item was worth. You may be the buyer getting a great

136

"Buy anything at the auction, Fred?"

deal today, but down the road you (or your heirs) are going to be the seller who feels cheated.

If you are dealing with either of the two major auction houses—Sotheby's or Christie's—the risks are lessened somewhat because these establishments are generally discriminating in what they sell, evaluating each item before it is included in a sale and representations are made about it in the auction catalog. They employ specialists in various periods and types of art, antiques, and other collectible items, although these people have as a primary goal to take in property to sell and get the highest price they can during the auction. These two auction houses also focus on the higher end of the art market, and a collector can learn a great deal observing and studying what is offered and how the process works. By going to the auction previews and studying the catalogs a collector can see a lot of higher-end items in a relatively short period of time. Smaller, regional auction houses do not generally scrutinize what is being sold with the same level of exactitude or expertise, and consequently the responsibility falls on the buyer to be very clear about what he or she is bidding on and assess the risk accordingly.

I highly recommend, when buying and selling at auction, that you enlist the aid of an expert such as an art consultant or advisor. The consultant or advisor can guide the collector to the most relevant marketplace to buy or sell the specific material the collector is contemplating purchasing or selling.

137

> ## Lessons to Live By:
> ## The Auction House Doesn't Know What It Has
>
> A Chinese vase was deaccesssioned from a Rochester museum and consigned to a regional auction house on Cape Cod. The auction house listed it as a "Famille Jaune Porcelain Palace Vase," described its "six-character Ch'ien Lung mark," dated it as 19th century, and gave a pre-sale estimate of $800 to $1200. The piece sold to a bidder who flew in from Taiwan for $23,000. This buyer consigned it to Christie's in Hong Kong who then sold it as a rare 18th century vase for $1.55 million—67 times the original price. The museum sued the regional auction house for wrongful appraisal and failing to advertise the sale to the international market. The parties settled the lawsuit, depriving the court of the opportunity to comment on the duty of the auction house.[7]

Buying At Auction—
Check It Out: Gather All the Information You Can

Generally, a whole spectrum of quality is offered in an auction sale. I've seen extremely fine items follow a lot of assorted pieces of low quality. I've seen auctions with nothing but the best hitting the block and ones where I couldn't believe that people wanted what was being bid on. For the eager auction neophyte who simply must get a deal on something, this range of quality can lead to expensive mistakes. But the knowledgeable auction veteran who has the patience to sit through the sale of things he is not interested in and possibly go home empty handed generally comes out ahead. This bidder has come to the auction having done his homework and consulted with his advisor ahead of time, hopefully minimizing the risk that he will overpay or bid on something that is not what he thinks it is. There are several opportunities to get information about the items offered in the auction prior to bidding.

If the auction house publishes a catalog advertising the items sold, this is your first opportunity to learn more about what you might be bidding on. Regional auctions generally do not publish a catalog but will sometimes have a booklet or sales sheet identifying the lots with descriptions.

The major New York auction houses publish and distribute magazine-like catalogs that contain photographs and descriptions of the items being sold that can include:

- The lot number which determines the bidding order.
- Artist or maker, dates of birth and death, nationality.
- Title of the work and its dimensions and medium.
- If the piece has a mark or signature, where that appears on the piece and how the name is presented.
- Estimated selling price.
- Whether the item is illustrated in the catalog.

Bidders are very much influenced by the photographs and the item descriptions within the catalog, and the resulting media buzz that is generated.

What an item is placed next to also can affect how it is perceived. A lesser piece displayed near a more popular piece may bask in the glow of its neighbor, or it can be lost in the shuffle and lay undiscovered in its shadow. (This is critical when you are the seller as poor placement can cost you money.)

Auction houses will open the gallery in advance of a sale so that you have the opportunity to view and closely examine individual items that will be sold. Use this preview time wisely. If possible, you will also want to research previous auction results for similar items to give you an idea of the upper limit of your bidding.

As with any major purchase, a smart shopper will independently research any auction item she is thinking of bidding on and find out everything she can about it and what similar pieces have sold for. Researching artists, manufacturers, and other representations made about the piece in the catalog ahead of time will help you understand the quality and character of what you are about to bid on. You may want to consult with a professional to carefully assess what the market is for a particular piece you are interested in and where it falls within qualitative ranking.

You can ask for a condition report from the auction house on specific pieces in which you are interested (note the auction catalog disclaimer on conditions and condition reports). An auction condition report is not an in-depth report; it generally consists of one line. Most of the time, there isn't a problem with the written representations, but when there is, the small print in the auction catalog becomes very important. You will also want to ask to see the provenance on a piece before you bid—if for any reason the seller is slow to show you provenance documents (or can't or is vague), you may want to think twice before making the purchase.

If you are contemplating purchasing a major piece at an auction, I strongly recommend you bring in an outside expert, dealer, or appraiser to evaluate the item before you determine a bidding strategy. He or she can spot issues of condition (overpainting, significant restoration, tears, relining of canvas, fake signatures, overcleaning) and quality that might not be obvious in the catalog photograph or even at the preview. You will want to examine the item closely to make sure it really is what the catalog says it is. Some bidders accept the auction house's word about the piece's condition, provenance, and other facts, but I feel this is very risky.

Buying "As Is"

> ### Lessons to Live By: Beware of Internet Photos
>
> If you are bidding based on a photograph of an item that you view on the auction website, please do so with utmost caution. Photographs shown on the Internet are necessarily displayed at a very low resolution—meaning not very much detail. Internet photos can be very misleading as to condition and specific features. If you are making a significant purchase hire someone to go to the preview, assess the item, and report back to you before you bid and get your heart set on something that is going to later disappoint.

141

When you are buying at auction, as opposed to buying at a private sale, you are generally buying in "as is" condition, without a guarantee or a return privilege. Auction houses almost always give you a "Conditions of Sale" document which contains the terms and conditions under which you are placing bids and making purchases. Generally, these conditions appear at the front or the back of the auction catalog in very small print. If you are bidding, it is very important that you review these policies carefully so that you understand what you are getting into. Here is an excerpt from a "Conditions of Sale" document we encountered recently:

> **"ALL PROPERTY IS SOLD 'AS IS.'** [Auction House], for itself and as agent of the seller, makes no warranties or representations of any kind with respect to any Lot. Buyer agrees that in no event shall [Auction House] be responsible for the correctness, description, genuineness, authorship, attribution, provenance, period, culture, source, origin, value or condition of any Lot. Nothing being said or done by [Auction House] shall be deemed a warranty of representation or an assumption of liability by [Auction House]."

What You Pay After the Hammer Falls

You must also realize that if you're the successful bidder on an item, the bid price is just the beginning of what you will pay. There are additional fees the auction house will tack onto your bid price, as well as taxes—these can total up to 25% more than the hammer price, or the price the item sells for at the conclusion of the bidding, once everything is factored in. These fees include the Buyer's Premium, usually 15 to 20%, up to a certain amount, plus state and local taxes. If you are paying by credit card, you are generally charged an additional premium for the privilege. Buying an object at auction for $100,000 can really mean $130,000 when you take into account the 20% commission and a sales tax of 8% (in New York City). It is best to calculate these fees in your head as you are increasing your bids by increment.

You're also expected to pay in full for your purchase before you leave the building, and you generally are required to remove your purchase immediately. You will need to make arrangements for shipping, if relevant, and if the shipper cannot accommodate you quickly enough, the auction house will charge storage fees. As soon as the hammer falls at the conclusion of the bidding process the risk of loss of the item passes to the buyer.

Some of the better auction houses will offer minimum price guarantees to the consignor in certain circumstances, and some states have special rules on return privileges. These will all be spelled out in the "Conditions of Sale" document.

Lessons to Live By:
The Winning Bidder Ships It Home—Oops!

An East Coast collector purchased several items, each in the six-figure range, sight unseen at an auction house on the West Coast. The auction house verbally assured him all items were in excellent condition. The collector never asked for a condition report and did not even know such a thing existed. (He was not represented by a professional art advisor.) It took several weeks before he could arrange for shipping, and the auction house began charging him storage fees. The works arrived at the collector's home damaged. The items had not been packed by a professional art shipper, although the collector retained the company recommended by the auction house. In transit, glass had broken and was shattered all over the packed items.

The shards of glass lodged themselves in the works of art and did substantial damage, ruining the pieces. The question now is are they worth saving? How much loss in value has occurred? Are they even worth sending out to the conservator for restoration? After restoration, what are they worth? One of the pieces, an oil on canvas, has several very small tears and significant paint loss in various areas of the canvas. Was the damage already there, prior to the shipment? Or did it occur during packing, shipping, and transit? How can it be proved? The collector has suffered a significant financial loss—how does he proceed?

Selling at Auction—
Where to Sell: The Venue That Fits Your Collection

Selling at auction involves completely different risks than buying at auction. In theory, by selling at auction, an item's "true market value" will be reached. When you choose to sell at auction you are literally making your object available to the general public, and the auction house is providing a way to sell and expose, or market, the item, hopefully to the broadest base of prospective purchasers.

The auctioneer is obligated to get the highest price possible for the piece that is being sold at auction. Auctioneering is regulated by state law, and so there is state-by-state variation in the laws and practices of auctions. You will want to acquaint yourself with the legal framework in your locality before you get too caught up in the frenzy of bidding or consigning with the expectation of making a killing.

When you are selling an item at auction, your first challenge is to determine the right venue. Auction houses come in all shapes and sizes. They have different specialties and strengths. Some specialize in certain types of property, some only take items that are of a certain quality, and some simply attract particular types of buyers making them more appropriate for your collection than others. Many auction houses will not accept art or antiques valued at less than a stated amount. Some of the New York auction houses will not accept items under $20,000 for particular sales. They also will not accept items they do not believe will sell. An auction house is very cognizant of its buy-in rate—the percentage of goods which go unsold—because this is often used as an indicator of their effectiveness.

145

While we have already discussed the two 10,000-pound gorillas—Sotheby's and Christie's—there are also other highly reputable auction houses outside of New York. Washington, D.C.; San Francisco; Philadelphia; Boston; Detroit; Chicago; and many other major cities have excellent alternatives if you do not want to or cannot sell through one of the biggies. Sometimes it actually makes more sense to sell outside of New York because sales histories support larger estimates in other locations. Regional artists, for example, may sell well in specific areas of the country but may go completely unnoticed in New York.

Where is the best place to sell your items and how do you find this information out? My recommendation is to work with an experienced art advisor who is familiar with the market for the items you want to sell. Which is the best auction house for your pieces? Is it best to sell in this country, in this part of the country, or is a regional auction best? Do they have major collectors in this particular collecting field who attend their sales and buy from them? What percentage of the consigned items do not sell? Do they have a good record selling this particular artist or maker? Are their specialists at the top of their fields? Will your collectibles fit in the overall theme of the auction? Are your items the best, in the middle, or at the lower range of the items being offered? Will the auction house accept the collection for consignment? There is a strategy for selling items and realizing the best value for the piece.

The location of the sale can make a tremendous difference in the sale price, and sellers should compare locations as well as the auction houses when deciding where to consign a particular piece. For example, in 2006, a Chinese or Russian work probably did better if it was sold outside of the New York market. Also, a mid-February auction in Maine runs the risk of depressed sales due to ice and sleet storms—people won't bid if they can't get there.

If you are looking to sell a diverse collection, consider splitting the objects between various auction house departments, locations, or auction houses in order to optimize the hammer price. Sometimes a regional auction house will perform better for certain types of art and objects (generally the "Ohs" and the "Oh Mys"). The auction house may offer its own solution which may or may not be in the best interest of the seller.

On the other hand, if the owner is a celebrity or a super-star collector, the collection may do better if kept intact and sold as a "single owner collection." When Sotheby's had the Jackie Kennedy Onassis sale, anything owned by her sold for many, many times what its real intrinsic value was. Her ownership catapulted everyday objects to new heights in the marketplace. A costume faux pearl necklace sold for thousands of dollars, a 20th century Chippendale chair for over $20,000—however, when this same chair came up for sale recently, it sold only for a few thousand dollars. An early 20th century piano once played by the Kennedys and their guests at Hammersmith Farm in Newport, R.I., intrinsically would be worth very little. However, with the Kennedy provenance and multiple photographs showing the piano at Hammersmith Farm with family standing around it, the piano sold for several thousand dollars. Remember John F. Kennedy's golf clubs I wanted to buy? The clubs were featured in the catalog and generated a lot of media buzz. After the dust settled from the resulting bidding war, the clubs sold for an astounding $800,000. Outside of the media buzz were the club covers—I thought I could snag these while no one was paying attention. They sold for roughly $43,000 (with the 15% auction fee and taxes)—not to me of course.

Don't take a "go it alone" attitude when choosing the venue to sell. Identifying the best venue to auction your collection is an area in which your dealer, appraiser, and other members of your art advisory team can provide tremendous value. Good advisors are generally very familiar with the alternatives available and are able to steer you in the right direction. They are also knowledgeable about other collections coming on the market, the timing and seasonality of the auction business, and can more than earn their fees by making sure that the right item is consigned to the right place.

After you have identified the proper venue, your next step is to enter into the negotiation process with the auction house to consign the items for sale. The wording of consignment agreements varies from auction house to auction house but certain issues are generally addressed in all of them. Generally, the collector is giving the auction house the exclusive right to sell, meaning the collector cannot change his mind later and withdraw the item from the auction unless the item fails to meet the reserve. The auction house on the other hand can withdraw an item from a sale if issues of authenticity or title are raised.

The auction house generally has complete discretion to determine the order in which items are sold at a sale and if and how they are grouped together in lots. However, your advisor/consultant can work with the auction house to assess where your piece should go and protect your best interests. The auction house also generally has full authority regarding the description of the piece that will be published in the catalog. Sometimes a seller can negotiate the amount of space the item will be given in the catalog and the size of the photograph, but beyond this most of these details are at the discretion of the auctioneer.

Auction houses charge the seller a fee to sell an item in addition to the fee they charge the buyer. This is how the auction house makes money—they get it from both sides of the equation. The seller's commission will be stated in the Consignment Agreement and is a percentage of the hammer price. The amount of the seller's commission varies from auction house to auction house and transaction to transaction. But keep in mind the amount of the commission is an item you can seek to negotiate. And, the more desirable your piece, the more leverage you will have negotiating with the auction company.

Pre-Sale Estimates and Setting the Reserve

The Headlines Speak for Themselves: When Painful Emotions and No Advance Planning Result in Bad Choices

On the front page of the Style section of one Sunday's *New York Times*, there was a photograph of people pawing through bins of clothing. The items had belonged to Elizabeth Tilberis, a fashion editor and society maven, who was a glamorous figure in the international fashion world for over three decades. These couture items were worth a great deal simply because they had been part of Tilberis' collection. These fabulous garments were being sold "in rural Maine, on a road dotted with convenience stores, bait shops, and a Veterans of Foreign Wars post." [8] All it took was a knock on the door by an auction "scout," and a bereaved husband was relieved to have someone haul the belongings away.

How could such a thing happen? This priceless collection of couture clothing and memorabilia could have been gifted to a museum, or used as part of a celebrity charity auction to raise funds for cancer, or so many other possibilities! This sad ending to a glamorous life could have been avoided with proper estate planning or a wise word from an informed advisor.

Lessons to Live By:
"Come into my web said the spider to the fly …"

Auction houses will cherry pick a collection and only take what they know will sell well. What is the collector to do with the rest of the collection? A carefully chosen and well-thought-out selling strategy is necessary to reach the highest revenue for the collector. Your advisor is trained and experienced in how to group the items in the collection so that they are offered in ways that will optimize the sales price.

Even sophisticated collectors sometimes think that if they invite representatives from the major auction houses into their homes to see their collections, they'll be able to impress the rep. Take, for example, the collector who invited an auction house representative to his home to view his collection because he wanted to sell a few of his best paintings, the cream of the crop. The rest of the collection, while certainly impressive, paled by comparison. But by showing the auction house the whole collection, he lost bargaining power that he might have had if he had not revealed the quality of what was left. An alternative approach would have been to meet with the auction house on their turf, armed with images and information about the paintings to be sold. In this way, the possibility of significant future business would be "in the air," and the level of service received, possible guarantees, and so

on would be in that context. In this case, the individual's desire to entertain the top experts from
the auction houses in his own home outweighed
negotiating logic.

Part of the consignment process is setting the pre-
sale estimates and the reserve. The auction house
will generally suggest a pre-sale estimate range, but
this is an aspect of the consignment process that
is open to discussion. Since the majority of collectibles sold at auction are unique, the pre-sale value
is judged by examining that specific piece's quality and condition and then comparing it to similar
pieces sold at auction and how well those pieces did
on the block.[9] Don't use this estimate to get out of
doing your own research! While the estimate may
look nice, keep in mind that auction houses aren't
just selling your work to a bidder, they're also selling
their services to you. Auction houses will sometimes
present a lower pre-sale estimate so that buyers will
show up to get a bargain. At the same time sellers
will want to work with places that regularly sell to bidders for more than pre-sale estimates of value.[10]

Occasionally the auction house will really miss the
mark in setting a pre-sale estimate. A very dramatic
example of this occurred in late 2006. Sotheby's
was selling a unique Indian weathervane that had
been sitting atop the Ford mansion in Grosse Pointe
Farms, Michigan for 35 years. They set the pre-sale
estimate at $100,000 to $150,000. The hammer
price was $5.8 million (including buyer's premium).
How could the hammer price be so far apart from
the pre-sale estimate? The winning bidder did not

What Is This Ring Really Worth?

The lifestyle consulting firm Ashton Pearl was asked to sell a diamond ring for a client which had been purchased at a major auction house five years prior for $200,000. She obtained four wildly varying bids:

- Auction estimate: 90,000
- Outright purchase: 140,000
- Outright purchase: 180,000
- Auction estimate: 240,000

The difference was quite remarkable. While the high auction estimate was enticing, the sale would have taken place in Geneva several months in the future. The expense and complexity associated with shipping the jewelry to Europe from the United States and the logistical difficulties if the ring did not sell in the auction, combined to convince the client to accept the higher of the two cash offers.

even enter the fray until the bidding reached $3.6 million. From then on it was a two-person contest between a phone bidder and Jerry Lauren on the center aisle of the salesroom. Mr. Lauren prevailed and after the sale commented that nothing touched the perfection of this weathervane.[11] He declared it a great work of art and the most perfect weathervane he had ever seen.[12] The other interesting thing about this piece is that its maker is uncertain and its provenance prior to Mrs. Ford's purchase in 1971 is cloudy. But the piece was so compelling that dealers agreed the folk art market moved up a notch.

It is also possible that the auction house will set the estimates too high, creating too high an expectation for the piece. When this happens the piece usually buys-in—meaning, the consigned item does not sell and the consignor "buys" the item back from the auction house. When this happens, the piece is hurt forever. It acquires the stigma "failed at auction" or "failed in a public forum." (The auction house will charge you even if the piece doesn't sell.) Much like the piece of real estate that was overpriced at the time it was listed, a year later, it is still on the market. This unfortunate result could have been avoided if the piece was fairly estimated at the time of the consignment.

The reserve is the amount designated by the seller below which the item will not be sold. In other words, if the bidding does not get up to this threshold amount, the item will be withdrawn from the auction for failing to meet the reserve or "passed." Setting the reserve amounts is another area where an art advisor can play an indispensable role in making sure the collector is preserving the value of the collection. The reserve amount, generally (according to most auction house policies), cannot exceed the low end of the pre-sale estimate. The amount of the reserve should be stated in the consignment agreement, and if any changes to the amount are made subsequently, these also need to be made in writing. The auction house will sometimes bid on behalf of the seller to get the bidding over the reserve amount. When the consignor has placed a reserve on an item in the sale, there will be an indication of this fact in the catalog.

The advisor or consultant can work with the auction house to market the items in the auction and heighten the level of interest among prospective bidders. Sometimes the reserve needs to be adjusted upward or downward after contracts have been signed for a variety of different reasons. Just a thousand dollars difference on the reserve can be the difference between cash or no cash, sale or no sale. Setting the reserve properly is a very critical piece of the puzzle in formulating a strategy to achieve the highest price possible at an auction sale.

Take, for example, the hypothetical sale of one of Rodin's lesser castings, which had not been properly advertised and was put up for auction during a time when there was just not a lot of buying going on. By setting a reserve on the piece the seller can ensure that dealers will not be able to snatch up the piece for hundreds of thousands less than what it's worth. However, if the sale doesn't meet the reserve, the seller still must face the fact that the piece did not sell and he or she has failed to convert the piece to cash.

That being said, there are times when a seller makes the strategic decision not to set reserves at a sale. This was the case when the Egan Collection was sold off at Northeast Auctions in August 2006. This collection sold for $5,952,000 (including premium)—a million dollars more than was expected. According to *Antiques and Arts Weekly*, the collection was sold without reserves or estimates which was considered a risky move, but the Egan's felt that estimates "can steer people low."[13]

The Consignment Agreement also should contain provisions detailing what happens if the consigned item buys-in—either it does not sell or fails to meet the reserve price. In this case the consignor will pay a buy back fee (usually a percentage of the reserve price) to the auction house to cover their expenses of cataloging, advertising, etc. Historically, 20% of items put up for auction are "bought-in" or go unsold. The collector is then faced with the dilemma of how to dispose of the unsold items. This is particularly troublesome in an estate sale situation because the estate tax return needs to be filed and the tax liability paid, but now the items are proving difficult to liquidate. Additionally, because of the public nature of auction sales, the whole world knows the item did not sell and this can affect the attractiveness of the piece and consequently its perceived value.

Costs for Shipping, Insuring, and Photographing the Work

Auction companies usually pass certain fees on to the seller that are associated with the consignment. The most common are photography, cataloging, and insurance. The auction house generally has the most important items in a sale photographed so that they can be featured in the catalog promoting the sale. Sometimes they will advertise in appropriate magazines and newspapers as well as on the Internet to create interest in the event and particular items featured. It is in the seller's best interest to have good photos made of the consigned item. The photography fee can sometimes be negotiated with the consignment of finer items.

The property needs to be insured against loss or damage during the entire sales process from shipment through public display in the gallery up to the handling on the day of the sale. Sometimes this can be a considerable length of time, up to two years. There is always the possibility that an item can get damaged on the auction premise. This can happen while the item is being stored, ready to go on the auction block, or after you have purchased it but have not yet picked it up. Obtaining insurance and keeping it effective while the piece is on the auction house premises is critical. Auction houses offer insurance to consignors; however, this is a profit center for them and they charge accordingly. The auction house customarily charges 1 to 2% of the hammer price or pre-sale estimate, but this is also an item that can sometimes be negotiated. Collectors are often better off obtaining their own coverage and making sure that it does not lapse.

Guarantees

In order to attract prime consignments, auction houses have, for over 30 years, offered certain sellers minimum price guarantees.[14] This practice has become increasingly prevalent and ensures that the seller will receive at least a minimum stated amount but also allows the auction house to share in the reward if the hammer price exceeds the guarantee. In order to attract the consignors of Picasso's *Dora Maar au chat*, Sotheby's gave the consignors a guarantee rumored to be in excess of $50 million. The amounts of guarantees are secret, but generally the higher the guarantee the larger the percentage of the overage negotiated by the auctioneer. The balance of the overage is paid to the seller. The *Dora Maar* sold for $95.2 million, considerably over the guarantee, and it is speculated that Sotheby's made about $17 million on the deal.[15]

The auction house can also lose on the deal. In 2005, Christie's sold Edward Hopper's *Chair Car* to a gallery that failed to pay the $14 million bid price, and subsequently filed Chapter 11 bankruptcy. Christie's paid the guarantee and took ownership of the painting. If the sale price does not make the guarantee, the auction house makes up the difference.[16]

Guarantees are generally used in estate situations with very high priced single pieces or with entire single owner sales.

Questionable or Over-Marketed Pieces on the Auction Block

It is fairly common practice for dealers to auction pieces that are problematic in some way—it could be a question of authenticity, an issue with the provenance, or some other issue relating to the marketability of the piece (a dealer's "mistake"—he has held the piece too long, it has been sold from dealer to dealer without being sold to a collector, it could relate to condition, poor subject matter, or not indicative of the artist oeuvre).

For example, the Hollis Taggart Gallery in New York put up two paintings for sale in an American Paintings auction. One was a Leon Kroll, which had been in their inventory for the past two years at a price of $55,000, and the other was a Thomas Doughty painting, also in the gallery inventory for over two years, with an asking price of $45,000. Both had been extensively marketed and shown at art fairs. Both works were fine examples of the artists' works, but for some reason remained unsold. In order to free up cash so they could put it into something else, the gallery put the paintings up for sale at auction. An interesting scenario occurred: the Doughty sold for $80,000 and the Kroll for $90,000. This irrational exuberance was great for the gallery, but was it good for the buyer, who most likely didn't know that the same paintings had been offered at the gallery for the past two years at half the price? What happens when the collector wants to sell them down the road and discovers that she overpaid for the works?[17]

Fakes, forgeries, and stolen art appear at auction. Reputable auction houses will not knowingly put a forged or stolen piece in an auction sale. There are instances, however, of auction houses selling pieces that insiders know are questionable. Most commonly these are pieces that have failed to gain certificates of authenticity from the artist's estates or the academic experts that resurface at auction houses —sometimes two or three times—before the item finally sells. When this happens, the winning bidder has purchased a piece that is virtually worthless.

There have been several widely publicized forgery cases exposed recently. These cases generally involve fairly sophisticated relationships between the people who deal in the forgeries and the artists who create them. One notorious case involved a dealer who would purchase the original work of art at auction, with a certificate of authenticity, and then have one or more copies made of the original with a forged certificate of authenticity. The dealer would sell the copy and wait several years and then sell the original. This crime was exposed when both the original and the copy of a Gauguin were in the catalogs at competing auction houses in New York to be sold during the same season.[18] This forger was sentenced to forty-one months in jail, ordered to pay restitution in the amount of $12.5 million to victims, and to forfeit eleven paintings, believed to be authentic works.

Sometimes it actually is not clear whether the item is fake or authentic. In May 2004, Taylor Thomson fought a battle in the British High Court after she sued Christie's alleging that two gilded 18th century Houghton urns she bought for £1.9 million were actually 19th century reproductions. The catalog had unequivocally described the urns as Louis XV 18th century urns. She won the first round of legal battles. The judge indicated that the pieces were most likely properly dated and authentic, but because she was a "special client," Christie's had failed to do enough to warn Thomson that 19th century imitations were also in the marketplace.[19] Within a year Christie's appealed the case and won. The Court of Appeal found that Christie's was "not negligent in dating and cataloging the urns."[20] In this case, authentication happened by the court.

The Headlines Speak for Themselves:

Stolen pieces also sometimes find their way into the auction house. The *New York Times* reported a sensational story in October of 2006: An intriguing man, whom very few people knew well and fewer visited in his home, died in his New York apartment. It came to light that he had been living under a fake name and had no will and no known family, so under the laws of intestacy his assets went to the government, who stepped in and proceeded to liquidate. Inside his apartment the Office of the Public Administrator for Manhattan discovered hundreds of works of art—portraits, paintings and miniatures. With municipal efficiency, they called two auction houses to manage the liquidation of the art. While researching the works, Christie's discovered that several of the pieces were stolen, including works by Fairfield Porter, Giacometti, Odilon Redon, and Kurt Schwitters. Christie's, of course, called the FBI who began an investigation. Then, in early October, a gallery owner purchased a painting from the estate at one of the auctions suspecting that it was a valuable John Singleton Copley. After the purchase the dealer looked into the painting's history and discovered that it had been stolen from Harvard University over 30 years earlier.[21] A second dealer who bought another piece from the estate at auction also discovered his purchase was stolen from Harvard.

The auction sales were voided, the stolen pieces are being returned to Harvard, and the entire affair is still being sorted out as of this writing. When the auctioneer was asked why the problems were not spotted prior to the sale he replied that they had assumed that the Copley was either a fake or a copy (he had set the pre-sale estimate at $1,500 to $2,500).[22]

A Fantin-Latour still life was sold for $1 million at a regional auction house in Connecticut. Prior to the sale, in compliance with his standard procedures, the auctioneer sent photos of the painting to Paris to confirm its authenticity and to the Art Loss Register in New York to confirm it was not in the database of stolen works. A certificate of authenticity was received and the painting was not registered in the database of stolen art, so the sale went forward in May of 2006. In September of 2006, the true owners of the painting returned home from an extended European vacation and reported the painting stolen out of their home. The auctioneer cooperated with the authorities and the thief was apprehended. The auctioneer voided the sale and returned the full amount to the purchaser.[23] Whose job is it to determine whether the items are stolen?[24]

Rescission of an Auction Sale

Under very unusual circumstances an auction house will rescind a sale. Generally the terms of rescission are stated in the Conditions of Sale and should be consulted before bidding. When consigned items have authenticity problems or are discovered to be stolen property a sale will generally be rescinded as we have previously illustrated in the stories above. A controversial case recently involved rescission of a Sotheby's sale of a flag banner with questioned authenticity. The banner was purported to have been used during the 1789 presidential inauguration of George Washington and was sold for $262,500 (including buyer's premium). The buyer discovered the authenticity issue and threatened litigation. Sotheby's rescinded the sale, gave the buyer his money back, and retook possession of the banner. Sotheby's demanded that the consignor refund the money, but he declined saying that the representations in the catalog contained enough "red flags" to make bidders cautious. Sotheby's has commenced litigation against the consignor as this book goes to press.[25]

Auction Sales Results

Headlines and stories about auctions often make it appear the auction house is delivering huge sales to its consigners. Take, for example, this *New York Times* headline: "A Solid Sale of $128 Million Opens Fine Art Auctions."[26] Very few people would think that was an unsuccessful outcome. The article goes on to say that "though there were no fireworks, the results were solid. Of the 58 Impressionist and Modern works on offer, 47 found buyers." And, "the sale totaled $128.2 million, after an estimate of $111.7

million to $157.9 million." At first glance, these returns seem great—the house appears to have estimated well and came within the spread, and many of the works were sold. But a closer examination of the numbers reveals a different story, one that's not as solid for the sellers. Included in the $128.2 million from this "solid" sale is the buyer's premium, which at the time was 19.5% for the first $100,000, and 12% for the remainder—this means that the actual sale came in at $112,808,500, only slightly more than the low estimate. Once the negotiated seller's premium is subtracted, as well as the cost to the sellers of the unsold pieces, the sales total falls short of the low estimate.

The Expert's Perspective:
Elizabeth Clement—
The Value of Obtaining an Expert Appraisal Prior to Buying or Selling an Item at Auction

Art, antiques, and collectibles have been appreciating at a very rapid pace over the last several years. In 2006, first half of the year art sales totaled over $4 billion at the two major auction houses alone, up approximately a billion dollars from the same time the previous year.[27] The art market is estimated to be a $30 billion-a-year business. Vast sums of money are being traded for fabulous works of art both in this country and internationally. There appears to be an unlimited amount of money to be spent on quality art, and each year new collectors enter the market driving up prices further still. The market is always about supply and demand. Over and over again, you hear from the art auction experts that there is a large pool of collectors who will spend whatever it takes to get the best of the best. There are new important collectors in Russia, China, and India adding to the globalization of the art market.

Sotheby's stock price (which has historically been a poor performer—Sotheby's is publicly traded, Christie's is privately held) has risen sharply in the last five years, trading initially at $13 a share moving up to $36 in early 2007, and was up 75%

in a year.[28]

The market is at an all-time high. The *New York Times*, commenting on the fall sales in New York in November 2006, reported, "These evening sales have the highest estimates in auction history. ... The auction houses have become so competitive for business that this season they have promised sellers larger and larger guarantees. ..."[29]

Amazingly, there seems to be no end in sight. This upward cycle has great staying power and continues its ramp upwards with no looking back. Many speculate that as more new collectors get into the market, there are fewer and fewer quality pieces coming up for sale. When quality items do come up, there are more collectors chasing these wonderful pieces, which drives the price up. It is all about supply and demand. There are many, many collectors and buyers of antique and collectibles properties now causing the supply for good to very good to exquisite examples in each collecting category to be harder and harder to find. The prices continue to go up, keeping pace with the demand for rare, unusual, and beautiful items.

The auction houses take in thousands and thousands of pieces each year; however, the auction houses' primary goal is to sell the works they are consigned. Buyers really need to be well educated to bid intelligently or hire an expert to do the work for them. It is a full-time job researching the marketplace and looking for the best of the best. Assessing condition, subject matter, size, date and time in the artist's career, provenance (if any exists) ... where does the piece fit into the overall picture? How much is it really worth? Is the current market overpriced? Is it over-inflated? Are collectors selling in this wave of current auction frenzy? Record prices are being realized. The greatest masterpieces from artists such as Picasso and Klimt are being offered. In any market, these pieces would achieve extraordinary prices as they are the best of the best and normally seen only in museums.

As studies, statistics, and, most importantly, the markets themselves illustrate, everyone in America seems to collect something these days. We are a nation of packrats—collecting and squirreling away everything from baseball cards, antique dolls, toys, ceramics, folk art, paintings, antique firearms, quilts, contemporary art, video, photography, pottery, Barbies™, textiles, historic documents, books, maps, stamps, and coins. The list goes on and on and clearly there are new markets created for new materials which all of a sudden become collectible and *hot*. Just look at the phenomenal success of eBay®. It is just amazing how many types of collectibles, art, and antiques trade every day all over the world via the eBay® auction system.

The success of PBS's *Antiques Roadshow®* has made the general public more aware of the possibility that what they have could be worth something. Most importantly, people are realizing the importance of calling in an appraiser before selling or throwing old things away that could indeed be very valuable. As helpful as the PBS show has been, the public perceives that an appraisal can be made in just a few minutes and the estimate is miraculously completed in seconds. Collectors must realize that this edited and compiled TV show is not the way appraisals happen in real life. The dealers/appraisers/auction house representatives on the show discuss the value of each piece as a group, and the appraisers in the segment have access to their laptops, enabling them to search the auction databases during the filming. They also bring some research books to the taping which assist them in their on-the-spot determinations of value. One member of the appraisal team is then selected to "present" for the cameras. Hours of research have gone into the assessment before you see the televised conversation with the owner of the object.

Collectors and the Appraiser

Working with a professionally prepared appraisal, whether you are buying, selling, insuring, borrowing, or lending, enables the collector to know what he or she has—the value, a clear and concise description, and how the item(s) ranks within the oeuvre of the artist. A good appraisal will educate you as to what your collection, or an individual piece, is currently worth and where the marketplace is, where it has been, and where it appears to be going. It is an opinion of value of what the items in your collection are worth at that particular moment in time—the appraisal date.

Is the piece one of the best examples of the artist's or maker's work, or is it a lesser piece and not that important? The price the collector is paying should reflect the quality of the art being purchased. For example a collector is seriously considering purchasing a Rembrandt etching—should she pay a high price because it is a Rembrandt? Is the collector educated enough to realize many Rembrandt plates have various states, some much more valuable than others? Does she realize how much the piece has been conserved over the years? An appraiser can identify any condition issues which may diminish the value. Is the collector aware of what similar pieces have been selling for at auction worldwide? Is she aware of the price last time one was offered for sale? Is the piece offered currently with multiple dealers and, if so, for what price? How does the condition differ on each piece being offered? Who has the most sought after and most desirable state? All of these questions affect value and, consequently, what the collector should bid or offer in a purchase transaction or how the estimates and reserves should be set in a sale.

The appraiser can analyze the marketplace both past and present and rank the collector's object with other similar objects having the same attributes, such as maker or artist, media, size, date, subject matter, condition, provenance, and exhibition history.[30] Auction records aren't the only "public records" available to the appraiser. They are only one piece of the appraiser's data. Market data is taken from various places, including dealer and gallery prices, private treaty sales, private dealer sales, trade shows, and trading between collectors. The appraiser must be knowledgeable in the marketplace he or she is researching and be able to call on dealers and

167

market insiders for pricing information.[31]

These days, there are so many collecting categories, including paintings, works on paper, sculpture, prints, photography, Americana, antique furniture, porcelain, hunting and sporting art, silver, nautical and marine art, firearms, Civil War memorabilia, dolls, toys, carpets, collectibles rare books and manuscripts, antiquities, vintage posters and movie cards, jewelry, teapots, Bakelite, textiles, and the list goes on and on. Each collecting category has its own corresponding marketplace where goods are traded. There are various levels of relevant markets. Market data research, qualitative ranking, and valuation expertise is mandatory in appropriately and comprehensively determining value based upon the purpose of the appraisal.[32] (For more on appraisals see Chapter 8.)

Often appraisers are called in to appraise "just a few items that we have been collecting over the years." The result is that these collections often have aggregate appraised values in excess of $1 million! This comes as a great surprise to the collector who never seems to think that his or her collection could be worth that much. Most commonly the collector has been acquiring over the years, never being fully aware of just how much the objects have appreciated in value. When the collector finally sees the appraisal report complete with descriptions, photos, and, of course, the values, he is often taken aback and in some instances in utter and complete disbelief!

Before getting an appraisal for any purpose, the collector should gather all relevant documentation for the appraiser. These documents include (but are not limited to):

- Any receipts or bills of sale

- Past appraisals

- Insurance schedules

- Conservation reports

- Inventories

- Publications, literature, catalogue raisonné material, and past exhibition history

- All other documents pertaining to the item and its provenance

Provenance is generally the history of ownership of a particular work of art. The provenance can refer to the artist's or maker's period in history and documentation of all previous owners of the object. The importance of who owned the piece previously can significantly increase the value of the item being appraised; the appraisal can also document rarity and other value-enhancing attributes.

A European painting with a significant provenance realized over $6.8 million recently in New York. It had the original wax seal on the verso side which had not been noticed by previous experts who had offered earlier valuations. The appraiser, who recognized the seal, proceeded to contact a group of recognized experts who conducted significant scholarly research which ultimately substantiated the provenance and increased the value of the piece substantially. This story perfectly illustrates why hiring and retaining an expert appraiser will save you headaches and make you money.

Whether you are about to consign some items or thinking of bidding on something in the most recent catalog, it just makes sense to bring in an expert appraiser so that you are making informed decisions.

Do You Need a Second Opinion?

On occasion appraisers will make an error. While these mistakes are rare, don't hesitate to get a second appraisal or to check your initial appraiser's references and work. Here's an example of what can happen when there is an appraisal error:

A law firm called in an appraisal group to evaluate some items in an estate before making distribution to the heirs. This appraisal group identified the pieces and valued them at a few hundred thousand dollars. The taxes were paid on the estate and the items were divided up between the heirs. Some of the heirs immediately sold their pieces and accepted offers based on the valuation in the appraisal. However, before selling his items, one of the heirs called in his own appraiser to reevaluate the items, wanting a second opinion as to value. The second appraisal valuation was for several millions of dollars. The heirs that had already sold some items now realized their mistake in relying on the first appraisal. Ironically, the heir who was more cautious and did not sell any items prior to the second opinion had been given, albeit unknowingly, all the items that had been undervalued and which were actually worth seven figures.

What went wrong with the first appraisal? The first thing that the law firm discovered was that first appraisal group was not a member of any professional organization, was not USPAP compliant, and had no Code of Ethics. (For more about these professional standards, please see Chapter 8.) Furthermore, they did not complete adequate market research on the items, nor did they conduct appropriate provenance research. They also failed to identify the relevant markets for the subject property, and the property was outside of their realm of expertise (yet they accepted the assignment anyway).

The current relationship between the appraiser, the heirs, and the attorneys is not a pleasant one. The attorneys had to reopen the estate to pay the correct amount of tax owed and there are still penalties possible with the Internal Revenue Service. In light of this new information, the heirs are requesting that the estate reallocate their share distribution to reflect the increase in valuation. Sadly for the family, all of the heirs are now not speaking to each other. The heirs who sold their items for the lesser values now want to cash in on the more cautious heir's proceeds and are trying to force a sale.

The law firm has now realized they need to revise their approach to how art, antiques, and collectibles are valued. The firm is putting a policy in place to utilize only appraisers who are members of the one of the three professional appraisal organizations. They have also decided as a matter of policy to have two independent appraisals completed on all items of personal property.

The Huge Price Paid for Failing to Appraise

A prominent collector with a very significant collection had strong family connections and ties to various cultural institutions. Although he had done an estate plan, the advisory team did not contemplate what would happen to the collection at the death of the collector. Various parts of the collection had been appraised whenever they were loaned to a museum as part of an exhibition but the collection was never appraised in its entirety. While the collector's advisors knew the collection was valuable, none of them had a handle on how much the entire collection was worth. They had done nothing to preserve the value of the collection or transfer the wealth to the next generation. Nor was any thought given to potential gifts to the institutions that were near and dear to the collector's heart.

The collector passed away unexpectedly. The collection was appraised for purposes of valuing the estate, and the appraisal revealed an enormous number, well into the tens of millions of dollars. The collector had been collecting for decades and bought the best of the best. The value of the art collection far outweighed the value of the real estate and other financial holdings combined.

The collection was sold at auction. By not including the art collection in the collector's estate plan and not doing any art succession planning while the collector was still alive, the heirs were effectively deprived of their inheritance. Almost all of the proceeds of the sale went to the IRS to pay the estate tax liability.

The unfortunate reality is that this situation is very common, even with the most sophisticated collectors who are working with the most highly respected advisors.

Bring the appraiser in yourself. Even you may be surprised at the cumulative value of all the things you have collected one at a time over the years. Your beautiful things may have appreciated more than you think. Don't wait for your advisory team to initiate the process. If you produce the appraisal and are proactive with your advisors about your intentions for your collection, you will be able to create an art legacy for yourself and increase the value of what goes to your loved ones.

173

Protecting Your Collection— Inventory, Preservation, and Insurance

The insurance sections of this chapter were contributed by Rebecca Woan

Franklin Silverstone contributed to the inventory sections of this chapter

"Collecting art is one of the great passions in life, an obsessive pursuit of objects that strike one's fancy, a tickling sensation of possession, lust, control, and fantasy."

–Carter B. Horsley,
The City Review

Over the years that Gael and I have collected, I've learned that like the three Ds (debt, divorce, and death) that often trigger hasty liquidations of collections, there are also three issues that are the mainstays of collection management—inventory, appraisal, and insurance. These three tools form a trifecta of important collection management issues that nobody likes to spend time on and, worse yet, many collectors ignore. In this chapter we will look at inventory systems, preservation and conservation of your collection, and the issues you need to be aware of when insuring your collection. Chapter 8 discusses valuation and appraisal.

It will never cease to amaze me when I meet an investment banker/collector who knows every single detail about her positions in the stock market but has never inventoried or insured her collection of Southwestern folk art. Or the attorney/collector who tracks his billable hours to the nanosecond, but has never hired a professional to appraise his collection of American sculpture. If you already are, or as you become, a serious collector, it's vitally important to keep good documentation about the items that you own and to insure them against loss or damage. It's really a preliminary step to art succession planning—if you don't know what you have and don't understand its value, how can you possibly formulate an informed plan for the ultimate disposition of your collection? Before you start to develop the plan for your collection or insure its value, you must create an inventory to figure out what, exactly, you have—especially if your pieces are strewn all over your house, boxed up in the attic, loaned to several museums, or "borrowed" for your daughter's new apartment.

Inventory and Cataloging

In the early 1950s, Michael Ventrist, an architect who dabbled in linguistics, and John Chadwick, a scholar of early Greek languages, managed to decipher the strange markings found on a series of clay tablets unearthed on the island of Crete. The text, called Linear B, is one of the two earliest known forms of written Greek. There was great anticipation among classical scholars about what the tablets might tell us about the lives of the ancient Greeks. The translation of the text turned out to be one of the most anticlimactic events in archeological history; what the tablets revealed was a detailed inventory of the contents of the palace.[33] The world learned that first century Greeks understood the importance of maintaining an inventory of what they owned.

177

There are several reasons why keeping an inventory is an equally important collecting practice in the 21st century:

- To know what you have and to be able to share that knowledge with others.

- To be able to see, when researching a potential purchase, if it will truly fit in with your collection.

- To organize your possessions and create a catalog of what you own.

- To create a "paper" trail in case of damage or theft for insurance purposes.

- To support valuation during the appraisal process.

- To document good title and authentication.

- To protect the provenance of a piece by keeping a history of it.

- To keep track of loans and gifts to institutions and individuals.

- To assist your advisory team during the estate planning process.

Getting Started

Most collectors do not begin the inventory process at the time they make their first acquisition, and so often they will need to retroactively set up a system that they can maintain and update as they acquire new items or divest previously recorded ones. If you have a very large or extremely valuable collection you will probably want to have the inventory and cataloging done by a professional. But for many of us, it is possible to capture and record the necessary information ourselves and maintain detailed files that will keep our thinking organized, support the efforts of our advisory team, and enable us to minimize our exposure to risks of loss.

There are lots of ways to organize and catalog your collection, but your first decision is whether you are going to do it on paper or on the computer. I strongly recommend creating the inventory document on the computer. If you don't have the skills yourself, this is a perfect project to do jointly with a child, grandchild, niece, or nephew who has a computer and would enjoy working with you on the project. In some cases, it may make more sense to find an art student looking for some extra money who would love a temporary assignment.

It doesn't matter if the collection is books, coins, scientific instruments, maps, or animation cells; there are several categories of information that you should keep a record of. Inventory records document the story of the collection—information on the artist or maker, the history of ownership and exhibition, conveyance and appraisal documentation, insurance records, and any other information that is relevant to the history or value of the piece. A thorough inventory record creates a trail proving ownership and documenting value should you decide to sell a piece or should theft or damage occur.

You are going to want to set up a paper or digital file for each item in your collection. In this file you will keep all of the paper documentation that goes with the item—the bill of sale, or cash or credit card receipt, a photo of the piece, any publications, historical records or other documentation that establishes the provenance, any appraisals you or previous owners have had made on the piece, and any other documentation relevant to this item.

179

In the inventory document itself you will want to first list every item in your collection as a separate entry. For each individual item you will want to indicate:

- The object type and media (oil portrait, watercolor landscape, metal sculpture, pearl earrings, Roman coin, Proust first edition, etc.).

- Other identifying information such as size, artist/author, manufacturer date, maker's mark, or any other details that would assist in recognizing the specific piece you are cataloging.

- A record of the date you acquired the item, how you acquired it (purchase, gift, trade, etc.), and either the price you paid for it or the estimated value on the date of acquisition.

- If the piece has been loaned for exhibition, note when and where it was shown and photograph any labels that appear as part of the exhibit.
- If the piece has been referenced in a book, magazine, film, catalog, or on TV, keep a record of the publication or broadcast details.
- If the item was part of another collection before it became yours, record any information you have about the prior ownership.
- For larger collections you will want to indicate the location of the piece—is it in a room in your home, at your office downtown, in your vacation home, in a storage facility, or on loan to a museum?
- If the piece has been promised as a gift to an individual or an institution, record details of your intentions.

If you are particularly ambitious, it can be very useful to record information about pieces similar to yours—part of the same series, by the same artist or maker, or from the same edition.

If similar pieces appear in an auction catalog, scan or document the information and note the sales price when it becomes available. You also will want to record when and where the lot was sold. These details can help substantiate the value of your piece and facilitate valuations and insurance claims.

Inventory Systems

Before computers and software programs, collectors and curators used index card filing systems to document a collection. Even today, many older pieces in museums or works that have been deaccessioned bear the imprint of previous tracking systems. These are seen as tiny slips of paper, glued to the backs of frames and on the bottom of ceramics or sculpture. Interestingly enough, these tracking marks have become integral to the history of the piece and they are generally left affixed and not removed. However noteworthy the remnants of the old inventory tracking may be, there was not much flexibility, making updates and changes very tedious.

With the advent of the personal computer, there have been several electronic inventory systems that have become available that are appropriate for collections ranging from museum-sized to the most modest personal collection. And, for those smaller collections, spreadsheet applications and a little computer know-how can fulfill most of a collector's needs. But, before you rush out and buy the most expensive system you can find or spend hours creating a personalized spreadsheet to manage your collection, there are some basic things that all inventory systems should have that you should know about. Also, there are some basic questions that you should be asking yourself before deciding on what system to adopt.

181

Picking the Inventory Management System That Is Right for Your Collection

When trying to decide between the self-made spreadsheet and commercial software, it's important to weigh the cost of the software against the investment of your time and the flexibility of what you create, as well as the time it takes to input the records of your collection. For example, if you happen to have a moderate-sized collection of signed first edition books (let's say between 20 and 100), it would take only minutes to create a spreadsheet that could store the title, purchase price, ISBN, and author. It would be fully functional and easy to sort. However, the hours spent tediously entering the individual information for each book could be dramatically reduced for an expenditure of about $70—the mid-price of a home book collection inventory system that checks the ISBN against Library of Congress and Amazon.com records to automatically fill in the remaining fields. In most cases, unless you have a lot of free time or a love of data entry, I usually recommend purchasing software or, at the very least, finding a spreadsheet template rather than making your own.

While pieces in art collections generally don't have unique identification numbers like (some) books or cars (and nowadays diamonds) do, commercial software usually includes several standard features as part of the inventory system that are much more difficult to replicate on a spreadsheet.

These features can include:

- Various filters through which to sort and view your collection.

- Wizards to create reports in electronic format or hardcopies for off-site storage, for your advisory team, your family, and your insurers.

- Wizards that make data entry simple and easy.

- Customizable data entry fields to accommodate even the most diverse collections.

- Search features that go online and pull data about the piece and its creator allowing you to cut and paste directly into the description field.

- Multimedia storage to include photos, videos, and sounds of the piece beside the inventory data.

- Fields to record information on all the objects of similar nature that have been sold.

When choosing software, take a good look at your collection and think about who needs access to the inventory. Is your collection all paintings or all sculptures? Probably not; most people collect in a variety of areas or will as the collection develops over time. It's important to choose software that can accommodate every facet of your collection. Do you want your dealer or your attorney to have a copy of the inventory? What about your daughter or members of your family office staff? As more and more people

---

Michael's Recommendations for Collectors: Collectify.com

I assume that the collectors reading this book will have collections that are as diverse as the one Gael and I have and probably don't want to spend too much of their valuable collecting time working on the inventory. Collectify,[35] which was conceptually designed by Franklin Silverstone, is an excellent software program used by many collectors whose inventory needs have grown beyond a do-it-yourself system. This easy-to-use software allows you to catalog, track, and share information with others, making it easy to get your advisory team the data they need to create an appropriate art succession plan and make sure you have the proper insurance coverage. It was developed according to the Getty Object ID™ Standards (www.object-id.com) and is suitable to manage any type of collection from poker chips and pens to fine wines to vintage cars. There are other software programs available as well; a few are mentioned in the footnote.[36]

become involved in your collection, a good inventory can save a lot of time and protect your investment. By sharing the files with your dealer, he or she can know what pieces would best fit the focus of your collection while at auctions or shows. And inventory records are vital for insurance, financial planning, and estate planning purposes.

A copy of the inventory should be kept in a secure location at a site separate from the collection so it can be preserved in the event of harm that may occur to the collection itself. Email a copy of the inventory, if you have it in digital format, to a friend or advisor every time it is updated. If your inventory is prepared by a professional, he or she usually will keep a copy of these records for you in secure storage. In the event of a loss, this information will be easily accessible. This is particularly true in the case of theft as the information can be quickly forwarded to the Art Loss Registry (www.artloss.com). You might also consider registering your collection with the Art Loss Registry before anything is lost. Collectors should also give copies of the inventory and the supporting documentation to a member of their advisory team or place it in a bank safe deposit box.[34]

Preservation, Conservation, and Insurance

Failure to take proper care of a prized collection can have tragic emotional and disastrous financial consequences. A major challenge for any collector is the preservation and protection of what you already have. And what a challenge it is! Improperly hung paintings can fall off the wall, fire can destroy just about any collection, and even just displaying the piece can result in long-term damage caused by exposure to sunlight and environmental pollutants. While these things all need to be considered at any point in a collection's development, it's particularly important when you start accumulating "Oh My God" pieces—if you can't live without it, how would you handle a situation in which it was damaged?

Cleaning the Collection[37]

According to the Master Guilder and Fine Arts Conservator at Bernacki and Associates, Barton Bjorneberg, many of the repair jobs he sees are brought to him not because of major disasters, but because of improper cleaning and handling techniques. Collectors are advised to allow only specially trained people to dust and clean the items in their collection. Even the best general house cleaning service may know little about fine arts. They may permanently damage a piece by applying polish, scratch the surfaces by using the wrong cleaning materials, or inadvertently damage a piece by brushing against it. I have a collector friend who actually has a seminar with her cleaning people when she acquires a new piece so that she is sure it is being handled and cleaned correctly.

Cleaning and Moving Guidelines[38]

- Don't over-clean; a little dust is not a bad thing.

- When cleaning wood, despite what the commercials may say, it does not need to be "fed." Small amounts of de-ionized or distilled water on a soft cloth is often all that is needed to clean furniture.

- Rub away from the center of the piece to avoid catching edges; wipe dry to minimize moisture. Always check first for any edges of the surface or finish that are lifting.

Lessons to Live By: What Could Happen—Will!

As we complete this book, construction work is being done at our home. When this project began we made a special effort to tell the workers to be very careful around the art, and attempted to impress upon them the fragility of the pieces, so hopefully they would be extra careful when moving around them. We were also very careful *not* to tell these temporary workers just how valuable the art really is. Unfortunately, I guess we didn't make enough of an impression, and almost paid the price. We left our prized Kehinde Wiley piece, (see Photograph 8) weighing over 100 pounds in its frame, hanging on the wall (our mistake), covered only by a drop cloth. One of the workers managed to put the corner of a ladder into the painting, almost puncturing the canvas. After reviving Gael from her fainting spell, we called a source who represents the artist and we were told to use a cloth and warm water behind the canvas. Miraculously the mark disappeared and now cannot be seen by any human eye, except Gael's.

Lesson learned: what could happen will!

- Use wax with carnauba (vegetable in origin), paraffin, or beeswax. Never use furniture polish with silicone! If you can buff to a shine you do not need to reapply wax.

- When cleaning ceramics, line the sink with soft cloth to avoid scratching.

- Be careful of "organic" and "citrus" cleaners. Some are as corrosive and staining as chemical cleaners and can cause permanent damage to a piece.

> ## Lessons to Live By: Take Extra Care!
>
> It's important to remember that loss to an artwork caused by deterioration is generally not covered by the insurance policy, so collectors are advised to work with experts to preserve their fine arts and collectibles.

187

- When moving a valuable or fragile piece, always use an experienced mover who will custom crate as necessary.

- When moving a piece, take the time to check for areas where finish or paint is chipping or worn away.

- Wear cotton gloves with polyester nodules that will improve your grip.

- Place items with fragile finishes in plastic bags before moving to save pieces that might fall off.

- Do not airtight seal with plastic wrap and do not store a long time in plastic.

Environmental Issues[39]

- Light is one of the most dangerous elements to which you can expose fine arts. Regardless of what the piece is made of, the UV rays in light will eventually break down all organic materials.

- You can filter sunlight with UV filters on the windows, in window shades, on framing glass, and on light fixtures themselves.

- Ideal lighting is most often incandescent, but can vary with different materials and finishes.

- Test artificial light to see if it is warm near the piece being illuminated. If you feel warmth, the light is doing damage to the work.

- Most importantly, avoid drastic fluctuations in temperature and humidity. Be careful of hanging paintings on exterior walls.[40]

Display of the Collection

Like most collectors, Gael and I love being able to share our collection with the friends and fellow collectors we invite into our home. When a piece of ours is off being cleaned or loaned, we put a photo of it in its place. But displaying a collection is fraught with risk. Sunlight can make those priceless pastels fade, or a spilt cocktail can ruin the upholstery on the Queen Anne loveseat. Even the most careful of collectors can have an accident—recall Steve Wynn's misplaced elbow when showing his Picasso to Barbara Walters and friends, which caused the cancellation of the $139 million sale of the painting in October 2006.[41]

The need to protect your collection must be balanced against displaying it in such a way that you can appreciate it. Our collections are like our children—we want to enjoy them and integrate them into our lives

It's a Family Affair: "Will the Thrill"

Right around the time Steve Wynn's elbow punctured a two-inch hole in his Picasso, "Hurricane Will" came through our house.

My daughter, Leslie, my first-born and the apple of my eye, and her wonderful husband, Chris, have expanded our family by three terrific grandsons and one beautiful granddaughter. We enjoy their visits immensely, and when the youngest, William, a.k.a. "Will the Thrill," learned how to walk—I mean, run—their visits got even more exciting.

One day as Leslie's family arrived, during the initial hugging and kissing in the kitchen, Gael said, "Where's Will?!" At this moment our valuable floor-to-ceiling lunch box collection had descended to the floor, blazing Will the Thrill's trail. We followed his path and found parts of our historic, irreplaceable, and virtually priceless Woodbridge figures knocked on the floor as if they were bowling pins. But, still no Will. We found him upstairs tossing Gael's exceptional collection of antique handbags into the air as if they were footballs.

Twenty minutes later, my daughter, her husband, and the three boys were checked into the Westchester Marriott Hotel. We had no choice. Part of our responsibility as collectors is to educate the little people in our lives about how to handle and behave around fine things. Will did not know that the Woodbridge figures were any different than all the toy figures he plays with at his house. Just as collectors learn connoisseurship,

189

children have to be taught to understand quality and how to respect fine objects. Otherwise, when they grow up they will behave like the Milwaukee crowd at the Martinifest! (See below.)

The lesson for fellow collectors who feel that insurance is too high-priced and not needed: damage to a collection can come in all sizes and shapes. Not only can it come from hurricanes, floods, theft, and delivery people, but also in the smallest and cutest way possible, in the form of everyone's own version of "Will the Thrill."

and not hide them away in warehouses, attics, or locked rooms in some overprotective shelter, but we also need to protect the beautiful things we have acquired and make sure they survive for the next generation of collectors. After all, we are only the temporary caretakers of the incredible things we own. But, since certain types of artwork are fragile and are not meant for regular viewing, and a collection on display does face increased risks, we have the additional responsibility to take steps to minimize some of those risks.

There are also some specific devices that you can purchase to make your home a safer place for your collection. These include smoke and CO_2 detectors, moisture/humidity detectors, and a sprinkler system. The detectors should be placed in the immediate area of the collection—smoke detectors within 100 feet of the collection and humidity detectors wired to set off the sump pump if needed. When installing the sprinkler system, due to the damage it can cause if it goes off accidentally, it's important to avoid placing valuable pieces in the direct path of the sprinkler heads. With the exception of a sprinkler system, most of these items are pretty inexpensive and should be in your home already.

Loss Prevention and Loss Control–Who Should Know about the Collection, and How to Manage High-Risk Visitors

Many collectors love to talk about their collection and open their home to visitors and sometimes journalists. Unfortunately, this generosity can increase the risk of art theft, which today is a $6 billion business and the second largest crime in the world, exceeded only by drug and gun trafficking.[42] While most collectors do not have the type of collections that will attract professional art thieves, access to their homes under the pretense of seeing the collection makes it easier for a criminal to learn the layout for a burglary. The collector is assumed to be wealthy and the criminal will be more interested in jewelry and silver than in the artwork. Particularly valuable artworks that might catch the attention of an art thief should be purchased anonymously at auction and should be lent from "a private collector."

All collectors should have background checks run on prospective household or family office employees. Some insurance companies are now offering this as a service for their clients. For large house parties, use an established catering company and inquire about their hiring procedures. It is not unreasonable to demand only senior employees with ten-

---

Lessons to Live By: Bragging Rights Can Lead to Difficulty

One of the most important things you can do to prevent theft is be mindful of what you say about your art to others, especially people you do not know well. Don't discuss the value of the art. Refer to it as "special," as having sentimental value, or having a great deal of importance to you but perhaps not having much market value. Bragging about the value of your collection can really get you in trouble.

191

ure of over a year and a clean background check be brought into your home.

Theft Prevention

Beyond these precautions, serious collectors should consider a theft deterrent like security alarms, surveillance systems, and safes. While no single one of these things will prevent theft from occurring in your home, the combination of them can help to minimize the loss and maximize your peace of mind.

Electronic security systems and surveillance systems are becoming increasingly sophisticated and the technology behind the devices is dropping in cost, making home security for the collector both appealing and economical. In an ideal setup, any movement of the art will be monitored through both wireless and wired sensors, exactly like the devices used in a museum. Some collectors even use exterior cameras with digital recording.

When choosing which alarm system is right for your home and collection, make sure that it includes window and door alarms, motion detectors, and wireless monitoring to send a signal to the alarm monitoring center if the wires to the main alarm are cut. You'll also need to decide if you want your alarm to be audible or silent. Audible alarms put the thief on notice that the alarm has been triggered and may prompt the thief to leave immediately. The silent alarm can aid in capture because the thief may not realize the alarm has been triggered. The downside is that an unsuspecting family member could be put in danger because he or she walks in on a robbery in progress or is at home and unaware that someone has entered the house.

And finally, should a thief break in, safes become the final protection for your valuables. Safes can come in many sizes, and entire rooms can even be retrofitted as vaults for those collectors who prefer to keep a large number of items at their home in a secure area. This way, even if the thief gets in, it's less likely that he or she will be able to take anything out.

Emergencies and Disasters

At the risk of sounding pessimistic, it makes more sense in today's world to speak in terms of "when," not "if" something will happen to endanger your collection. Hurricane Katrina showed us that even major cities are not immune to damage caused by large-scale storms, and Sept. 11 saw the previously unimaginable destruction of not only an incredible amount of human lives, but also of priceless works of art, including several Louise Nevelson pieces.

193

Here are some emergency preparedness procedures for the collection:

The Headlines Speak for Themselves: What If …

When New York Yankees pitcher Cory Lidle had his tragic flying accident in October 2006, I could not help but think of a "what if" scenario. Years before I had visited the home of some prospective clients who resided in the building Cory hit —right around the floor where he made impact. These collectors had millions of dollars of uninsured and uninventoried art. When I asked the couple what was to become of their collection, they gave each other a knowing glance and told me that some of the pieces were "earmarked" for their children. During the course of my visit with them I stressed the importance of art succession planning. They informed me that they would think about all I had said and would contact me. I never heard from them again.

When Cory's plane hit this building, I thought to myself—what if the apartment he crashed into was this same couple's? All the art in that apartment would be gone. It represented a significant percentage of this couple's net worth. This couple's approach to transferring their collection to their children was the moment when I first came to understand the "empty hook," as I have now labeled it (see Chapter 9), approach to art succession planning. The number of collectors I run into who are "going bare" (self-insuring) and not insuring their art assets is staggering. The number of those who have failed to implement a planning strategy for their art is even more shocking.

- Make sure that your insurance agency subscribes to the Art Loss Register (www.artloss.com), an international database that helps track stolen art in the event it is resold. This increases the chances of recovery and will also strengthen your claim should the item be sold to a good-faith purchaser.

- Hire a professional conservation expert to do a disaster-preparedness survey. This survey will include not only a general inventory of the collection but also an analysis of the structures that house it, the security features currently in place, and the necessary steps to ensure proper emergency response should a disaster occur. It will also establish the safest areas where artworks are least likely to be damaged by wind and water.

• Establish a standing arrangement with a nearby art storage facility to pick up and care for your works in the event of a natural disaster warning. Keep a supply of cardboard and packing material on hand to ensure items are properly wrapped during transport and storage.[43]

The Assurance of Insurance

It is almost axiomatic that the individual who is thrilled and impassioned by the hunt of collecting is not someone who readily embraces the comparatively humdrum task of protecting what he or she has acquired. And now, as insurance rates are skyrocketing, even diligent collectors are finding more reasons to avoid this supremely important component of collection management. During these times of increased risk due to hurricanes, terrorism, earthquakes, brush fires, and other external events, it is imperative for collectors to realize what they have at risk and the consequences of failing to act.

Accurate inventory and appraisal, appropriate conservation, and effective loss prevention are all important elements of protecting a collection and making for better "investment" results into the future. But, if and when disaster strikes, the only thing that will give you financial relief is insurance. Bringing in a qualified insurance broker as a member of your advisory team is a crucial decision that should be made as soon as a collection becomes established. Insurance protection for valuable collections would seem an obvious requirement, but many collectors have either no fine

Lessons to Live By: You Don't Have to Be a "Collector" to Be a Collector

A colleague introduced me to a wonderful elderly couple after I spoke at a presentation on how art holdings can result in charitable donations to non-art related charities. I was invited to their home, which was filled with beautiful blue and white Dutch Delft pottery, and said it was a pleasure to meet fellow collectors. I was met with a pleasant but gruff, "You're in the wrong house, sonny! We are not collectors!" I replied, "Then someone must have snuck into your home last night and placed all these beautiful objects here."

Here is a case of a couple that "accumulated" this marvelous collection over their 50-some-odd years of marriage. Since they didn't consider themselves collectors, their collection had never been inventoried, insured, authenticated, or appraised. Working with their advisors, we assembled a team to accomplish all of the above. The Dutch Delft objects were worth well in excess of $1 million. Upon passing this information onto the couple, I was met with my second pleasant but gruff response, "Is that all? We thought it would be worth much more!" Now that they know what they have and its true value, we are beginning to develop philanthropic plans to allow their best pieces to remain in public view and the remainder of the collection to help the many charitable organizations they personally support.

art coverage or a collection that is significantly underinsured. Why does this happen?

Often, the collector started with a few relatively insignificant pieces and then got caught up in the excitement of collecting. Before long he had amassed a valuable collection that he had still not insured. Or, a collector has collected for years and may have been good about gathering information in the beginning, but has let that part drop off—the appraisals have not been updated, she has failed to tell her insurance agent about her new acquisitions, and the agent has never bothered to ask. The good news is that it isn't difficult to insure a collection. It takes an appropriate insurer and a diligent broker who is willing to take the time to make sure the documentation is in order.

How Is Art Insured?

Insurance companies offer several different ways for insuring valuable pieces in your collection, and even the collection as a whole.

These methods include:

- Insuring the pieces in your collection as part of the contents of your home.

- Insuring the pieces in your collection as "scheduled items."

- Insuring your collection through blanket coverage.

The Advisor's FYI: Asking the Right Questions

It's not uncommon for your client to not know what's valuable and what isn't, particularly if he or she recently inherited the property in question. That's why it's important for the advisor to go beyond the question, "Do you have any valuable collectibles or fine art?" When the client responds negatively, the advisor will want to follow up with, "Do you have any items in your home that you have had appraised or you feel we should maybe have appraised?" The advisor should maintain a list of reputable art, antiques, and collectible appraisers (see Chapter 8 for pointers on this) that can be called in to assess a collection when there is uncertainty as to value, title, provenance, or authenticity.

198

Lessons Learned: Change in Value Coverage

One of the most dramatic examples of change in value that I've encountered happened when a single drop of water ruined a piece of contemporary art. The collector suspected that the damaged happened when a drink splashed as someone added an ice cube to his carbonated beverage at a party. Fortunately, the collector's insurance company covered change in value. Otherwise, the insurance company would have asked for a repair and the work would have been returned to the collector, although with a drastically reduced value.

Insuring the pieces as contents. When pieces in a collection are insured as contents of the home, their coverage is included within the "contents" section of the collector's homeowner's insurance policy. This means that items are not individually listed—or scheduled—but are treated like other valuables in the home. On the plus side, this is usually the least expensive and simplest option. However, this method provides the narrowest coverage. Depending on the insurer, claims on fine arts and antiques may be settled at actual cash value or "functional value," which means that the insurer will not provide replacement cost coverage even if the policy is a replacement cost policy. In other words, a 17th century antique map will be settled at the price of a newly-made reproduction. Also, because many perils, including flood and earthquake damage, are excluded from virtually every standard homeowner's insurance policy, this ostensibly helpful coverage option is usually of no use in the event of natural catastrophes.

Insuring the pieces as "scheduled items." A fine arts schedule, like a personal articles floater on a homeowner's policy, offers broader protection for the collector. For starters, scheduled items are covered in the event of flooding, earthquakes, and wind damage—although some states may charge an additional cost for this coverage. Also, many of these plans include coverage for losses due to temperature change.

And, in the event of a loss, there's no deductible that needs to be met.

However, scheduled items require a bit more work from the collector. Each item scheduled will need to be appraised and listed separately, a cost in time that will be worth it for the more valuable pieces in the collection. When you schedule items in your collection, it may be worth getting your additional coverage from an insurer that specializes in fine arts rather than the same company that provides your homeowner's policy.

Insurance companies that specialize in the fine arts market generally offer a broader spectrum of coverage for scheduled pieces that includes automatic coverage for 90 days for newly acquired items. This is especially helpful when clients make new purchases; it gives them some time to contact the insurance agent to schedule their new acquisition. These specialty insurers also offer three other different forms of coverage, not found elsewhere:

> ## The Advisor's FYI: Insurance Considerations When Buying a New Piece from a Dealer
>
> The dealer is responsible for the artwork until it is delivered. If the collectors are responsible for shipping the new purchase, they should use a specialized art shipper. The collectors should notify the insurer in advance and request that the new acquisition be added to the schedule and provide the insurer with the shipping details. If the collectors have concerns about art purchased but not yet delivered, they can ask the dealer to provide evidence of insurance on the item.

199

Change in value, resulting from a partial loss. Often an item can be repaired, but the value of the work might be significantly reduced because of the damage. Sometimes even the best conservation cannot erase the damage. Contemporary art, especially, is considered to have lost much of its integrity with any damage. "Change in value" covers any decrease in value as a result of damage, and for particularly valuable pieces, it's important coverage to have in place.

Replacement cost protection, or Market Value Protection. This means if the market value of the items has appreciated, the insurance company will pay up to 150% of the agreed value of the item. Not all fine arts appreciate at the same rate. Just like the stock market, there are certain categories of fine arts that are "hot," and others that are not. It's easy to see how the value of a piece of art might appreciate 50% or more in a year, but it's very difficult to constantly monitor the market and maintain updated appraisals. The 150% Market Value Protection eases the insurance burden for the client who owns rapidly appreciating works.

This protection is also helpful in the case of a total loss, when a client might prefer to replace the lost work with something else. Since art and antiques are often one-of-a-kind, it's impossible to purchase an exact replica. Market Value Protection affords the insured the luxury of being able to purchase something similar to the item that was destroyed.

Blanket coverage. An alternative to scheduling each item is to obtain blanket coverage, which means the items are not listed separately. If clients frequently buy and sell items or have a collection with many items of relatively low value (such as wine, stamps, collectibles, or china), they may find it difficult and tedious to schedule each item. This option allows them to determine the maximum amount of coverage they will need and make this the blanket limit. The insured has a greater burden of proof, however, because the values are not agreed upon in advance.

Good documentation is needed to support a claim. Annual renewal reporting to the insurer will facilitate the claims process because the insurer can review the values and request updated valuations or appraisals for items that appear undervalued. Renewal reporting requires discipline on the part of the collector, because the inventory must be updated and the values made current. For significant collections, it is recommended that a curator or cataloger be engaged to maintain a collection database.

The Headlines Speak for Themselves: The Milwaukee Martinifest

Museums occasionally rent out their space for private parties as a way to raise revenue and increase the visibility of the museum in the community. Generally, these events are attended by sophisticated people who respect the surroundings and food and drink are kept away from the exhibition space. Sometimes, however, things do not go as planned.

In early 2006, the Milwaukee Art Museum provided the venue for the $30 all-you-can-drink Martinifest. Almost 1,900 people showed up (the museum claimed they were expecting capacity to be limited to 1,400). The crowd was young and the martinis flowed. Witnesses told stories of people throwing up next to priceless works of art and resting their drinks on sculptures. According to one account, a group of guys climbed on Gaston Lachaise's Standing Woman, groping her breasts and taking pictures with a cell phone![44]

Fortunately for the museum, this incident, fraught with the potential for physical damage, actually saw very little. Acidic drinks took off some of the patina on two bronze sculptures, but that was about it.[45] The lesson here: check out the museum's event policies before you loan a piece.

"Forget the artwork. Who made the martinis?!"

When Lending Art Outside Your Home

If you are loaning the collection to be displayed in a location other than your home, there are two things that you need to be aware of. First, if a museum wants to borrow a piece from your collection for an exhibition, they should arrange and pay for an insurance policy covering the art during shipping and for the entire duration of exhibition. (Even though they are providing this coverage, it is most important that you keep your individual coverage in place.) The museum's insurance company may ask the collector to sign a waiver of subrogation. Subrogation is the right of the insurance company, having paid its policyholder for a loss, to assume the rights of the policyholder and to try to recover some of its money from any other party that may be liable. It's highly recommended that collectors decline to sign this waiver.

It is not uncommon for pieces to be damaged while on loan, and the collector's insurance policy often responds more favorably than the museum's commercial coverage. By retaining the right to subrogate, the collector is likely to receive better claims settlement options, and his or her insurer can then subrogate against them if the institution has been negligent. Also, if you plan on regularly lending your collection, it can be effective for your lawyer to create your own loan form for museums, which will include things like subrogation and even terrorism insurance.

The second thing you need to be aware of is shipping. Shipping fine art items demands special skills, especially when it comes to valuable pieces, which should only be handled by a qualified art shipper. A fine art shipper will have skilled personnel who will provide a condition report before and after the shipping, have climate controlled vans to move the artwork, and specially trained packers who custom-make crates to house the artwork during the move. Extremely high-value artworks may require a professional security guard to accompany the art throughout its journey.

If you are wondering just how important it really is to use a qualified art shipper, take note of one collector who sent a significant painting through a commercial freight shipping company. The painting was appro-

203

priately crated but, while picking up the crate to move it, the shipper's workman drove a forklift right through the canvas! Needless to say, the results were devastating. Unfortunately, the painting was not insured on a fine arts schedule. It was covered under the "contents" portion of the homeowner's policy, which covered the repairs but not the substantial loss in value on the work itself. The shipper's insurance only provided the standard cargo insurance of a few dollars per pound, clearly not enough to compensate the owner for the loss.

Lessons to Live By: Who to Call Should Movers Turn a Mermaid into Guppies

Since Gael and I believe in sharing our collection, we promptly said "yes" when asked to lend our "truly monumental" Mermaid (as Gerry Wertkin, the then-director of the Museum of American Folk Art called it) for a retrospective of William Edmondson's work touring five cities over a two-year period. At the time, our insurance agent was a friend who provided us with a policy from a company that did not specialize in fine art coverage. The Cheekwood Museum in Tennessee, Edmondson's hometown, asked us if it would be okay to insure the Mermaid for $750,000 while it was traveling. I said "yes" and then mentioned it to my agent, who advised us to drop our coverage on the piece since the museum would be paying for it for the next two years. This sounded like good financial advice.

When the movers arrived to take the piece from our home, I was on the putting green, across the street from our house (the benefit of living in a golf community). Gael came running out of the house screaming for me to come right away. When I arrived, I saw that the movers had wrapped our priceless, irreplaceable Mermaid (see Photograph 3) in a *towel* and were carrying it to their truck! I told the movers to immediately return the piece to the house and instructed them to have a crate built, which was to be approved by me, Gael, and Fred, and only then would we allow the Mermaid to travel around the country. I do not know which policy—the museum's insurance, my discontinued insurance, or the shipper's insurance on the item—would have been responsible if (God forbid) the movers had stumbled and turned my monumental Mermaid into a school of guppies. These are important questions that I had not thought to ask my insurance agent.

The moral of this story is that you need a professional insurance advisor who works with art and can coordinate your personal insurance with the shipper's and museum's insurances to at least alleviate the financial part of a disaster happening to one of your prized "Oh My God" pieces.

One Collector's View:
Norma Roth–
The Perils of Off-Site Storage–
A Rainy Day Story

When you have a sizable collection and need to store some items outside your home, there are challenges related to the condition of the property where your pieces are stored. Here is a horror story about what can happen when you least expect it. Norma and her husband Bill are Top 100 Collectors (as designated by Art & Antiques *magazine) and have a large collection of beautiful art objects, ranging through many forms and styles, which they have been assembling for the past 25 years. They store part of their massive collection in a 5,000-square foot building affectionately called the "studio"—a facility that has served them well for many years. But one small leak that appeared one day while the studio's roof was being pressure-cleaned led Norma and Bill down a nerve-wracking path and jeopardized many items in their world-class collection!*

After discovering water dripping down one wall of the studio, we quickly hired a roofer with a very good reputation. Before work began, I took him on a tour of the studio in order to impress upon him the nature of the items stored inside the building: textiles, beadwork, ethnographic objects with delicate feather work, piles of Oriental rugs, stacks of paintings, areas filled with antique furniture piled to the ceiling, and shelves with ceramics and glass. After assuring me that he had plenty of insurance coverage, the roofer agreed to install a new state-of-the-art roof.

There was a complication. The roofer needed a full week for the project, and the weather was not cooperating. It was a complex roof to install, and it would additionally entail moving both air conditioning units from the roof, at different times, with the assistance of HVAC professionals, so the humidity control and air temperature would never be at risk. Due to the unusually active rainy season that year, we agreed to wait two months before starting the project. A week of sunshine was needed. So in the meantime, the leak was patched and items were moved away from the problem areas and Bill and I waited anxiously for work to begin.

Then a new problem presented itself. A sample of the roof was taken and revealed that several earlier roof jobs had been layered, one upon the other, throughout the years without stripping off the old ones. In order for the state-of-the-art roof to be installed, all the old layers had to be removed, at an additional charge. So the roofing crews began work in earnest, bright and early the following Monday. The project was finally underway.

Each day presented a new challenge. Between the constant noise and the falling particles of debris loosened by the roofers' hammers, both Bill and I were on edge. We were constantly shifting pieces from one place to another, wrapping them in protective material and trying desperately to keep our precious things out of harm's way.

After working all week, the roofers weren't able to finish the job by the end of the day on Friday. They assured us that the roof was fully secure for the weekend, and would be fine until they were able to finish the last 20 feet on Monday. With a clear weather forecast for the weekend, everyone was confident that the job would be completed without a hitch.

That hope was dashed on Saturday morning. A typical Florida downpour—fast, loud, furious, without warning, and out of nowhere—descended. Because of the intensity of the storm, we decided to do a quick check of the studio, just in case. What we found was nothing short of a disaster. The front room, which held many of our best Chinese textiles and robes (because the room had a drywall ceiling) had water running down our magnificent Stueben chandelier as though from an open faucet. Bill threw all the textiles that were under the fixture into a pile on one side of the room and ran to get buckets and plastic containers, which he placed everywhere water was dripping. Had he not moved so quickly, everything would have been a total loss. Instead, only one Chinese embroidery was totally ruined, and three others suffered damage. Several fine American pieces were severely stained by the brackish water. These were eventually cleaned but their original pristine condition was ruined.

Bill and I moved from the front room to the back room, thinking things were under control. I glanced at the outside wall. This wall had been covered in beautiful patterned Chinese wallpaper, but now had a peculiar watery sheen across its entire surface. And the black carpet squished as I hurried across it to a platform filled with priceless headdresses. As I tried to grab objects off the platform, I realized there was nowhere to move anything. There were objects everywhere. There was not an inch of space without a piece of art already in it. African art, kimonos, paintings, headdresses, textiles; on the floor, on the tables, in boxes, everywhere! Finally, the roofer arrived to check things out. Oh my goodness! They'd made a mistake. "The boys forgot to cover the edge of the roof so the open blocks are exposed along the roof's border." Therefore, when it rained, the water poured down to the foundation through the wall, creating the perfect nightmare.

209

With the exposed areas covered, and the rain over, the water eventually stopped seeping into the building. For hours, Bill used a large wet/dry vacuum while I moved objects and dried things that had been splattered. What had been an organized confusion of objects was now total chaos. An area of approximately 50 feet had been affected by the moisture. Even though the long-term damage to the objects was minimal, the studio looked like it had been hit by an explosion.

The roofer came a few days later to ask for payment. He seemed surprised when I asked him for his insurance information in return. Since he had done work for us satisfactorily in the past and he complained about outstanding expenses related to the job, I gave him a partial payment, telling him that full payment would come after the cleanup costs had been assessed. But we had one more huge surprise in store—the roofer's insurance only covered residential jobs. Since our studio was a commercial building, it wasn't covered by the roofer's policy. Needless to say, the roofer did not receive the rest of the payment and negotiations ensued.

Bill and I are still struggling with the cleanup more than two years later. We have learned about the value of insurance in all facets of our collection—not only for the pieces themselves, but for anything that involves or affects (or has the potential to affect) the pieces of our collection.

Appraisal and Valuation

With Contributions From Charles Rossoff, ASA, and Aleza F. Tadri

"Your motivation ... must always be to please yourself. Follow your intuition and buy what sings to you. The objects you acquire should give you pleasure and fellowship."

–Richard Faletti,
Tribal Arts Autumn 1997

For many individuals, art collecting is much more than a simple hobby—it is both a passion and a serious financial investment. However, oftentimes the pleasure of acquiring new works and the enjoyment of the collection takes precedence over more pragmatic concerns such as insurance and estate planning. Luckily, art advisors, lawyers, and appraisers can help you navigate the intricacies and nuances of the art world.

At first, the art market can seem complicated and daunting. There are retail art dealers, secondary market art sellers, auction houses, appraisers, art advisors, decorators, collectors, and art consultants, all of whom impact the market differently. What can be a hot commodity one day can almost overnight become undesirable. Conversely, an unknown artist whose piece was purchased for a few hundred dollars can become the art world's next superstar, exponentially increasing the value of the art object. Part of the excitement of collecting art, antiques, and collectibles is searching for the new great investment, the next Picasso, and training one's eye to discern the ordinary from the extraordinary.

The art market, like the stock market, is a place to invest money for both short term and long term returns. For instance, sales records for contemporary art keep being broken at each subsequent Contemporary Art auction at Christie's and Sotheby's. Considering that some of the pieces being sold are less than 10 years old, you can have an amazing rate of return on what can be a recent, low cost investment. On the other hand, some art investments, like fine wine, take years to reach full maturity. Patience can be a virtue in deciding to buy and sell art in today's art world.

Knowing the value of your collection can help you in many ways. It will help you make informed decisions on whether to buy or sell a piece of art. You can see how purchasing new works can increase the prestige and value of your current collection. You can ensure that your family will enjoy the artwork for generations to come. And, finally, you can learn when to acquire a piece simply for the joy it will bring you.

A professional appraisal provides a description of the properties and an objective assessment of their values at a specific point in time. The appraiser analyzes both historical and market related information in order to create a document that you can rely upon. Building a relationship with your art advisor and appraiser will allow you access to areas of the art world unavailable to the general population. You can play an active role in this process by providing information to these professionals, and by consulting with them before buying and selling art in order to maximize your investments and profits.

213

Important Value Characteristics

The professional appraiser's most valuable service is his or her ability to identify value characteristics through detailed knowledge of connoisseurship, materials and methods, construction, the effects of age, condition, and art history. Through research, appraisers select comparable properties in the appropriate market that become the basis for their value conclusions. It is necessary for the appraiser to not only catalog the object according to the Getty ID, but also to determine which characteristics of the property have the greatest effect on the item's value. While each property is unique, the following information should be included for each item being appraised:

214

Descriptive information: This includes (but is not limited to) the maker/artist, title, year, medium, dimensions, markings, signatures, stamps, inscriptions, and a short narrative description of the property.

Provenance: This is the ownership history of the item. This can have an extreme positive or an extreme negative impact on the valuation of the property. For instance, Jacqueline Bouvier Kennedy Onassis' faux pearls estimated at $500 to $700 sold at Sotheby's on April 25, 1996 for $211,500. This price far exceeded any other sale of costume pearls sold at auction solely due to its association with the former first lady. On the flip side, collectors must be wary of purchasing items without a history of ownership, as this lack of provenance could be a result of theft, fakes, and forgeries. It is also more difficult to resell a piece without a documented provenance for the same reasons. The International Foundation for Art Research (IFAR) and the Art Loss Register regularly publish stolen art updates, and the Art Loss Register maintains a listing of stolen art available to the general public.

Authenticity: Appraisers are not authenticators; however, they can assist you in the process of authentication. If the authenticity of an item is in question, for example, as a result of lack of provenance, this can affect the value of the item. In this scenario, the appraiser can direct you towards the appropriate experts before continuing the valuation process.

Condition: While appraisers are not conservators or restorers, they are trained to recognize condition problems as negative value characteristics. If a detailed condition report or proposal on how to restore the item is necessary, an appraiser can assist you in finding the specialist conservator/restorer for your property.

Lessons to Live By:
How Authentication Affects Value

Authentication is a separate process done by museum curators, academics, conservators, artists' estates and foundations, and other specialists who are both qualified and accepted within the art community as having the expertise and authority necessary to issue a certificate of authenticity. The authentication process can be both time consuming and challenging.

Appraisers do, however, sometimes need to consider authentication issues. Here's a story that demonstrates how appraisers can help collectors determine what they have:

An appraiser was asked to submit an appraisal of the fair market value of an Old Master painting that was assumed to be worth several million dollars. The painting was part of an estate that was embroiled in a grossly expensive multi-state lawsuit and was considered to be the principal asset. The appraiser first examined the painting from photographs, and then the painting was made available for inspection at a storage facility. The appraiser found the painting suspicious—it did not stylistically match authenticated works by the Old Master. The appraiser decided that the best way to proceed was to consult with an art historian who specialized in the time period and to send the painting for conservation examination. The consensus reached by the expert specialists was that the painting was a later copy done in the style of the Old Master, but was not in fact a work by the Master himself.

The correct attribution drastically reduced the value of the painting. The litigation was no longer over a multimillion dollar estate, but over an estate worth only a few thousand dollars. Had the painting been appraised before the litigation began, perhaps this correct identification of the painting would have served to better distribute the assets of the estate to the heirs and avoid the expense of litigation entirely.

What Is the Intended Use of the Appraisal?

The first question to answer in the appraisal process is also the most straightforward: why do you need the appraisal? The answer to this question determines the scope of work of the appraiser, the intended users of the report, and the type of value conclusions placed on the objects. For instance, if you need an insurance appraisal, the appraiser will value your collection differently than if you need an estate planning appraisal. Establishing the intended use of the appraisal from the outset will allow the appraiser to complete the appraisal accurately and correctly to best meet your needs.

Who Is a Qualified Appraiser?

The IRS requires all appraisals to be written by "qualified appraisers." In 2006 the IRS defined a qualified appraiser as:

> "an individual who (I) has earned an appraisal designation from a recognized professional appraiser organization or has otherwise met minimum education and experience requirements set forth in regulations prescribed by the Secretary, (II) regularly performs appraisals for which the individual receives compensation, and (III) meets such other requirements as may be prescribed by the Secretary in regulations or other guidance."[46]

This newly revised definition stresses the importance of having an accredited appraiser prepare all your documents for IRS review. Should there be an audit, having your appraisal prepared by a qualified appraiser will lend credence to the determinations of value. While a qualified and an unqualified appraiser may arrive at the same value conclusions, as the taxpayer, you should avoid giving the IRS any reason to question the validity of your tax return, and should strive to hire a qualified appraiser with the required designations.

Most collectors will work primarily with personal property appraisers. Personal property is defined in *Uniform Standards of Professional Appraisal Practice* (USPAP), the recognized standard for appraisal practice, as "identifiable tangible objects that are considered by the general public as being 'personal' and that are not 'classified as real estate'."[47] This includes paintings, prints, books, cars, residential contents, computers, and farm equipment—basically any object one can touch that is not land or architecture. However, a collector may also need the services of other disciplines in specific situations. For example, if an artist were to donate the intellectual property and copyright along with a painting, this would require a fine art appraiser for the tangible property (the painting) as well as a business valuation appraiser for the intangible property (the intellectual property).

It is important to note that due to the breadth of property included under the heading "personal property," personal property appraisers are often divided into classes, such as machinery and equipment, fine art, decorative arts, antiques, collectibles and memorabilia, gems and jewelry, etc. In certain cases, such as fine art, these classes are further categorized into subclasses such as Western art, Asian art, ancient art, African art, etc. It is necessary to find an appraiser with expertise relevant to your collection. If you have a large Japanese print collection, you must find a specialist in Asian art as an appraiser who works only in European and American art would not be qualified to catalog and value your collection. An appraiser who is highly qualified to appraise one collection therefore might not meet the criteria of a qualified appraiser for another collection.

Appraisal Organizations

The three largest appraisal organizations in the United States are the American Society of Appraisers, the Appraisers Association of America, and the International Society of Appraisers. The American Society of Appraisers is the oldest of the three organizations, founded in 1936, and is the only major appraisal organization representing all of the disciplines of appraisal specialists. Its members are regularly tested in both subject specialty exams and valuation science, are required to adhere to the American Society of Appraisers Code of Ethics, and must adhere to USPAP. Additionally, to maintain membership status, there is a mandatory continuing education requirement. The Appraisers Association of America was founded in 1949 and is comprised of personal property appraisers of fine and decorative arts, jewelry, and household contents. The International Society of Appraisers, founded in 1979, is also specific to personal property appraisers. All three societies provide referrals of members by location, discipline, and specialization.[48]

The Role of the Appraiser

When selecting an appraiser, it is important to understand that appraisers are not advocates; an appraiser is not allowed to ignore valuation science and research because a collector wants a bigger tax break. An appraisal can have long lasting monetary, legal, and emotional repercussions, and because of this the collector will want to carefully discuss his or her expectations and insist on compliance with appropriate ethical standards during the scope of the engagement. The most important ethical requirement is that the appraiser may not have a vested interest in the properties being appraised.[49]

An appraiser is not allowed to be paid a percentage of the value of the item or base his or her fee on the outcome of an appraisal valuation. This type of situation could influence the appraiser's conclusions, as it is in the appraiser's best interest to place high values on the properties being evaluated. Appraisers also have an obligation to state all relevant facts that influence value. For example, if you own a painting from the School of Rembrandt, the appraiser is not allowed to identify the painting as a "Rembrandt" as this is misleading to the intended users of the appraisal. Another example would be the non-disclosure of restoration and conservation work, which can be either a positive or negative value characteristic depending on the situation. The ethical requirements

Lessons to Live By: An Appraiser by Any Other Name

Aside from appraisers, there are many other professionals who state opinions of value. Many people go to the auction houses for appraisals or back to the dealer who sold them the art in the first place. However, obtaining an appraisal from someone other than a qualified appraiser is risky. These third parties often have a self-serving interest in a particular valuation outcome. A dealer representing an artist may try to inflate the value of a piece to enhance the status of the artist. Auction houses are trying to persuade you to consign your property for sale, so they also tend to place the highest value possible on a piece. Many dealers are not qualified to write fair market value appraisals for donations, as they work primarily in the retail market, which may not be the most appropriate or common market for a particular piece. Only professional appraisers who adhere to recognized standards can guarantee impartial valuations without any vested interest in the property.

in USPAP or those found in the Code of Ethics of appraisal organizations protect both the appraiser and the collector.

How Does an Appraisal Work?

When conducting an appraisal, the appraiser must have knowledge not only of all markets relevant to the type of property in the collection (auction, retail, wholesale, etc.), but also how to access sales information and how to correctly apply the information to the appraisal issue at hand. Even the most straightforward appraisal has its own facts and circumstances, and it is only by applying the appropriate valuation methodology that the appraiser ensures that the value conclusions in the report are accurate. These methodologies boil down to three standard approaches to valuation:

221

The Income Approach: valuing an item based on research and analysis of the present worth of anticipated income.

The Cost Approach: valuing an item based on research and analysis of the cost of a substitute property with equivalent function and desirability, providing an estimate of the depreciated reproduction, reproduction new or replacement cost new of the property.

The Market Comparison Approach: valuing an item based on research and analysis comparing sales of property similar enough to the property being appraised to permit detailed comparison, estimating value by comparison with properties sold in the relevant market, with adjustments made for all differences which affect value, such as differences in characteristics of value and in time.[50]

When Do I Need an Appraisal?

Since we commonly think of appraisals as solely estimating the cash value of a piece or a collection, it is easy to forget the wide variety of situations when an appraisal is an important prerequisite to another objective.

These situations include:

- Purchasing insurance coverage.
- Making an insurance claim.
- Donating and gifting.
- Consigning an item for or bidding on an item at an auction sale.
- Making estate planning decisions.
- Acquiring a piece through a dealer, show, or trade with another collector.
- Equalizing and ensuring fair distribution to heirs.
- Obtaining a loan secured by the collection.

Appraisals For Insurance

Most homeowners' insurance policies cover general residential contents along with the real estate. However, while a policy may cover the replacement cost of the home, the personal property is only covered for its actual cash value, a fraction of the replacement cost. Additionally, many homeowners' insurance policies have exclusions for fine art, antiques, collectibles, silver, etc. For additional insurance, the collector has two options: to buy blanket coverage, which extends the limits of the policy but retains the same exclusions; or, to purchase a separate all risk floater policy either in place of the blanket coverage or in addition to the blanket coverage[51] (for more information about insurance coverages, see Chapter 7). When purchasing supplemental insurance on excluded property, most insurance companies require the property to be scheduled, which requires an insurance scheduling appraisal. This benefits the collector in two ways:

- There is a clear record of the item including cataloging, a photograph, and an agreed upon replacement value. In the case of loss, if there is a question of whether the piece was in your possession, the insurance appraisal can act as a record of ownership.

- The cost of insuring scheduled items is a fraction of that for blanket coverage.

Should you ever have to make a claim, a damage loss claim appraisal will be necessary. Whenever damage or loss occurs, appraisers are hired by the collector (the claimant), the insurance company, and/or the party responsible for the loss in order to value the damaged property prior to damage, after damage, and after treatment.

There are two main types of damage loss claims, those for scheduled items and those for unscheduled items. If the item has been scheduled on your policy, both you and the insurance provider have agreed to the value of that item beforehand. You have been paying premiums for the item based on this agreed upon value. At the time of loss, once the damages have been assessed, the insurance company will either pay for restoration or write you a check for the agreed upon value, assuming there are no other

223

extenuating circumstances. Receiving payment on claims for scheduled items often takes less time than for unscheduled property, as the appraisal and assessment of value have previously occurred.

If the damaged property is unscheduled, the first step is to determine the condition and value of the item before damage and how much of the loss of value was incurred due to the immediate incident and how much loss of value resulted from other conditions such as age or sun-bleaching. This is usually a much longer process, as it involves not only a determination of loss of value, but forensic appraisal work to determine the value of an item which may, in the worst-case scenario, no longer even exist. The settlement amount of the claim is determined by your insurance policy, so it is beneficial to insure items at the highest valuation level. Scheduling items is not a fool-proof way of ensuring quick payment on a claim without litigation, but it serves as an important step in proving your own consideration of the property as well as the condition and value of the item in its undamaged state.

The estimation of diminution of value due to damages and the resulting treatment is never a straightforward process. Different property types and collector classes forgive conservation and restoration work to varying degrees, sometimes, as in the case of modern prints, not at all. It requires extensive knowledge of multiple market levels, as the treatment will often change the appropriate market level for the valuation of the property. It also requires forensic appraisal skills in determining the condition and the value of the item before loss in order to assess the diminution of value caused only by the particular action being claimed. As a result, reliance upon accredited appraisers with experience in determining diminution of value is extremely important in damage loss claims. Retaining the services of a qualified and certified appraiser in damage/loss actions can result in the claimant receiving compensation he or she would not be awarded without the services of the accredited appraiser.

Appraisals for Donation, Gifting, and Estate Taxation

Whether you are dividing your estate, minimizing potential tax burdens, making a charitable contribution, or structuring layered PowerGifting™, your advisory team will need a professional appraisal during the planning process. For example, by IRS guidelines, any gifts you structure estimated at $5,000 or more require a qualified appraisal and Form 8283.[52] Furthermore, if the gift is valued at $20,000 or more you will need to attach a complete copy of the signed appraisal to your tax return.[53]

225

Take, for example, a donation of art, antiques, or collectibles valued over $20,000. In the event of a valuation dispute, the donation will be reviewed by the IRS Commissioner's Art Advisory Panel. This panel meets a handful of times a year to review submitted cases, reviewing 250 to 300 items at each meeting. The 2005 Art Advisory Panel consisted of twelve dealers, eight curators, and six IRS staff members. (There are no appraisers on the Committee due to the requirement that prohibits participants from appraising while they are serving.) According to the Summary of 2005 Panel Reviews issued by the Art Advisory Panel, in 2005:

- "There were 2,274 items with an aggregate tax-payer valuation of $217,981,879 on 105 taxpayer cases under consideration."
- "The claimed value of the average charitable contribution was $317,500 and the average estate and gift item was $95,579."
- "The Panel recommended total adjustments of $62,852,328 on the reviews now concluded for these meetings."
- "On the adjusted items, the Panel recommended adjustments amounting to an 86% reduction on the overvalued items in charitable contribution claims and a 56% increase on the undervalued items in estate and gift appraisals."[54]

Lessons to Live By:
The Benefit of Hiring an Experienced Professional Appraiser

An estate clearance company was asked to pack and clean an apartment in New York. The estate clearance company felt that some of the artwork in the apartment might be valuable, and recommended to the executor of the estate that he hire a professional art handler to crate the specified paintings. The executor decided that before hiring the art handler, he would have an appraiser come and perform a walk-through of the apartment, to decide whether the extra shipping and insuring expenses were necessary.

When the appraiser walked into the apartment, the executor informed him that he believed most of the residential contents were not valuable, but that the art might require additional insurance for the period it was in transit. The appraiser questioned why an estate tax appraisal had not been written. The executor replied that the estate fell beneath the federal requirement and there was only one heir. His tax attorney advised him that an estate tax appraisal was not necessary. The appraiser began walking around the apartment, checking to see if any antiques or artwork should be separately packed and insured. The executor and appraiser decided that a handful of paintings should be specially crated and insured, while the bulk of the contents could be handled by the estate clearance company.

The appraiser wrote a USPAP compliant appraisal with research, sales comparables, and photographs, and insurance was purchased accordingly. When the beneficiary received the artwork, one of the pieces was damaged, probably from having been dropped during handling. Since the appraiser was able to prove the condition of the painting before shipment and insurance had been purchased, the beneficiary was able to successfully submit a claim and receive money to purchase a new frame and conserve the painting back to its original state.

227

As there are monetary penalties for incorrect valuations of appraised items, it is important to choose an appraiser who meets the IRS requirements for a qualified appraiser who has the expertise necessary to properly evaluate the items you are submitting.

Appraisals of Estate Property

Professional appraisals of tangible personal property belonging to an estate enable individuals to derive the full benefits of estate planning without overpaying taxes, and can help prevent disputes from inequitable distributions. Estate litigation, either among heirs or against the IRS is costly, time-absorbing, and a hassle. The correct identification of the items in an estate both lessens the possibility of questioning the contents of the estate as well as quickens the resolution process should a problem arise.

There are three main types of estate appraisals— estate planning, estate taxation, and estate distribution; all are fair market value appraisals. As of a given date, regardless of the type of estate appraisal being written, there is one and only one fair market value for any given item. So, theoretically, if an appraiser was working on an estate planning appraisal on August 15, 2005 of a Dali print, it would have the same fair market value of another Dali print from the same edition in the same condition in an estate taxation appraisal with an effective date of August 15, 2005 or an estate distribution appraisal with an effective date of August 15, 2005. Incidentally, this fair market value would also be accurate for a donation appraisal of the same print with the same effective date of valuation.

Estate planning appraisals give individuals the opportunity to have control over the division of their estate with full knowledge of the fair market value of their property as of the effective date of the appraisal. These appraisals also enable individuals to place assets within trusts, partnerships, and other entities that serve to lessen the estate's tax burden. If you decide to rely upon an estate planning appraisal, it is important to keep the information up to date; you should regularly revisit the valuation of the items as well as update any items you may have bought or sold during the intervals between appraisals.

Estate taxation appraisals are required by both the federal and state governments. Each state has its own estate tax regulations. The federal government requires items with a fair market value of greater than $100 to be listed individually. Items with a fair market value of less than $100 can be grouped into lots.

Audits

Sometimes the IRS issues a general audit of the art and antique appraisals when they perceive a problem exists in the valuation of other assets within an estate, including business valuation and real estate. Other times the personal property is audited when the IRS agent questions the valuation methodology and/or authenticity of the items in the report. An accurate appraisal written by a qualified appraiser where the items are correctly cataloged, and there is a clear rationale for value, serves as the best defense against these types of audits.[55]

Lessons to Live By: Why Not Use the Insurance Appraisal?

While the IRS does have the right to request copies of insurance policies, it is common knowledge that fair market value differs from replacement value. If you only submit your insurance appraisal to the IRS, the IRS will happily rely on the higher values to estimate taxes. By submitting a properly prepared estate appraisal, the IRS will at least consider the fair market values submitted rather than using the replacement market to determine taxes owed, considerably lightening the estate's tax burden. While the IRS may disagree with fair market valuations submitted by the appraiser, the values in question can usually be negotiated to a point that is fair to both the estate and the IRS agent.

229

Special Rules for the Artist: Valuation of an Artist's Estate

Valuation of artist estates can be problematic for inexperienced appraisers. The IRS recognizes that it is reasonable for specific types of artwork within an artist's body of work to vary greatly in value and marketability. Experienced appraisers calculate blockage discounts by dividing an artist's estate into value and marketability segments. These appraisals enable tax attorneys, CPAs, and financial advisors to craft the most advantageous plans for the estate and its beneficiaries. Appraisals also assist the estate and its beneficiaries in maximizing present and future income.

Estate distribution appraisals can be written either using fair market value or marketable cash value depending on the needs of the estate. When the estate distribution appraisal is written using marketable cash value, the marketability of the items is taken into account, as this affects the resale and liquidation of the property. Regardless of whether the appraisal values the property using fair market value or marketable cash value, the estate distribution appraisal enables the estate to fairly divide the personal property according to the guidelines set forth in the will. Estate distribution appraisals can also eliminate (or settle) disputes among family members that can arise over a perceived bias towards a particular heir, or over fine art and antiques items that are believed to be valuable. The items that are being fought over can be found to be fakes or forgeries, which are usually of negligible value. Having an accurate appraisal that the heirs can rely upon with confidence can help avoid this unpleasant experience.

Other Roles of the Appraiser

Due to the constant handling of art objects as well as the professional appraiser's extensive knowledge of current trends in the art market, professional appraisers are excellent art advisors, collections managers, and expert witnesses. Often appraisers will act in more than one capacity for a client, such as writing insurance appraisals for the collection that they are overseeing. As long as a conflict of interest does not arise (for example, making a commission on the sale of an object and then appraising the same piece for the transaction), both you and your collection will benefit from the appraiser's knowledge and expertise.

Collections Manager: Collections Managers handle all aspects of exhibiting, maintaining, storing, shipping, and documenting a collection.

Art Advisor: Art advisors ensure that their clients pay reasonable and commensurate amounts of money for the works they purchase. They also handle research, exhibition loans, and publishing materials on a collection that serve to enhance value.

231

Expert Witness: Appraisers regularly serve as expert witnesses in damage loss, tax, trust and estate, donation, divorce, and dissolution cases.

Things Are Not Always What They Seem

Appraisers seek and find value. Often times, the appraiser will arrive at conclusions different from his or her clients' expectations. Sometimes, the appraiser is lucky enough to uncover a hidden treasure, much to the delight of those involved with the appraisal process. However, sometimes appraisers discover misattributions or other negative value characteristics that result in an object having only decorative value instead of having blue chip collector value.

An appraiser was hired to perform an estate planning appraisal for his client and her children. The children were particularly interested in the furniture in the household, because their mother had always led them to believe that she had a premier collection worth hundreds of thousands of dollars. The appraiser walked around the house with the bickering heirs, examining all the pieces they believed to be valuable. Before completing his inspection, one of the prospective beneficiaries asked him to review a table that the family believed to be of considerable value. In order to properly examine the piece, the appraiser cleared the items off the table's top to better see the veneer and to flip the table on its side to analyze the construction methods used.

As he was clearing off the table top, the appraiser picked up a small statue of a female dancer. His first attempt to pick up the piece was unsuccessful, as the weight of the statue exceeded his expectations. Moving the statue from the table top, the appraiser examined the table, which proved to be a 20th century reproduction of little value. Placing the statue back in its place, he decided to take a closer look at the piece that, up to this point, had gone unmentioned.

The appraiser spotted a Degas signature next to a foundry stamp on the back edge of the sculpture's base. Having a suspicion that the bronze sculpture was an authentic work, he asked if anyone in the family knew anything about the piece and how it had been obtained. The daughter answered that no one in the family ever thought anything of the sculpture, and that all they knew was that it was given to their grandfather in lieu of a debt. He then asked if anyone knew about the signature and attribution because it was signed "Degas." Everyone in the room fell silent and stared at the appraiser in disbelief. After the piece was authenticated, the small, previously unnoticed dancer was valued for several hundred thousand dollars, by far the most valuable piece in the collection. The beneficiaries had previously decided to sell the statue to an estate liquidator. Had the appraiser not been called in to perform the appraisal, the beneficiaries would have unwittingly given away the one item that was actually worth fighting over.

What Happens If You Don't Get the Collection Appraised?

A few years ago, there was an estate of a collector with an important art collection. During the collector's lifetime, he had loaned various pieces of his collection to museums; as a result, he felt he had gained a sense of his collection's worth from insurance appraisals the museums had taken out on the pieces while they were on loan. The collector had drawn up a will with his lawyer, thinking that he had accounted for all the assets in his estate. Only individual pieces of art were appraised and listed in his estate plan, not the entire collection.

233

After the collector's unexpected death, an estate appraisal of the art collection was necessary. The appraiser conducted an inspection, researched the fair market value of the pieces, and submitted his report to the attorney who had drawn up the will. While the lawyer, the collector, and the collector's family thought they knew the value of the collection, they were shocked at the final valuation based on recent comparable sales found in the appraiser's report. The value of the art collection exceeded the value of the real estate and the financial holdings.

In order to pay the imposed taxes, the collection was sold at auction. By not considering and planning for the value of the art collection in its entirety, the beneficiaries of the estate were deprived of the majority of their inheritance. Unfortunately, almost all of the proceeds of the sale went directly to the IRS, certainly not the intended beneficiary of the collector's estate.

This situation is more common than most collectors realize. It is important to have a knowledgeable art advisor and appraiser upon which you can rely when making important decisions. Even you might be surprised at the cumulative value of your collection.

Making assumptions about the value of your collection without hiring an appraiser could lead to serious financial repercussions: tax penalties, unequal distributions, and incorrectly priced sales. Making decisions about the value of your collection without an appraiser is similar to paying your taxes without consulting a CPA or tax advisor—you might pay your taxes accurately; however, it is possible that you will underpay and still owe the government money or, more likely, overpay and never see that money again. You have spent time and money building your collection, why not ensure that it is properly appraised, protected, and planned for so that future generations of your family can benefit from your good judgment —first in acquiring the special piece but then in maintaining its value? You should have complete control over your assets and collections, and by planning correctly based on accurate appraisals, you will create a legacy for yourself and your loved ones.

Appraisal Checklist

Before you call an appraiser:

- Assemble receipts, past appraisals, and any documentation you may have on your collection.

- Count up the approximate number of items you would like appraised (this will enable you to receive a more accurate fee quote).

- Inform the appraiser of any time restrictions you may have.

- Honestly discuss and disclose all possible uses for the appraisal.

- Honestly discuss and disclose everything you know (including family stories, where it was purchased, any prior attributions, etc.) about your collection.

- Understand that professional appraising and valuation science is a lengthy process which is based on in-depth research; expect the appraiser to take a reasonable amount of time researching and writing your appraisal, especially for large collections.

- Be wary of individuals who have past, present, or future interest in the properties being appraised.

- Openly discuss any opinions of value anyone might have about your collection.

When hiring an appraiser:

- Ask if he or she is a member in good standing of one of the three professional appraisal associations.

- Ask to see a copy of the person's resume or CV, which includes his or her society affiliations, memberships, publications, and any other relevant credentials.

- Ask if he or she complies with Uniform Standards of Professional Appraisal Practice (USPAP).

- Ask if the person catalogs according to the Getty ID system.

- Ask to be sent a written agreement with a fee proposal and description of scope of work.

- Ask to be provided with a fee structure that includes the person's hourly rate and additional expenses, such as travel, color photos, additional research, extra copies of the report and the like.

- Ask what experience the appraiser has in valuing a collection like yours.

Michael and Gael with their dogs Muffie, Minnie, Maggie, and Sushi

#1 Michael standing in front of painting by Morris Hirshfield,
American Beauty, 1942, oil on canvas, 48"H x 40"W

#2 Kitsch Room Installation in the Mendelsohn's home

#3 William Edmondson, *Mermaid*, ca. 1935-40, carved limestone,
13.25"H x 35"W x 5"D

#4 Cecil B. White, *Scenes from American Life*, ca. 1925,
mixed fabrics, 77"H x 66"W

#5 G.P. Ailers, *Desk and Chair* from Sussex, New Jersey, 1878,
wood with polychrome, desk: 78"H x 38"W x 45"D;
chair: 35.5"H x 15.25"W x 12"D

#6 Thornton Dial, *Flowers of the Blue Things*, 1997, enamel and mixed
media on canvas mounted on wood, 83"H x 60"W

#7 Michael and Gael

#8 Michael sitting in front of *Woodbridge Figures,* ca. 1920-40, wood with polychrome, ranging in size from 4.5"H to 7.75"H and Thornton Dial's *Smooth-Going Cats Going to the Top,* paint and mixed media on canvas mounted on board, 71"H x 88"W

#9 ©Kehinde Wiley, courtesy of Conner Contemporary Art

#10 *Campeachy Chair* attributed to John Hemmings of Monticello, walnut frame with original finish, oil cloth upholstery filled with cotton batting

#11 John Anster Fitzgerald (1823-1906), *Rabbit Surrounded by Fairies*, British mid-19th century, watercolor with body color and gum arabic, 21.5"H x 30"W

Kendra and Allan Daniel Collection

PART II

Planning for the Disposition of Your Collection

The second part of this book is about planning for the disposition of your collection when you are ready to transfer individual pieces or the collection as a whole to a charitable organization, the next generation of your family, or to someone else in a purchase and sale transaction. This part of the book prepares you for the conversations you will need to have with your advisory team in order to properly carry out an art succession plan. When you are working with your attorney, accountant, insurance professional, or financial planner, this part of the book will acquaint you with various planning options that are appropriate in particular situations. This material is intended to provide you with enough information so that you are asking the right questions and to enable you to become a full participant in the planning process.

Obviously, any time we are discussing particular planning techniques or legal tools these need to be discussed in detail with your advisory team to determine the suitability of these approaches to your particular circumstances. Throughout this part of the book we offer some general suggestions as to when particular strategies might be applicable, but of course the facts of your individual circumstances could alter the appropriateness of a planning tool. It is also possible that we have not discussed a planning strategy that might be an ideal approach for your particular circumstances. It is most important that you have a full and open discussion with your attorney about any of the legal strategies we have talked about. This book presents a broad overview of an array of planning options that may or may not be appropriate in your situation. Your attorney and the other members of your advisory team will be able to guide you through an appropriate analysis of the ideas we have presented in this book and focus your thinking on the strategies that are best suited to your individual situation.

The High Cost of Denial—
How **Not** to Lose 70% of
the Value of Your Collection

"It is possible to provide security against other ills, but as far as death is concerned, we men live in a city without walls."

—Epicurus

According to the Center on Wealth and Philanthropy (formerly the Social Welfare Institute) at Boston College, $41 trillion in assets will be passed intergenerationally by 2052.[56] Based on a conservative estimate of leading dealers, auction houses, and major trust companies, $4 to $6 trillion of this amount is projected to be in art and antique assets. The *New York Times* reported recently that "one in every 325 households had a net worth of $10 million or more in 2004, the latest year for which data is available, more than four times as many as in 1989." [57] And of this number it is generally thought that one in three is a collector of something. Yet, despite the vast amount of wealth in the area of art and antiques, advisors rarely work with their collector clients to create a disposition plan for their collections, and generally these assets are glossed over in the estate planning process.

Developing a succession plan for a collection may take months, and implementing it could take years. Nevertheless, the pleasure of finalizing your wishes during your lifetime, even though they may not be fully carried out until after your death, shouldn't be undervalued. Careful planning can ensure that your artistic vision will survive for generations.

Failing to plan can end up costing your heirs as much as 70% of the value of your collection at the time of your death if items are sold through traditional public sales channels without the proper planning. Advisors have a fiduciary responsibility to protect and preserve the value of your assets. My prediction is that it is just a matter of time before an advisor is called on the carpet by an angry heir, who, if motivated and knowledgeable, is willing to sue based on the financial loss of the collection's value.

" And don't go auctioning off my collections!"

243

The failure of the advisory community to contemplate arts and antiques assets is an odd phenomenon. I have examined the data intake questionnaires of several of the top estate planning law firms in the United States and, without exception, there has not been a line item inquiring about art, antiques, or collectibles. I did find one questionnaire that asked the client to disclose any item for which an appraisal had been done in the last year (this usually refers to real estate). Art and antiques assets are traditionally lumped into the tangible personal property line item on the intake questionnaire.

The problem is exacerbated by the reluctance of collectors to discuss these assets with their advisors. This happens sometimes because the collector does not view herself as a collector—she thinks she has just accumulated "a bunch of stuff." A study by a leading financial services firm shows that 50% of families worth in excess of $10 million may not call themselves "collectors," but have lots of "stuff" sur-

The Advisor's FYI: Moses-Mei Art Index

Two economists, Michael Moses and Jianping Mei, have created the Moses-Mei Art Index, which tracks sales of art from 1875 to 2002, and demonstrates that investing in art compares favorably with stock market investments. The index tracks the value of artwork that has been auctioned publicly twice. The Moses-Mei index shows a 12.56% annual return for postwar and contemporary art, their newest index, and a 7.14% return on their All Art Index. Their research concludes that art outperforms fixed income securities as an investment, but slightly underperforms stocks in the U.S.[58]

The Moses-Mei index provides an important tool for the investor/collector who wants to diversify his or her portfolio. During the boom years of the 1990s, and the crash that followed the dot-com bubble, their index rose

rounding them in their homes. In other situations the collector is reluctant to discuss these assets because she prefers to keep them under the radar screen, because of "empty hook" estate planning that has gone on in previous generations (as discussed below).

Most collectors don't view their art or antiques as investments, or as assets that have long-term financial value. Most of us collect because we love the piece, not because we're looking at the future internal rate of return or how much we'll make at the time of the sale. In fact, the very idea of selling a piece in the collection at any time during our lives is like asking to sell a child! At the very least, even though many collectors don't see the collection as an investment, they need to be aware of the financial value of the collection—and how it can be used to create wealth for loved ones, cash for themselves, or a legacy into the future. If properly planned for, a collection can become as good an investment as anything else you will invest in—maybe better, because you can enjoy the beauty of the art while it appreciates in value, free of current taxes.

As with all of the other things we own, art and antiques assets need to be protected and ultimately planned for to maximize their full financial value. Art succession planning accomplishes more than just the mitigation of tax liability. If done correctly, it can be used to generate philanthropic capital for charities, structure gifts to museums, and create cash that collectors can use to buy better pieces or to live on. (More about the role of art succession planners in Chapter 14.)

and fell independently of the stock market, offering investors a non-corollary investment option.[59]

Failing to Plan Is the Most Expensive Approach

Let's look at the usual scenario when an estate that includes art and antiques assets that were *not* contemplated in previous estate planning comes into an attorney's office. A file shows up on the lawyer's desk that looks neat and clean at first glance because there is a will, a competent executor has been appointed, and the initial assessment looks like a $5 million estate with most of the assets in stock, an insurance policy, a single-family residence, and the proceeds of a 401(k).

Then an inventory arrives. It turns out the decedent's significant other was the chair of the art history department at the local college. The inventory discloses collections of pre-Columbian art, South American textiles, and advertising posters from the 1920s and 1930s. There is also a 1957 Karmann Ghia coupe on blocks in the garage and a lot of French wine in the basement. The house is furnished in the French Modern style with original pieces by Ruhlmann, Breuer, Herbst, and Jourdain. It is later determined that the items were acquired one by one, here and there throughout the professor's career—approximately sixty years—and they have never been appraised or insured. The items have always been in the home of the professor and his significant other (now the decedent). After the professor's death his partner continued to live in the jointly-owned residence with all of the furnishings in place. The attorney who did the estate plan for the professor retired and moved to Miami ten years ago. The professor's estate required only a simple probate because of the prior planning, and was handled by the decedent's nephew, who had just graduated from NYU law school with a LLM in tax. A federal estate tax return was filed two years ago, which did not disclose any art or antiques assets.

The attorney handling the current estate is now looking at an inventory that reflects a sizable collection of something—he's not sure what—and he has no idea what it is worth. Conventional wisdom dictates that he should have his paralegal call an auction house and get somebody to come over and look at the stuff and give him an idea of its value. The auction house representative calls back a few days later and reports that several of the pre-Columbian items are quite extraordinary and worth many thousands, the South American textiles have been very well cared for and are probably worth a great deal, the car is choice, the wine collection is quite significant, and the furniture and posters are a gold mine. Now what?

The attorney gets on the phone and calls the senior partner at the largest law firm in town, who he knows socially. The senior partner says that in his firm, in situations like this, they just turn the whole thing over to the auction house, who sells it all and the cash goes into the estate. He cautions the attorney that he needs to get the process moving quickly, because he has only nine months to file the estate tax return and sometimes you really need to hustle to get everything resolved within that period.

Whether he likes it or not, the attorney has just become the involuntary curator of several very significant collections. He doesn't know anything about art or antiques, but his intuition tells him that dumping all this stuff in the lap of the auction house for a hasty sale may not be the right answer.

Well, I applaud his intuition! If he takes the advice of his sage colleague, the beneficiaries stand to lose up to 70% of the value of the collections. By the time estate taxes, seller's premiums, undervalued sales, and unsold items are factored in, the collection would have been liquidated for a fraction of the estimated value. On the other hand, if the attorney put a little effort into the thoughtful disposition of these assets, much of the value of the collection can be preserved and the heirs will benefit meaningfully from his foresight. If the attorney doesn't want to become an expert on these matters, there are consulting firms that specialize in art succession planning. Here is an overview of the issues that must be resolved:

- Estate taxes—the value of this decedent's estate is quite significant because of the highly appreciated items in the collection. The challenge here is that most, if not all, of the assets will need to be liquidated in order to fund the estate tax liability. So what is the best way to sell off the assets so that the heirs are certain to have enough to pay the taxes due?

- The art and antiques assets were not reported on the federal estate tax return that was filed at the time of the professor's death—does that Form 706 tax return need to be reopened?

- Is the auction house that the attorney has been working with the right venue for the sale of these items? He is dealing with several different types of collections. He might be able to get significantly more for the French Modern furniture in New York than he can in Atlanta or Indianapolis.

- Does the attorney understand the pre-sale estimates and reserve issues that affect the net sales proceeds when items are sold at auction? Does he know that he needs to get his own opinion of value to help in the negotiations with the auction house? Does he know how to set the reserves so that he is not squandering the value of choice items? What will he do with the items that do not sell at the auction?

- Does the estate have good title to the South American and Mayan pieces? Travelers could purchase art and antiques in the flea markets and on the back streets of certain cities of Mexico, Colombia, and Peru in the 1950s and early 1960s that may have title problems.

- Are there condition concerns and should they be addressed prior to the auction?

- Is a public sale (auction) the best way to dispose of the items in the collection? Would it be more advantageous to identify dealers who specialize in the items in this collection? These dealers would have contacts with high-end collectors (private sale) who would be willing to pay top dollar for some of the better items he is liquidating.

- If he is going to sell the entire collection at auction, does it make sense to sell everything in one sale, or could he realize more if the items were grouped with similar items in a specialty auction that attracted collectors who focused on this area of collecting?

- If the decedent's nephew (the NYU graduate) is his only heir, is there an issue because the nephew failed to include the art and antiques on the Form 706 tax return filed at the time of the professor's death?

These issues are just a snapshot of the kinds of problems that can arise when the advisory team has failed to plan for the art and antiques assets in conjunction with planning for the other assets in the estate. Postmortem planning offers far less flexibility than lifetime planning.

249

The Empty Hook Syndrome

Sometimes the failure to plan for the disposition of art and antiques assets is the result of a family history or practice of removing desirable objects from the home of a newly deceased relative before an inventory of the household effects is made. In this manner, valuable family heirlooms can pass from generation to generation without any documentation of assets transferring. This strategy is referred to as the "empty hook" syndrome. When the collector passes away, the art is quickly whisked off the wall, leaving an empty hook. The daughter thinks: "No one knew Dad and Mom owned it!" She re-hangs the painting in her own home, and never gives it a second thought. What if this painting became her biggest nightmare rather than a great tax-free windfall?

Because of its very nature, art cannot ever truly disappear. And, according to the law, it's part of the collector's estate and should be taxed as such. Hiding art along the generational ladder can unleash a series of inopportune events in which one error compounds another to snowball into a truly nightmarish predicament.

Unfortunately, collectors who try to sweep their artwork under the rug to outwit the IRS are blithely unaware of the following:

- **There is no statute of limitations for estate tax fraud under Code Section 6501(c)(3).** This fraud will follow inheritors for generations to come.

- **There are unforeseen personal circumstances that may necessitate the sale of the artwork down the line, bringing its existence into light:** the triple Ds of death, divorce, and debt. When the art is sold and the funds are deposited into a financial institution and subsequently throw off interest and dividends, the IRS may inquire as to the source of the funds and then how the art was acquired.

250

How will the next generation or future generations get caught under the microscope of the IRS? Take the case of Bill and Joanne Morton.[60] Back in 1928, Bill and Joanne decided to spend their fifth wedding anniversary in Paris, where an unusual portrait of a woman caught their eye in the window of a curio shop. They bought it and hung it in their bedroom. The painting followed them from house to house, finally coming to rest in the living room of their last house, which they purchased after the birth of their only child Jake.

It wasn't until Jake studied art history in college that the Mortons discovered that their curio shop find was nothing less than an original Picasso—and therefore worth a great deal! Over the years, the Morton's Picasso was kept strictly under wraps. It was never displayed publicly, never shown in a museum, and never insured. In fact, other than close personal friends, no one knew it existed. The Mortons never discussed their Picasso with their trusted advisors for tax and estate planning purposes. When Bill and Joanne passed away in the early 1980s, Jake took the painting and hung it in his own home without discussing it with anyone. When Jake himself passed away two years ago, his son Trent, well aware of the family's empty hook art plan, followed suit.

Shirtsleeves to shirtsleeves in three generations.

However, Trent is more interested in buying Lamborghinis and vacationing in Tuscany than putting in hours at the family business, and consequently has squandered the wealth he inherited. He has made a series of poor decisions regarding his finances, while maintaining a lavish lifestyle, and has fallen deeply into debt (sound familiar?). He needs money, a lot of it, and the sooner the better. Trent speculates that in today's art market the Picasso is worth somewhere in the area of $20 million. The sale of the Picasso would sure come in handy.

When Trent is forced to sell the Picasso, he will have a major problem on his hands: he has a piece of art without any provenance! Collectors and dealers are understandably worried about buying a piece that hasn't had some kind of positive paper trail documenting ownership, and because of inherent concerns about the authenticity of the piece. Questions will arise about stolen art, good title, and, in this case, where the Picasso was during the years 1936 to 1945. Moreover, the fact that the piece hasn't been validated by having been part of a museum show or included in a catalogues raisonnés, is very much to its detriment, and will likewise depress the sales price when Trent attempts to sell it. It is also possible he may not find a dealer or auction house willing to represent him.

Because Trent must sell the Picasso, he's also in for another rude awakening. Selling a work anonymously (as a private collector) at auction is no guarantee that the painting won't be traced back to him. Moreover, what will he do with such a huge sum of cash? If the income is reportable or traceable (as wire transfers are), the IRS will certainly wonder where the money came from, triggering a likely audit. If the IRS gets on Trent's case, penalties and back taxes could wipe out the actual value of the painting and cause audits of previously filed tax returns.

Trent Morton's no-win situation is an illustration of what happens when families are in denial about the importance of a proper art succession strategy. Simply passing artwork down from generation to generation under the 706 radar is like playing the old game of "hot potato" with a Picasso. Nevertheless, it happens with astonishing frequency, even with the most sophisticated of collectors.

The Advisor's FYI: Understanding Authentication and Provenance

Provenance is a documented ownership and exhibition history of an individual piece. Provenance is a chain of title, if you will, and a record of when the piece has been shown or displayed and by whom. Good provenance almost always increases the value of a piece of art. Like trust, provenance is a quality that, once broken, is extremely hard to restore. And while the idea of provenance is easy to explain, it can be extremely difficult to come by, as a particular painting at the Portland Museum of Art in Portland, Maine demonstrates:

In 1983, Henry H. Reichhold gifted *La Gioconda* to the museum—not the one currently hanging in the Louvre, but a copy of it attributed to either one of Leonardo da Vinci's students, or the master himself. It's likely, according to the museum, that the piece is a study for the more famous *Mona Lisa*, rather than a copy. After receiving the gift, the museum sent the painting to the Straus Center for Conservation and Technical Studies at Harvard University, where they determined that it was painted prior to 1510. But, due to the painting's lack of provenance, it cannot be unequivocally attributed to da Vinci. To prove its origin beyond a doubt (i.e., to restore the painting's provenance) the Portland Museum of Art would need a qualified authority, for example an art historian and scholar who has published several papers on da Vinci, to create a document authenticating the work. If authentication happened, the Portland Museum would own a piece that would fall into the category of "priceless." Until then, it has an exceptional piece that no one really knows quite what to do with.

But, when questions of provenance arise with today's collections, many collectors believe that the word of their dealer, or the certificate of authenticity that their dealer gives them, is enough to establish provenance. Quite often, this is not true. One of the more unsavory tactics unscrupulous dealers use, when they have a piece of art whose provenance is in question, is to sell it with only a certificate of authenticity. To be sure of an established provenance, collectors should make sure that they have some of the following:

- A signed certificate or statement of authenticity from a respected authority or expert on the artist.

- An appraisal from a recognized authority or expert on the artist.

- Letters or papers from recognized experts or authorities discussing the art.

- An exhibition or gallery sticker attached to the art.

- An original sales receipt.

- A film or recording of the artist talking about the art.

- Names of previous owners of the art.

- Newspaper or magazine articles mentioning or illustrating the art.

- A mention or illustration of the art in a book or exhibit catalog.

- Verbal information related by someone familiar with the art or who knows the artist.[61]

"The Kids Will Love It" and Other Delusional Justifications

Collectors often delude themselves into thinking that their children appreciate their collection as much as they do. Frequently, however, the children do not want the collection; they want the cash the collection represents. I have heard many collectors who do not want to deal with the issue of lifetime planning say, "I'm just leaving it all to my kids and they can sort it out." What these collectors are missing is twofold. Number one—the kids may not want it. Number two—even if they do want some or all of it, if the transfer is made as an outright bequest in the will or passes under the residuary clause, the kids may have to sell or liquidate all of the assets in order to pay the estate taxes due on the collection.

Marni is our youngest child, so she grew up living with our collection and experiencing the excitement as we acquired new things and our rooms were increasingly dominated by contemporary folk art. She was there when we had art-related events in our home to raise funds for charities. Her friends had to be instructed that they could not touch. We have taken her to museum openings of shows at major museums that included our things. Marni is the only one of our three children who had our collection as an active force in her life.

Several years ago, I asked Marni if she could choose any five things from our collection, what would she take with her? She went around the house and, about a half hour later, came back with a list of five of the most important pieces in our collection. I was thrilled, thinking she appreciated the finest pieces in the way that Gael and I did. Since I write and speak on this subject and am always asked by fellow collectors how to pass their passion for collecting onto their children, I asked Marni how she came up with these five pieces. She clarified that she chose these pieces because she'd make the most money when she sold them. This was an incredible blow and an invaluable lesson to us that has affected the planning we have done for our own collection. The kids don't love the stuff the way we do. It's painful to accept, but it's just not their thing. They want the cash. If we do not plan correctly during our lifetime, the many intermediaries between the art and the cash seriously deplete the value of our children's inheritance.

256

The lesson here is that you must have a conversation with your children to determine if they want all or any specific pieces in the collection. If any of the children indicate they want particular items, these preferences need to be included in the planning process. You will need to strategize with your advisor on how to make the transfer in such a way that your child does not get clobbered with taxes, taking all of the joy out of the gift. You will also need to factor these gifts into your overall estate plan, so that your children are treated in the manner that you intend.

In addition, you will want to have a more general conversation with your kids about the collection. Have you told them how much the collection means to you, what you want to happen to it, who you want to have certain pieces, or where you want it to wind up? Have you told them how it should be sold, which dealers will know what's it's worth, and where the records and insurance papers are? Without this information, your kids won't know how to answer the attorney when he asks, "What should we do about your parents' art?" Assume your kids want the cash, not the collection, but at least prepare them to make the right choices about disposing of it.

Appoint an Art Trustee

A collector should appoint an art trustee—a dealer or friend who knows enough about the pieces in the collection to help the advisor or children make better decisions. Gael and I have appointed Fred Giampietro, our dealer and family friend for more than twenty years, as our art trustee. If anything happens to Gael or me, Fred knows what to do for the benefit of our children and to put our art legacy into place.

Loss of Control

If your collection passes to your estate without specific direction as to its disposition, your intentions for the collection are thrown out the window. Several years ago we met with a wonderful guy who owned one of every Corvette model made for the last 50 years. He had an estate plan that contemplated every other asset he owned, but absolutely no plan in place for the car collection. He heard me speak at an event and wanted to set up a meeting to discuss planning options with his family and advisors. We started talking to him about creating a Museum Without Walls (more about this in Chapter 13), which would enable him to tour some of his cars for exhibition purposes, to help raise funds for his favorite charities, and create a family legacy. We had a meeting scheduled, but several weeks before, his office called to cancel, saying he wasn't feeling well and had to reschedule. Over the next few months, I followed up with him and found out the illness had taken his life.

If the man had lived a few months longer and we had put the plan we were discussing in place, he could have controlled and determined what happened to his collection. In contrast, I was told the family was selling off the cars in the collection one by one, with the proceeds going to family members. It should be pointed out that capital gains taxes, both federal and state, as well as dealer's fees, can deplete the proceeds by almost 50%, and then there will be estate tax considerations. His family ended up with a fraction of the value of this collection in cash. A well-designed lifetime plan could have provided funding for the family and charitable family legacy for future generations. This is an example of 40 years of collecting passion wasted.

Avoiding the "Family Art War"

The unfortunate but all too frequent byproduct of failing to plan is litigation. Witness the complicated, messy, and embarrassing courtroom drama that has fractured the McCartney/Eastman family.

Following his death, Christie's auctioned off the legendary art collection of Lee Eastman (Paul McCartney's father-in-law from his marriage to Linda) and his wife Monique Eastman, with the proceeds being split seven ways between their children and grandchildren—including a share to fashion designer Stella McCartney, daughter of Paul and Linda McCartney. But then, in January of 2006, three children from Monique's previous marriage filed a suit, claiming a portion of the proceeds of some works sold at auction.

When commenting on the case for the *Wall Street Journal* Ralph Lerner, an attorney specializing in art law, noted that the case could be "tough to prove," because Monique had signed documents dictating what was to happen to the paintings before her death in May 2005.[62] And a marital deduction trust established by Monique and Lee before his death in 1991 excluded the children who brought the suit. This is fortunate for Monique's intended heirs. But this case illustrates that even when lifetime planning has taken place, if it is not well executed, the family can still end up in a family art war.

When family members do want specific pieces from your collection, this can present another set of problems if not properly planned for. If the collector has not inventoried, cataloged, appraised, or insured his pieces and there are no records of acquisition or any documentation of what he has, the lack of record-keeping can result in unfortunate consequences. Here are two stories that illustrate particularly bad results.

A collector died, having kept no documentation of the existence of his significant collection of Russian Impressionists. At the time of his death, the collection was put into a storage facility and the collector's son and daughter were each given a key to the unit. Since the interfamily transfers of the art collection were never documented (the "empty hook" strategy), the children were told to wait several years before doing anything with the pieces. About 20 months later, the daughter went to the storage facility to have some of the pieces appraised. When she entered the storage unit, it was completely empty. She called her brother inquiring about the paintings, and he said to her, "What paintings?" She asked the probate attorney and he said, "What artwork? I have no records of any artwork." Other than her key she had no proof that any art was ever in the storage unit. Worse yet, she may end up paying penalties for artwork fraudulently transferred if she blows the whistle on her brother. Unfortunately, legal fees, penalties, and interest will eat up a good portion of the value of the collection, if she ever sees any of it again, and the siblings will never talk to each other as long as they live. This definitely was not the legacy the father intended.

Similarly, take the furniture collector who collected Federal period pieces over his lifetime. He had placed the name of each of his children under one of his three special pieces so that each knew which item to take upon his death. When he passed on, each child took their designated piece to their own home. Within the first year, one daughter sold her Rhode Island highboy through a dealer for $910,000. (I'm sure she also omitted paying capital gains tax since the piece never existed for tax purposes.) Two years later, the collector's second daughter sold her painted blanket chest to the same dealer for $1.3 million. The son had an emotional attachment to his piece and lived with it for many years. When it was time for him to retire and downsize, he figured that he would make out well, too, so he offered his tall case clock to the same eager dealer. The dealer called and broke the news that his piece had been poorly restored and was worth only $12,000. The son initially tried to negotiate a financial settlement with his two sisters. When that failed he blew the whistle on them for not paying estate taxes on the transfer of the inherited furniture pieces. Now, the family is in an art war and the siblings do not speak to each other and most of the value of the antiques has been depleted by litigation costs, back taxes, and penalties.

It's terrible to watch something that speaks to the greatness of humanity, like art, destroy family relations. That's why Gael and I have proactively discussed the future of our collection with all of our children, put our intentions down in writing, and have implemented detailed lifetime planning, including the appointment of an art trustee.

261

The Headlines Speak for Themselves: Brooke Astor's Childe Hassam

Art can also trigger huge intergenerational disputes and misconduct driven by greed and selfishness. One of the most shocking examples of this is the tragic civil and criminal proceedings surrounding Brooke Astor's estate.

It has been reported that Brooke Astor's most beloved piece in her art collection was the painting

Flags, Fifth Avenue by American Impressionist Childe Hassam. It hung in a place of honor, above the fireplace in her library. In 2002, Brooke's son, Anthony D. Marshall, who was handling his mother's financial affairs, sold the painting to a Santa Fe art dealer for $10 million and took a $2 million commission for himself. The painting was then resold for twice what the dealer paid to a private collector. It all went relatively unnoticed until September 2005, when a lawsuit alleging neglect, brought by Brooke's grandson, Philip Marshall, sent the sale of the painting and the Astor family to the front pages of newspapers around the country. Friends of Brooke, who passed away in 2007, and unidentified sources questioned whether she was even aware of the sale and indicated that she intended to gift the painting to the Met, where she was trustee emeritus.[63]

The situation is complicated by the recent disclosure that Anthony Marshall inaccurately reported the cost basis of the painting to the IRS on a 2002 tax return, overstating the basis by millions of dollars ($7.425 million versus $172,010), which significantly reduced the tax liability on the transfer.[64] Further questions involve revisions to Brooke Astor's will made in 2003 and 2004, after she suffered a marked decline in her health. These revisions redirect millions to Anthony. As we go to press with the 2nd edition of this book, Anthony Marshall and his attorney have been indieted on charges that they conspired to have the $198 million estate left to Anthony.

Planning for the Ohs, the Oh Mys, and the Oh My Gods

We introduced you to our three-tiered rating system —the "Ohs," "Oh Mys," and the "Oh My Gods"—in the first chapter of this book. We use this system not only for acquisitions but also for strategic planning when we are contemplating the disposition of a piece in our collection. We have separate approaches, generally, for the different strata of pieces. The "Oh" pieces are those to which we are not attached and will liquidate easily. These might be a lesser quality duplicate of a piece that we have since acquired in better condition, or things we acquired in the very early days of acquisition before we developed our "eye." The "Oh Mys" are better pieces that round out our collection and are consequently used for different purposes in the planning process. And the "Oh My Gods," obviously, are the pieces that we would not consider letting out of our home as long as we are alive and so we will put a plan in place that allows us to retain possession of these until we are gone.

Categorizing your collection into these three groups helps the collector make good decisions during the process of planning for the disposition. Pieces at the "Oh" level can either be sold to create liquidity that will fund another planning objective, or gifted to a related use charity and sold by them, creating much-needed philanthropic capital. A collector could also sell these and use the cash for living expenses, retirement, to buy more art, or to fund an estate planning objective. The "Oh My Gods" are often very good pieces that could form the basis of a traveling exhibit using a Museum Without Walls strategy (more about this in Chapter 13) or the piece may be sought after by a museum curator and the subject of a promised gift with an accompanying endowment.

In the chapters that follow, we will discuss planning options available to collectors and the factual circumstances that make these particular strategies appropriate, given the collector's objectives. As we discuss these various planning options we will also make reference to the "Ohs," "Oh Mys," and the "Oh My Gods," because some of the strategies we will discuss are particularly useful for pieces in one or the other of these categories.

10

Working with Your Advisory Team

**With Contributions From
George Kasparian, Esq.**

"Teamwork is the ability to work together toward a common vision. The ability to direct individual accomplishments toward organizational objectives. It is the fuel that allows common people to attain uncommon results."

–Andrew Carnegie

Although most collectors *should* be highly disciplined about researching, finding the right pieces, and negotiating prices for their collections, they are often very negligent about planning for its ultimate disposition. My thoughts are that, given all the time and energy we put into assembling our collections, we owe it to ourselves, and the many people in the world who also care about the things we love, to see that the collection is dispersed in a way that fulfills our intentions.

If your family does not want any of it, then give some thought to who might want the items in your collection —a museum, historical society, college or university, hospital or nursing home, library, or trade association might be thrilled to house and display the items that mean so much to you. For instance, Boston's South Station periodically mounts exhibits in its center court simply for the enjoyment of the thousands of commuters who pass through this hall every day. The exhibits have ranged from electric trains (which stop hundreds of busy workers in their tracks), to photographs, to architectural plans and models, to a Martin Luther King, Jr. retrospective, to children's art. A family's name is often attached to these collections, making future generations of these families very proud indeed.

In contrast, you may feel that too much of your net worth is tied up in your collection, so you need to sell off parts of it to have some cash to live on or to leave to your kids. Regardless of your planning objective, the bottom line is that there are right ways to do these things and wrong ways that could result in losing much of the value of the items you have collected. I have always preferred to try to do things the right way. Doing things the right way usually requires me to spend a little time thinking and planning and a little money up front so that I am executing my plan in a way that will optimize the value of the item I am transferring or selling. The investment frequently involves a discussion with one or several members of my advisory team.

Assembling Your Advisory Team

My advisory team consists of financial professionals—my attorney, my CPA (tax advisor), and my investment advisor, who is also my financial planner; and art professionals—my dealer (Fred, whom I have mentioned in earlier chapters) and a whole network of other people that come in and out of the picture depending on the transaction I am working on. These include, first and foremost, the appraiser, who is an expert in the type of art we are dealing with, my contacts at any number of museums and galleries, someone at the auction house where I am looking to consign an item, a planned giving officer, or even another collector who has had experience structuring a particular type of transaction similar to a deal I am contemplating. You cannot put together a successful art succession plan by yourself. You need to surround yourself with experts who bring professional judgment and perspective to your decision-making.

267

If I am making a gift to a charitable organization, I am going to want to run it by my tax people to make sure it makes sense given everything else that is going on in my relationship with the IRS. If we decide the gift makes sense, then I need to have a conversation with my attorney about how to structure the gift so that this strategy fits in with the rest of my estate plan. I also want to talk to an appraiser to get a sense of the value of the piece and I may need to speak with my insurance agent because the gift might require an accompanying endowment that could be structured with a life insurance policy. The financial planner might also need to be consulted because we need to monitor my cash position and consider the possibility of structuring this gift in a way that could create some income for me in the short-term.

In my experience, I have always come out ahead when I have made the investment in consulting with my advisors before I make a major move with any of my assets. I have also learned that planning for art is a little different than, say, planning for the disposition of something in my stock portfolio. It is possible to determine the value of stocks and bonds at any given point in time using the Internet. It is also possible to find an almost immediate buyer who will pay a market price for the equities. Try doing that with art.

"Well, we're not quite sure what it's worth ... a similar piece just sold in London for $880,000, but it had been exhibited and mine was in a private collection and hasn't been loaned for over 100 years ... and this artist has recently had some authenticity issues like the Dali problems ... and this piece has a lot of overpainting and needs to be restored ... and we think it might sell better in New York than here on the West Coast, although a dealer in La Jolla thinks she has someone who might want it for around $150,000 —that's an insult. ..." You see the problem. It is essential that we bring in the experts to give current market value for sales purposes. Value can be difficult to pin down and a buyer willing to pay what you think the piece is worth can be difficult to locate, especially if there is a timing issue. These and other issues related to the uniqueness of art, antiques, and collectibles require special planning in order to fully realize the value of the piece.

How Art Succession Planning Relates to Your Overall Estate Plan

Planning for your art and antiques assets needs to be fully integrated with the planning you are doing for your other financial assets. Your estate planning attorney has probably done a beautiful job planning for your real estate investments, your stocks and bonds, the proceeds of your life insurance and re- tirement accounts, and your partnership interest in the business you own. But just think for a moment —I'll bet that same attorney didn't ask a whole lot of questions about your art and antiques assets at the time all this other planning was done, and I would venture to say that you didn't bring it up either. He or she probably asked you about the tangible personal property in your home and suggested a round num- ber that generally suffices to cover furnishings and other personal property items in people's houses. For most clients this is probably a perfectly accept- able approach. But not for those of us who collect.

Most of us who are collectors may have a high per- centage of our net worth tied up in our collection— the items hanging on our walls or sitting on pedes- tals and the things we have stored in the garage, in the summer house, in the attic, or even in the wine cellar. If your attorney is not a close friend and has never been to your home, he or she does not know that you have an Andy Warhol in your living room. So the first lesson from this chapter is, tell your advi- sory team about your collection and its approximate value so they can factor these assets into the plan- ning process. Be proactive in making sure they understand exactly what you have, that it comprises a significant percentage of your net worth, and that you have specific intentions for the disposition of some of the items in the collection.

So the first lesson from this chapter is, tell your advisory team about your collection and its approximate value so they can factor these assets into the planning process.

Some collectors believe that they have taken care of the disposition of their art and antiques assets because they have had a conversation with their children and told them who should get what at the time of death. Other collectors have gone through their home and put little stickers on the bottoms or backs of items indicating who should get the item when the contents of the home is dispersed. I can not emphasize this enough: *this is not an art succession plan* (it may in fact be an invitation to the IRS to audit!).

My view is that the advisor has a duty to inquire regarding these assets. Admittedly, there are clients who will have nothing worth reporting. But even moderate-income people can have collections that have been in their family for years that they may not even realize have significant value. Examples are electric trains and old toys, which have become very valuable. Antique jewelry, Bakelite, and copper pieces from the 1920s and 1930s have escalated tremendously in value. Old books, maps, historic documents, stamps, coins, and medallions can all have significant value. Guns, musical instruments, sporting goods, and scientific equipment can be worth tens of thousands of dollars. You have probably heard the famous story about the violin that was only worth a few thousand

270

dollars, but the bow was extremely rare and worth hundreds of thousands.

Advisors generally are not sensitive to the fact that most high net worth individuals accumulate something. My recommendation is that the collector needs to engage the advisor in a discussion about the collector's personal interests. Talk about what's in the attic and the basement, your grandmother's beautiful silver serving pieces in the dining room, the display cabinet of Fabergé eggs, the garage full of antique cars, or the wine cellar full of vintage Bordeaux.

At the time of your death, everything you own goes into your estate, and—unless you have done some lifetime planning—is subject to federal estate taxes if your net worth exceeds a particular amount ($2 million in 2006, 2007, and 2008). You also may have to pay estate taxes at the state level, depending on the state in which you reside. In addition, without proper planning, your assets, including art and collectibles, could get tied up in probate with all of the associated delays and costs. So having your kids go into the house and remove objects, particularly valuable ones, is a prescription for disaster. ("Empty Hook" estate planning is discussed at length in Chapter 9.) If you want to give particular pieces in your collection to members of your family or friends, or even charities, you need either to provide for this in your will or do some lifetime planning. Planning for these assets during your lifetime offers considerably more flexibility and more options for creative ways to accomplish your specific intentions for your collection. Hoping everything will fall into place after you are gone is simply not realistic and almost always fails to maximize the financial value of your collection.

271

For Collectors Only: What Is Probate?

Probate is the legal process conducted by a state court that manages the distribution of your assets after you die. The probate process generally consists of the following main steps:

- Filing the will with the court and appointing an executor to oversee the estate.

- Inventorying all of the property owned at the time of death.

- Paying the estate's debts, claims, and taxes, if any.

- Settling any disputes.

- Distributing the remaining property to beneficiaries according to the will.[65]

When cataloging and inventorying the collector's property, the court will only consider property that is owned by the collector at his or her death that does not otherwise "have a landing place," or, in other words, pass by designation or ownership.[66] For example, if the collector had a home and a bank account that were held jointly with his spouse, generally speaking, these items would be transferred directly to the spouse and not pass through probate.

The probate process is generally fairly straightforward. The executor/administrator of the estate, who is usually named in the will, will go before the court to present the will for validation (if no one was named in the will, then the probate court will appoint an administrator to fulfill the same function).[67] The probate court will make sure that all legal formalities were followed and that there are no objections to the will. The executor also will provide the court with an inventory of the collector's property and a list of the beneficiaries to whom the property is being given.[68]

Sometimes, a will may be contested during probate. Disgruntled or omitted family members may contest the will because they feel that they did not receive a large enough share of the estate or because they received nothing at all. The claims may include the following:

- The collector was improperly influenced when drafting the will.

- The collector lacked sufficient mental capacity when executing the will.

- Legal formalities were not followed when drafting the will.[69]

In most instances, the will is not contested, and the collector's wishes are carried out. However, there are some situations in which an instruction in the will can be overridden. For example, most states allow for a spouse to receive a portion of the estate, regardless of whether he or she was included in the will. In addition, creditors may have claims to the estate, and the executor or administrator generally must honor these.[70]

The probate process can be long and expensive, which is why many people try to avoid it. With proper estate planning, property may be passed immediately upon the collector's death to the in-

273

tended beneficiaries without going through probate. Here are some examples of assets that enable your beneficiaries to avoid probate:

- Assets, such as real estate, held as Joint Tenancy with Right of Survivorship.

- Assets with a Designated Beneficiary (i.e., life insurance policies, retirement funds, and IRAs).

- Bank accounts that are Payable-on-Death (POD).

- Securities with a Transfer-on-Death (TOD) provision.

- Any property held in a Revocable Living Trust.[71]

One very important consideration about probate is that all documents filed in probate court are a matter of public record. Details about your finances are publicly accessible. If you have assets or matters that you do not want disclosed to the general public (for example, you do not want certain family members to know what paintings you have or to whom they are being given), discuss with your advisor the possibility of using various estate planning tools to pass these assets and avoid the public disclosure of probate.

"We'd like to extend our deepest sympathies on your loss. By the way, would the estate have any of the early Renaissance masters that you'd like to auction?"

Unintentional Consequences of a Gift

If you choose to leave items of personal property in your will to various recipients, you also face the prospect of giving these people a gift they cannot afford to receive. If your estate is taxable—and most collectors have taxable estates (we will assume so for purposes of this discussion)—the items you are leaving to your family are included within your estate and are subject to the federal estate tax. The federal estate tax rates are from 41% to 46%, in 2007.[72] So depending on the value of the item you are leaving to your son or daughter, the estate is going to need to be able to write a very large check in order for the kids to be able to receive it (unless you have done some lifetime planning ahead of time). Often the result is that the family member will have to make a very hurried sale of the object, in order to meet the tax filing date, which severely compromises the value of the item you left in the will. So in spite of your intention for them to have the object and their desire to own it, if they cannot come up with the cash to pay the taxes, they will be forced to sell the piece. I do not believe this is how you wanted this story to end.

This nasty outcome can be completely avoided, however, if you involve your advisory team and undertake some lifetime planning. Your attorney can help you structure your gifts in such a way that you will be able to give the art to the family member and also give a source of funds to pay the tax liability— generally in the form of a life insurance policy held in a trust. But there are other ways to create the source of funds as well. The key point here is that you can give the cake to your kids and let them eat it too, if you bring your advisors into the planning process while you are still alive.

For Collector's Only: Federal Taxes—Gift, Estate, Income, and Capital Gains—And the States Get In On the Act Too

Collectors should be aware of the potential tax issues they face when transferring art or other collectibles during their life (gift tax), passing the assets after their death (estate tax), or selling the assets (capital gains tax). It is extremely important to monitor transfer tax developments in light of the significant changes passed by Congress in 2001 and the continuing uncertainties these changes have created.

The Gift Tax

A gift tax is a tax you pay when you transfer assets (real property, money, art, etc.) to someone else during your lifetime. The gift must be accepted for it to count as a valid transaction. Once the gift is given, the gift-giver assumes primary responsibility for any taxes that need to be paid. Under the current law, you are allowed to pass a total of $1 million worth of assets to others tax-free.[73] This level has been set by Congress and is expected to remain the same for the foreseeable future. There are several special gift tax exemptions that do not count against the $1 million lifetime cap:

Annual exemptions: You are allowed to gift $12,000 per recipient every year without paying a gift tax (married couples are allowed to gift $24,000 per recipient). If you make gifts above that amount, you must file a gift tax return (known as a Form 709). Only gifts above $12,000 will count against your $1 million lifetime gift tax exemption.[74]

Example: If Cliff Collector has two children, three grandchildren, and one nephew, he could give each of them $12,000 in one year without filing forms or paying taxes on the total gifted amount of $72,000. If Cliff decides the next year to give his painting, valued at $800,000, to his two children, Cliff would have to file a gift tax form because the value of the gift for gift tax purposes would be $776,000 ($800,000 − (2 x $12,000)). The $776,000 would reduce his $1 million lifetime exclusion to $224,000.

Spousal exemptions: You are allowed to gift an un-limited amount to your spouse without paying a gift tax as long as your spouse is a U.S. citizen and you are legally married at the time of the gift. If your spouse is not a U.S. citizen, you are only allowed to transfer $100,000 per year without it counting towards your lifetime gift tax exemp-tion.[75]

Life insurance exemptions: You're allowed to trans-fer a life insurance policy to someone without paying gift or estate taxes as long as the cash value of the policy (whatever has been earned from its investment component) is under $12,000 and the policy is transferred at least three years before you die. If you die within three years of transferring your policy to someone else, the pol-icy's benefit is includable in your estate for estate tax purposes.[76]

The Federal Estate Tax

The federal estate tax is a tax based on the value of total property you transfer at the time of your death. Unlike an inheritance tax, which draws di-rectly from the beneficiary, or person inheriting property or money, the estate tax is paid from the value of the estate itself, before the assets and property are transferred to the beneficiaries. Even if your property avoids probate and passes directly to your beneficiaries through a trust, it is still subject to the federal estate tax.

Determining your Gross Estate. To find out how much you are going to pay in estate taxes, you need to first determine the value of your gross estate (i.e., the total fair market value of all your assets and property at the time of death). The following types of property are included in your gross estate and are therefore subject to the estate tax upon certain conditions:[77]

- All property owned exclusively by you at the time of your death, including tangible (paintings, furniture, antiques, jewelry), intangible (stocks, bonds, mutual funds), and real estate.

- Insurance, if owned at death or transferred within three years prior to your death.

- Annuities, unless they are straight life annuities, which terminate upon death.

- Property where you have a retained life estate (i.e., property that you have transferred to another person but have retained a right to possession during your lifetime).

- Property owned with your spouse. If you own property jointly with your spouse, 50% of that property is taxable as part of your estate. However, when the property is owned by tenants in common (father/son, boyfriend/girlfriend, etc.) the entire property is subject to estate tax, unless the surviving tenant in common can provide evidence that he or she made contributions to the purchase of the property.

Estate Tax Deductions. There are certain deductions that allow you to limit the amount of estate tax liability by reducing your gross estate:[78]

- Marital deduction: The marital deduction allows you to pass an unlimited amount of property to your surviving spouse tax-free.

- Charitable deduction: The charitable deduction allows you to transfer assets to a charity without being subject to an estate tax. Most museums, colleges, libraries, and hospitals qualify as charitable organizations.

- Estate expense and liability deductions: Estate expenses (cost of funeral, lawyers, probate) or liabilities such as debts are also treated as deductions that can be subtracted from the total amount of your gross estate.

Estate Tax Credit. The estate tax credit refers to the value of assets you can pass on to family and friends after your death without paying any estate taxes. In 2007, it allows you to pass on up to $2 million in wealth without paying any estate taxes on the transfer. Any amount of your estate that is transferred after your death over the $2 million maximum will be subject to taxation. In 2009, the federal government is set to increase the estate tax credit to $3.5 million. In 2010, the estate tax is scheduled to phase out all together, only to reemerge again in 2011 at the $1 million level.[79] What happens after that will be up to future Congresses, which unfortunately makes planning now for your estate that much more uncertain.

Estate Tax Rates. Estate tax rates are determined by the total value of your estate. Generally, they tend to be higher than income tax rates. Like estate tax exemptions, estate tax rates change frequently. In 2007, federal estate tax rates range from 41 to 46% (46% being the maximum rate applied to any estate). In 2009, the maximum tax rate will decrease to 45%. In 2010, the rate will temporarily drop to 0% when the estate tax disappears, before jumping up to 50% beginning in 2011.[80]

Sample calculation: To see the estate tax in action, here is a sample calculation based on 2008 tax rates.

Suppose a single man named Cliff Collector owns the following property at the time of his death:

House	$1.8 million
Bank Accounts	$900,000
Stocks	$1.3 million
Art Collection	$1.2 million
Life Insurance	$1 million
Total Gross Estate	$6.2 million

Because there are deductions that factor into the estate tax equation, Cliff's estate does not have to pay taxes on this gross amount. If Cliff donates $300,000 to a charity, owes $175,000 on his mortgage, and his estate winds up paying $25,000 for funeral costs and lawyer fees, this $500,000 would be deducted from Cliff's gross estate to produce a final taxable amount of $5.7 million.

Based on the prevailing IRS estate tax rates, an estate worth $5.7 million would end up owing $1.7 million in taxes after the $2 million estate tax credit is deducted from the total.

State Death Tax. Like income taxes, estate taxes are also paid on the state level at various rates depending on the state in which you reside. With the passage of the 2001 tax bill, the federal government phased out the state death tax credit in 2005, which had tied the state death tax to the federal. This "decoupling" of the state death tax from the federal estate tax has resulted in states determining their own estate tax systems as well as the need for more tax planning.

Capital Gains Tax

A capital gains tax is a tax on profits earned from the sale of investments, including art and collectibles, which are taxed at 28% (some advisors are unaware of this fact). They are included as part of your annual income tax return. To compute capital gain, you subtract the cost basis (or cost of buying the asset) from the selling price (amount realized). Capital gains are triggered by a realization event—typically the sale of the asset. It is important for collectors to note that capital losses on the sale of the art and collectibles are deductible against any gains from the sale of art and collectibles in the same tax year (these assets comprise the "28% rate group basket").[81] The cost basis of an asset (used to calculate the gain) is determined by how you acquire the asset. There are three ways you can acquire an asset:

1. Purchasing the asset: If you purchase the asset, the cost basis is the price of the asset at the time of purchase, including any commissions and associated expenses.

Example: If you purchase a painting for $300,000 plus a $30,000 broker's commission, your cost basis would be $330,000. If you subsequently sold the painting for $900,000, your capital gain would equal the selling price minus cost basis, which would be $900,000 - $330,000 = $570,000.

2. Receiving the asset as a gift: If you received the painting as a gift, there are four situations that decide the cost basis and tax liability:[82]

a) If you are selling the gift at a gain, you use the carryover basis, which means you take the donor's cost basis (what the person making the gift paid for it).

Example: If Cliff's father gives him a painting that the father originally purchased for $400,000, but is now worth $900,000 at the time of the gift, then Cliff's cost basis is $400,000. If Cliff later sells the painting for $1 million, he has a $600,000 capital gain.

(b) If you receive the gift at a gain, but are selling it at a loss, the cost basis for the person receiving the gift is the carryover basis (the donor's basis).

Example: Cliff's father gives him a painting worth $900,000 at the time of the gift, which he originally purchased for $400,000. The paining turns out to have dubious provenance, and Cliff later sells it for only $250,000. The loss would be $400,000 - $250,000, or $150,000.

(c) If you receive the gift at a loss and sell it at a loss, you use the fair market value (FMV) of the asset at the time of gift to compute the loss.

Example: Cliff's father gives him a painting worth

$300,000 at the time of the gift, which his father originally purchased for $400,000. Cliff later sells the painting for $250,000. Using the fair market value of the painting at the time of the gift, the loss would equal $300,000 - $250,000, or $50,000.

(d) If you receive the art as a gift from the artist, you would use the artist's cost basis, which is the actual cost of the materials involved in creating the item. In this case, the gain would be taxed as ordinary income rather than at the capital gains rate.

Example: Suppose Cliff's friend Mark Rothko gave him an original painting in the late 1950s. The painting cost Rothko $40 in paint and supplies, plus a $100 canvas and $860 for framing and mounting. Cliff's cost basis would be $1,000, and if he subsequently sold the painting for $10 million, his gain would be $9,999,000.

3. Inheriting the asset: If you inherit the asset, you receive what is known as a "stepped-up basis," which means that your cost basis is the fair market value of the asset at the date of the death of the person who left the asset to you.[83]

Example: Cliff's father bought a painting in 1970 for $50,000. When Cliff inherits the painting in 2003 upon his father's death, the painting is now valued at $400,000. If a year later Cliff decides to sell the painting for $475,000, under current tax law he only has to pay taxes on a capital gain of $75,000 (he is taxed only on gains since his father's death). On the other hand, if Cliff's father had gifted that painting to Cliff while he was still alive and Cliff sold it in 2004 for $475,000, Cliff

> would have had to pay taxes on all gains earned between 1970 and 2004, or $425,000.
>
> From now until 2010, there will be no limit to the amount of stepped-up cost basis any beneficiary can receive when inheriting an asset. In 2010, when the estate tax temporarily phases out, the stepped-up cost basis will be limited to $3 million for the surviving spouse and $1.3 million for all other beneficiaries. Congress will have to decide what to do after 2010, so stay tuned!

Working with Private Family Offices

Some collectors are in situations where the family has employed or retained a group of professional advisors and concierge service providers who support multiple generations of the family. The goal here is to achieve continuity in the management of the family's assets across the several generations and to avoid situations where advisors are working at cross purposes. These advisors work in what are called private family offices and provide all the same services that individually retained advisors provide, but they are generally planning for and providing services to several members of the family simultaneously.

Historically, private family offices have been the purview of the super-wealthy; they dealt with names like Rockefeller, Morgan, Carnegie, and Kennedy. They are very private businesses—unless you need one or are brought into the circle, you probably will have not even known about them. As the number of ultra-wealthy families has increased and affluence has become increasingly concentrated in the United States and a small group of other countries, the number of family offices has experienced explosive growth, with at least 4,000 operating in the U.S. alone. And while they are still very private, making exact statistics hard to determine, their rising popularity has led banks, trust companies, investment firms, and financial services companies of all varieties to diversify their service offering into this area.

A family office is exactly what it sounds like: it is a separate legal entity established to manage the business affairs of multiple generations of a family. The office generally employs several professional advisors who work together to support all the members of a family (or in some cases more than one family). The typical scenario is this: Great Grandpa started a textile business that became very successful and, by the time his son came into the business, had multiple locations—manufacturing in the deep South, distribution in New York, and administrative offices in Chicago. Grandpa became President, diversified the company, and took it public. The family has always retained a controlling interest. Daddy came into the business, refocused the company on luxury goods, and took the company global. Daddy's daughter, Jill, became Executive Vice President in 2002. Jill's husband is VP of Marketing. Jill's daughter has just graduated from the Rhode Island School of Design and is working part-time in the design department. In March of 2005 the company was acquired by a French firm that dominates particular segments of the luxury goods market. Grandpa, now in his late eighties, has just stepped down as Chairman of the Board, Daddy is CEO, and he and his two sisters sit on the board. The family, which was always wealthy, has now received a huge infusion of cash—hundreds of millions of dollars.

Families in this situation first of all need professional management of the money and the business affairs of the family. They are dedicated to keeping the wealth in the family and passing it to the next generation using well-structured estate and financial planning services provided by the top firms in the country. Many families in these kinds of circumstances set up a private family office to run the legal, financial, and business affairs of the family.

Generally the family office is staffed by financial advisors, investment professionals, attorneys, and people who provide concierge services. The family office might also employ a domestic staff and people to take care of yachts, planes, cars, and, in many cases, art. Family offices also generally work with a network of other service providers in whom they have complete trust and confidence. These can include insurance representatives, interior designers, party planners, PR firms, and art consultants.

As the Baby Boomer generation approaches retirement and comes into control of more and more of the wealth of this country, their values are beginning to affect how family offices are managed. Family cohesiveness is being recognized as a core value that must be promoted by the office. The staff is expected to be on call and available 24/7 to each family member. There is also an increasing focus on philanthropy. Members of the office staff must be familiar with the charitable interests of their family and able to facilitate involvement in these causes and special interests.

The family office has two key principles that drive them. First, families should remain in control of their wealth. This means that families should be fully involved in and able to completely customize the management of their assets. They should have full transparency on the fees that they are paying as well as having a private view of their entire asset base. Families should also have complete knowledge of any conflicts of interest and a clear understanding of the risks that they are taking.

Second, families should be able to align their wealth management plans completely with their values and interests. This means their advisors should hear and be receptive to those values and reflect them in their wealth management strategies, and that families should be able to understand their investments and plans after discussions with their advisors.

288

The Family Office and the Collector

For collectors, this means that the staff in the family office need to provide effective collection management and to help plan and structure innovative charitable gifting strategies. It is often important to these wealthy families that the art and antiques be kept in the family and so the advisors will need to coordinate interfamily transfers and provide financial methods to address the tax issues. In other situations the family will want to gift an item to the institution where they sit on the board and the advisors will need to negotiate the transfer and prepare the documentation required. The result is that lawyers, accountants, and financial planners are finding themselves filling the role of impromptu curator and art advisor when the family comes to them with wishes to gift or dispose of parts of their collection.

In this situation the family office will generally add an art advisor to the composition of the family office, either as an independent contractor or, if the collection is large enough, as an employee of the office. By adding an art advisor, the family office now has a person who can work with the dealer, the auction house, the receiving institution, the advisory team, the appraiser, and others to coordinate the details involved with the sale or gift of the piece. Additionally, an art advisor can help maintain the inventory of the collection, and can oversee insurance, transportation, and other logistics when items are loaned for exhibition; the restoration of damaged pieces; and various other aspects of collection management that the collector may not have the time or interest to do.

How This Book Helps You Work with Your Advisory Team

289

In the chapters that follow we discuss an assortment of planning tools that are commonly used by estate and financial planners. None of the approaches discussed in this book involves pushing the envelope with the IRS, fancy offshore techniques, or anything other than tried-and-true methods that are within the generally accepted practices of most professional advisors.

What is somewhat innovative in the planning options discussed in this book is this—professional advisors are accustomed to looking at classes of assets in bulk. Advisors will generally address all of your stocks and bonds as a block or all of your investment real estate as a single asset and plan for them in bulk. In order to optimize the value of art, antiques, and collectibles assets, individual pieces require independent consideration in the planning process. Unlike stocks or other types of financial holdings, every piece of art is

290

unique, and the process of establishing the value of the piece is not as easily determined as establishing the date of death value of 100 shares of AT&T.

The history, condition, provenance, and acquisition circumstances of a piece of art often necessitate special planning on an item-by-item basis. For example, a very good piece acquired inexpensively in the early days of acquiring may have appreciated tremendously through the years, triggering a huge capital gains issue. A charitable remainder trust could be the perfect planning strategy for this asset, particularly if you need to generate some income for living expenses. Another equally good piece may have come to the collector with a stepped-up basis or was purchased for more than the current market estimates and would be appropriate for a very different treatment in the estate plan. A third piece may be a gift from the artist and require another treatment entirely. You may also have a group of "Oh" level items that can be sold to raise cash to pay insurance premiums or given to a non-related use charity to be sold to raise funds for operating expenses. The point is that you want to encourage your advisory team to look at your art assets individually and make separate determinations as to the appropriate planning strategy for each, particularly at the "Oh My God" level.

The second somewhat innovative approach to the recommendations in this book is that we are often recommending that commonly-used legal tools be used in combination or in phased or layering techniques so that you have more than one legal tool in use in a planning strategy for a single piece or grouping of pieces. This approach is illustrated by some of the more sophisticated plans we discuss in the case studies in Chapter 14. In these case studies we will offer some fact patterns, based on representative situations we have drawn from our planning experience, that illustrate how you can bring all of these planning tools together and create an integrated strategy that enables you to do what we call PowerGifting™. PowerGifting strategies insure that the planning team has preserved as much of the value of the collection as possible by:

1. Reducing what is paid to the IRS.

2. Creating an art legacy through charitable gifting.

3. Transferring as much wealth as possible to the next generation.

But before we get to the fancy stuff, we need to spend some time looking at your various planning options in isolation to make sure you understand how all of the component parts work. Then we will bring it all together in an integrated plan compiled from a broad range of client experiences. Our goal here, remember, is not to turn you into an estate planner, but simply to give you enough information so that you can have an informed conversation with your advisory team and articulate your specific intentions for each item in your collection.

11

Charitable Giving and Fulfilling Your Philanthropic Intentions

**With Contributions From
George Kasparian, Esq.
and Daniel Waintrup**

"The manner of giving is
worth more than the gift."

–Pierre Corneille

Whenever you are thinking about the disposition of your collection and having a discussion about it with your advisory team, it is inevitable that you will eventually touch upon the question of charitable donations. Some collectors may not initially want to give any of their collection to museums or charitable organizations, but the issue should at least be explored as an option so that you understand how gifting can be used in conjunction with other strategies to preserve the value of your collection and give even more to your kids, if the plan is properly structured using our PowerGifting™ approach. Philanthropy is an important alternative because charitable gifting offers excellent options that are beneficial to the institution, the collector, and the collector's family.

The Framework for Charitable Giving

In 2006 Warren Buffet gifted $37.4 billion to charity. In the course of the estate planning process Buffet is quoted as saying, "It [planning an estate] is a much tougher problem, frankly, than amassing money."[84]

A whole array of questions will come up when you begin to think about giving some or all of your collection to charity:

- How much of a deduction will I get for this gift?

- Should I donate my photography collection to the local art museum or the hospital capital campaign?

- What do I do if the Smithsonian says no to my PEZ® Dispenser collection?

- What if I'm not ready to fully give up ownership of my grandmother's Weisweiler secrétaire?

- The painting was given to me as a gift by the artist—does that affect anything?

Your team of advisors can help you with the answers to many of these questions. The material that follows will give you a basic understanding of the framework behind a charitable gifting strategy, and then will show you how to use some of these strategies in order to accomplish specific objectives as you plan for the disposition of your collection.

Tax Deductions

Whenever you are focusing on the tax ramifications of a charitable gift, you will want to immediately bring your tax advisor and/or attorney into the conversation. The professional advisor's role when it comes to this aspect of charitable giving is to provide guidance and help you navigate the tricky waters of tax deductibility under the Internal Revenue Code. As a general rule of thumb, the collector who gives a work of art to a museum is entitled to deduct the fair market value of the piece when computing his or her taxable income.[85] Deductions based on contributions of personal property, like a collection, are limited to 30% of the taxpayer's adjusted gross income as defined on the tax return.[86] However, unused deductions may be carried forward and used over the five succeeding years.[87]

There are eight key issues that you need to consider when you are contemplating making a charitable gift:

- The type of receiving (or donee) organization.
- The qualified appraisal requirement.
- The willingness of donee organization to accept the gift.

- The appropriateness of restrictions on the gift.
- The potential for deaccession by the receiving institution.
- The related use/purpose rule.
- The five-year carryover provision.
- Charitable Remainder Trust and Fractional Gifting options.

Types of Donee Organizations

While the collector is free to give property to whomever he or she likes, only organizations that fall under specific guidelines can accept a charitable contribution without being subject to capital gains or income taxes. The IRC §501(c)(3) lists these types of donee organizations and the guidelines they must follow. To qualify as one of these donee organizations, the organization must:

- Meet the "organizational test": the articles of organization that created the charity must require it to engage in one or more exempt purposes. Also, the charity must not be allowed to participate in activities outside of the exempt purposes that it was designed to promote.[88]
- Serve a public, rather than private, interest and not engage in lobbying (attempting to influence legislation) or promoting/opposing candidates for public office.[89]

In terms of the type of activities that qualify for tax-exempt status, an organization may be exempt from paying capital gains or income taxes on a donation if it is organized and operated for one or more of the following purposes:

- Religious
- Charitable
- Scientific
- Testing for Public Safety
- Literary
- Educational
- Prevention of cruelty to children or animals.[90]

Therefore, as long as the above requirements are met, you may donate the artwork or collectibles to any charity you choose, and you will receive a charitable income tax deduction. The amount of the deduction can be a little trickier to determine —read on.

297

The Qualified Appraisal Requirement

If you are structuring a gift with a value greater than $5,000, the IRS requires the collector to obtain a qualified appraisal, and if the gift is valued at more than $20,000 a complete copy of the signed appraisal must be attached to the tax return.[91] For purposes of qualifying for a charitable income tax deduction, the IRS defines a "qualified appraisal" as follows:

1. Is made not earlier than 60 days prior to the date of contribution of the appraised property.

2. Is prepared, signed, and dated by a qualified appraiser.

3. Describes the property and its physical condition.

4. The date (or expected date) of contribution.

5. The terms of any agreement or understanding entered into (or expected to be entered into) by or on behalf of the donor or donee that relates to

the use, sale, or other disposition of the property contributed.

6. The name, address, and taxpayer ID of the appraiser.

7. The qualifications of the qualified appraiser who signs the appraisal, including the appraiser's background, experience, education, and membership, if any, in professional appraisal associations.

8. A statement that the appraisal was prepared for income tax purposes.

9. The date (or dates) on which the property was appraised.

10. The fair market value of the property and method of valuation used to determine the fair market value.[92]

The appraisal must be received by the collector prior to the due date of the tax return. This requirement is extremely important because the deduction can be completely lost if this provision is not complied with.

Will the Charitable Organization Accept the Gift, and Are There Any Restrictions on It?

Just because a collector has offered to donate some or all of his or her collection to a particular charity does not necessarily mean that the charity is obliged to accept it. Many collectors do not understand why a charity —for example, a museum—would refuse a generous gift of a piece of art. Well, there are several reasons why. Firstly, it might not fit in with the flow of the permanent collections that the museum has accumulated. If the collector has spent a lifetime focusing on pre-Columbian art and the museum showcases contemporary pieces, then the museum is not going to want to add the collector's pieces to its collection, no matter how rare and valuable. It simply does not fit. (For more on why gifts are declined see Chapter 5.)

Secondly, the piece may be declined for quality or because the museum may have a similar or exact duplicate of the piece. Museums, libraries, and almost all other charitable institutions that the collector may consider gifting to will have a focus that dictates how the institution builds its collection. This focus determines both the scope and the quality standards of items that will be accepted into the permanent collection. Sometimes the museum will accept only a few pieces from the collection that meet their acquisitions criteria and reject the rest. What do you do with the balance?

With art, particularly in the "Oh My God" category, not only is the quality of the piece important, but it must also come with a clean chain of ownership and well-documented paper trail. Issues of origin and authenticity, tax liens, criminal investigations, and claims from foreign nations or previous owners are sometimes out there waiting to cause trouble. Without the paper trail, institutions run the risk of showing a forgery or possessing something removed illegally from another country or that rightful heirs are searching for. Currently, this is a major issue for museums. Nazi-purloined art coming into the market from South America; archeological pieces purchased illegally through private transactions in Guatemala, Italy, and Egypt; and pieces with unexplained gaps in the chain of title are causing serious issues at museums throughout the world, and can cause a curator to summarily reject a piece. If a museum thinks that there is even a remote chance that the provenance or authenticity of a piece is in question, it is not going to accept the gift.

One of the most popular covers of the *Saturday Evening Post* was a painting by Normal Rockwell, "Breaking Home Ties." Run on the September 25, 1954 cover, the painting depicts a boy and his dog on an old truck, the boy about to leave home for the first time. American cartoonist Don Trachte bought the painting directly from Rockwell in 1960, for just $900. "Breaking Home Ties" became Trachte's most prized possession. When he and his wife divorced a decade later, he secretly made a replica of the painting. He then hung the replica instead of the original above the fireplace in the living room of his house in Vermont, and stored the original in a secret compartment behind a wall of the house, and told no one.

After Trachte entered an assisted-living facility, his four children lent what they thought was the original to the Norman Rockwell Museum in Stockbridge, Massachusetts. While on display, however, art scholars noticed some subtle discrepancies between the painting and the tear sheet of the *Saturday Evening Post* cover. They dismissed the discrepancies, however, as bad conservation because the provenance of the painting was perfect. After Trachte's death in 2005, his sons discovered the original "Breaking Home Ties" behind the secret sliding wall panel, and believe he hid it to protect their inheritance. The copy traveled internationally as part of exhibitions throughout the 1960s and 1970s and was loaned to the Norman Rockwell museum for display from 2003 to 2006. The original painting was sold at auction in

November of 2006 for a record-breaking $15.4 million. This is a very strange incident, and illustrates that even in a situation of perfect provenance a museum can exhibit a forgery.

The Headlines Speak for Themselves: A Question of Provenance at the Getty

Museum policies regarding the provenance of a piece have been tightening up, particularly since foreign governments have gotten more aggressive in reclaiming illegally-taken art and antiquities. These issues made headlines recently with the sensational story of Marion True, a former curator for the Los Angeles J. Paul Getty Museum.[93] In May 2005, Marion was indicted by the Italian government on the charge of conspiring to traffic in looted antiquities. As summer and fall wore on, articles about Marion's misconduct—including photos of the Getty's prized marble Griffons in the trunk of a car—were splashed over the front pages of major newspapers and all over the Internet. As of the printing of this book, the case was still before the Italian courts, but the Getty has agreed to return a significant cache (approximately 40 objects) of artifacts to Italy.

An Endowment to Support the Gift of Art

It is an increasingly common practice for a museum to conditionally accept a piece into its permanent collection, requiring a supporting curatorial or endowment fund to accompany the gift. This fund is a second gift of cash that accompanies the gift of art and is used to cover the ancillary expenses of storing, preserving, transporting, insuring, and generally caring for the piece by the museum. If the museum will accept the art only if it comes with some money, then you have several options:

1. A cash gift can accompany the piece.

2. A plan for cash payments over a period of time.

3. A bequest of other artwork that can be sold to create a fund.

4. A life insurance policy or annuity can be structured to create the endowment by naming the museum as the beneficiary.

5. A trust can be structured leaving the corpus to the museum.

The first and second options are very straightforward, and if the collector has the liquidity, outright cash gifts will often greatly simplify the negotiations with the museum. Not everyone will have the requisite liquidity, however—very often, the collector's assets are almost completely tied up in the collection. If this is the case, the remaining options become more feasible and allow the collector to fund the donated piece by paying for life insurance premiums, which can be financed by selling off lesser pieces or borrowing against better ones found in his or her collection. The museum (or other charitable organization) needs to be named the owner and the beneficiary of the policy. If this is done correctly, the premium payment(s) become fully deductible to the collector. Similarly, a museum can be named as the beneficiary of a trust or a retirement plan, and if the gift is not to be made until the collector's death, these can fund the endowment.

Restrictions on Gifts

Sometimes collectors will want to put some kind of restriction on the gift; for example, "the sculpture must always be displayed and never put in storage." While these kinds of restrictions were sometimes accepted in the past, particularly if a museum was very interested in the piece or the piece was first-rate, it is a practice that is increasingly avoided today. A museum is generally considered a public trust and as such owes a duty of loyalty to the community—its beneficiaries. By accepting a gift with restrictions, the museum places itself at risk for a conflict of interest. For this and other reasons, museums are increasingly disinclined to accept gifts with strings attached. Courts are cooperating by terminating or revising restrictions that came with past gifts, freeing the current museum staff to act in accordance with the current vision and focus of the organization.[94]

Take, for example, Miriam Collector, who has decided to give a Louis XVI wardrobe to her local art museum. The museum curator is a French furniture aficionado who would love to see the wardrobe as part of the collection. So, the curator accepts the piece with the condition, made by Miriam Collector, that the piece will never be sold. Flash forward twenty years. The Francophile curator has retired and the museum

Special Rules for the Artist: Valuing a Gift of the Intellectual Property of an Artist

There are circumstances where the advisory team may need to bring in the services of other personal property appraisers with specialties in areas other than art. For example, if an artist were to donate the intellectual property and copyright along with a painting, this would require a fine art appraiser for the tangible property (the painting) as well as a business valuation appraiser for the intangible property (the intellectual property). In the alternative, if the artist wanted to donate the work to charity at her death and retain the reproduction rights for her heirs, this would also present a valuation issue.[95]

(Contributed by Elizabeth Clement)

has changed its focus to American folk art. They now have no place for a Louis XVI wardrobe in their gallery space and storage is prohibitively expensive: the "Oh My God" wardrobe has become an "Oh God" albatross. Now, does the museum honor the donor's wishes or the public's interest in the new collection?

To avoid this problem, the collector's advisor will want to use suggestive language instead of mandatory language when structuring the gift. That way, the collector expresses his wishes for the piece, and the museum can oblige in good faith to follow his wishes, but will not be stuck if it cannot comply. In the future, if the museum decides that the family's gift no longer fits into the current museum holdings and they want to deaccession it, they will most likely allow the family to find another appropriate home.

Offering the right pieces to the right museum so that you have a reasonable degree of certainty that the gift will be accepted is a challenge that both collectors and professional advisors do not generally anticipate. Structuring the gift in a way that makes it an attractive offering can be even trickier if you do not have experience working with curatorial staff and planned giving departments. These are situations where an art succession planner can greatly enhance the negotiation process by working in full partnership with the advisory team in order to accomplish the intentions of the collector. In complicated situations like these the succession planner becomes a member of the advisory team, serving as a liaison with the museum staff and assisting during the negotiations on matters having more to do with museum practices and culture than strictly succession planning issues.

305

The Expert's Perspective:
Joe Jacobs

The Barnes Foundation in Merion, Pennsylvania owns the great Modernist collection of Dr. Albert B. Barnes, which was opened as a private museum in 1922. Barnes's will required the collection to remain untouched as he displayed it in his mansion in Merion. The works were never to be loaned, and reflecting his belief that the poor color reproductions of his day grossly distorted the original works of art, his paintings were never to be reproduced in color—only in black and white. Faced with bankruptcy, the foundation appealed to the courts to abandon the Merion location and move the museum to a new facility in downtown Philadelphia, located near the Philadelphia Museum of Art and the Rodin Museum.

The court saw the need to empower the foundation to act outside of the original intentions of the collector so that the collection could survive and continue to be shown, studied, and appreciated by the public. The court ruling enabled the financially beleaguered foundation to raise money for its survival. The trustees arranged for a major international tour of highlights from the collection, such as Henri Matisse's *The Joy of Life* and *The Dance*, and the works are now reproduced in countless publications in color, reproduction rights and transparency rentals generating significant income. While little remains of Barnes's vision as it was articulated in his will, the collection remains intact today, and can be enjoyed and appreciated by the public.

Deaccessioning Art Assets

In the last few years, a difficult situation has shown itself that deserves some reflection by collectors planning for the disposition of art assets. It has become increasingly common for museums to deaccession, or sell off, pieces that were gifted to the museum and a fair market value tax deduction taken. Sometime after the gift is accepted, the museum puts the piece on the market to be sold at public or private sale, with the proceeds coming back to the museum to be used either for general operating expenses or new acquisitions.

The Headlines Speak for Themselves: The New York Public Library— Nice Work If You Can Get It

The New York Public Library, a city landmark with over 50 million books, declared itself in financial distress three years ago due to city and state financing cuts. A campaign to raise $18 million privately was established and the library sold off many important works of art for $52 million to help shore up the endowment. The library has also reduced its tuition assistance plan for employees, again citing budget constraints. However, during this financial distress, the library's president and chief executive increased his annual compensation to over $800,000, an increase of more that $221,000 from the previous year. Other senior level new hires received

significant pay increases from their predecessors in the equivalent position. Board members stated that it was necessary to increase the compensation of these individuals in order to attract top-flight managerial talent to this "unique and complex" organization.[96]

A museum is a repository of local, national, and global treasures and the idea of a museum selling off an item in its collection may seem counterintuitive. "Why would any museum want to sell off a Calder or any other work?" you ask. The reasons are as varied as the art itself. Most often, a museum will deaccession lesser pieces to raise money to purchase other works of art for the collection. Sometimes, however, they will sell off a masterwork in order to generate a large amount of cash to fund a new building or wing. It is also common for museums to trade works of art that are thought to be of equal value in order to round out major collections in the other facility. Also, as curators change and collections evolve, it may be that this institution's permanent collection is no longer the best place for the piece in question.

The Metropolitan Museum of Art in New York, for example, has a longstanding policy of consulting with a donor before deaccessioning a piece it received in the last 25 years.[97] In 2006, however, they had a bit of a mishap when the museum consigned an Eduardo Chillida sculpture to Sotheby's which had been given to them in 1986, without consulting the donor. The donor learned that the piece was being sold through a friend who saw it on the Sotheby's web site. The donor immediately complained to the *New York Times* and *ARTnews*. The Met withdrew the sculpture from the sale but not in time to avoid a barrage of criticism. The donor was highly offended and the museum received a great deal of bad press because of the snafu.[98]

One of the most dramatic examples of deaccessioning was the Armand Hammer Museum of Art and Culture's 1994 auction sale of one of Leonardo da Vinci's Codex manuscripts to Bill Gates for $30.8 million.[99] Similarly, in 2005, the Met sold off an important group of photographs, the Los Angeles County Museum of Art sold major Impressionist and modern works from its permanent collection, and the New York Public Library deassessioned Asher Durand's well-known *Kindred Spirits* and two signature portraits of George Washington by Gilbert Stuart.

The Advisor's FYI: Note to Professional Advisors —Due Diligence

As of this writing, the practice of charitable organizations selling off pieces received as a tax deductible gift has not been challenged by the IRS, but I believe it will come under scrutiny in the near future. I believe the professional advisor has a responsibility to inquire as to the intention of the related use organization in accepting a charitable gift. If a deduction is posthumously disallowed because of use changes, the collector's heirs are in a very difficult situation. Obviously, we do not know the answer to this question, but, with proper planning and due diligence on the professional advisor's part, the situation can be avoided and the potential exposure circumvented.

Related Versus Non-Related Use

When donating to any type of charitable organization, it is imperative for the collector to consider how the donation will be used, because this determines the tax treatment of the gift. The distinction that must be made when donating art or antiques to a charitable organization is whether the art will be used for a related use or a non-related use. If the donation is for a related use, then the collector is allowed a deduction for the fair market value of the donation. If the donation is for a non-related use, the collector can only deduct the cost basis of the item, which is defined as the collector's acquisition cost.[100]

To a degree, the difference between types of usage is subjective and it's important for the collector to inquire how the piece will be used after its donation in order to maximize the tax deductibility. The Internal Revenue Code (IRC) defines a related use as being "related to the purpose or function" of the charitable organization. Whereas a non-related use is defined as one that is "unrelated to the purpose or function" of the charitable organization under §501.[101]

While this sounds pretty straightforward, it raises important questions. For example, let's revisit Miriam Collector and her Louis XVI wardrobe—an "Oh My God" level piece. Assume Miriam paid $38,000 for the piece 25 years ago and it is now worth $1.5 million. Miriam has the choice of giving her piece to either the art museum or the community hospital. Assuming the museum accepts the donation with the intent of displaying the piece as part of its permanent collection, it qualifies as a related use gift and she can have an income tax deduction equal to the current fair market value ($1.5 million). If the hospital, on the other hand, intends to sell the wardrobe to raise funds for its capital campaign, this is a non-related use and her tax deduction would be limited to her cost basis ($38,000). Although this sounds simple now, confusion can result when it's unclear if the museum intends to display the piece in its galleries or if the planned giving department intends to put the piece in the auction at the annual fundraising gala. The collector needs to be very clear on the intended use of the gift at the time the gift is being structured in order to be sure that the intended tax benefit of the gift is realized.

Sorting Out the Use

For the collector to get the most benefit from his or her donation, the professional advisor and the collector need to approach the charitable institution thoughtfully. What may seem to be an non-related use can in fact be related, allowing for a larger deduction, assuming the item has appreciated since its purchase.

An innovative approach can be used if the collector wants to donate a piece to a fundamentally non-related use organization, but the organization will use the piece for a related use purpose. Take, for example, the collector who donates some "Oh" level (bottom tier) pieces in the collection to a hospital which then displays the pieces in a children's ward within the scope of an art therapy program. While the purpose of a hospital could never be confused as being the same as an art gallery, the inclusion within an art therapy program allows the collector a related use deduction to a non-related use organization.

A prospective donor should request documentation from the organization (including letters from the IRS) confirming that the IRS made a determination that the organization qualifies for tax-exempt status under Section 501(c)(3) of the Internal Revenue Code. In addition, the donor can ask for written certification that the charity intends to use the art for an appropriate purpose.

The charity must file IRS Form 8282 if, within two years of the date of the gift, the charity disposes of an item valued at $500 or more. This form shows the disposition date and the amount of proceeds received by the charity. It is intended to help the IRS track discrepancies between the claimed value of non-cash contributions and the amount eventually received by the charity.

Giving to a Non-Related Use Charity

Despite the difference in tax treatment, a collector may want to use his or her collection to benefit non-related use charities. Donations of this sort can be leveraged to increase the benefits for both the collector and the organization, beyond just a simple donation with the collector taking the cost basis deduction. Ways to do this include:

1. Giving the pieces to a related use space, freeing up tax savings to make donations to non-related use charities.

2. Creating a charitable remainder trust with the remainder interest going to a non-related use charity, taking the cost basis deduction but creating income for the collector.

3. Taking a loan against the artwork and donating the funds to a non-related use charity.

4. Leaving the art as a bequest in the donor's will to the charity, which then can sell the pieces to create philanthropic capital.

Sorting out how to benefit both a related use and a non-related use charity can be done. I saw the benefits of these different approaches when a family called me in to evaluate some collectibles in the grandfather's home. The family wanted to structure a gift for a special needs center, raising money for operating expenses. Inside the grandfather's home I saw a wide array of antique cameras, stereoptic cards, viewers, and old photographs. Despite the grandfather's protests that he was not a collector, the outside appraiser I brought in informed us that several pieces in the collection were worth a substantial amount of money.

Special Rules for the Artist: What Is the Artist's Basis for a Charitable Gift?

If the donor of the piece is the artist, the question of tax deductibility becomes even more complicated. The current code section allows an artist to deduct only her actual cost (for paint, clay, canvas, wire, etc.—whatever the artist has used to create the art) rather than the fair market value of a piece she has created. This, obviously, results in a huge disincentive for artists to gift their works to museums. The reasonableness of this code section is currently being challenged by the Association of Art Museum Directors, who believe that the public would be served by creating an incentive for such persons to make their creations and papers available to the public while the donor [artist] remains alive.

314

Since no one in the family was interested in retaining the collection, we structured a gift that benefited the charity as well as the collector. If we had just donated the collection to the special needs center, the collector could only have taken the cost basis of the pieces as a deduction. Instead, the collector made a gift of the relevant pieces in the collection to a children's museum for a related use, i.e., displaying the pieces. This allowed the collector to take a charitable tax deduction for the full fair market value of the donation. He then used the tax savings to benefit the special needs center by taking out a life insurance policy on himself with that charity as the beneficiary. By taking these extra steps, not only was the family able to make a donation to the special needs center, but they were also able to give portions of the collection to the children's museum that fully recognized its value and would make the collection available for public viewing. The remaining pieces in the collection were sold by the special needs center to raise money for operating expenses.

The Five-Year Carryover

In some situations the collector will want to gift an item that is worth a great deal of money, such as a family heirloom, that results in a very large tax deduction, especially as it relates to the collector's current income level. When this happens the collector is confronted with IRC §170, which limits the amount of a charitable income tax deduction to a percentage of current income. If the donation is made to a museum, and the gift is considered a related use, the collector can deduct the current fair market value up to 30% of his adjusted gross income. If the donation of art goes to a non-related use charity, then the collector's deduction is limited to his cost basis up to 50% of adjusted gross income.[102] The good news is that the code allows an individual to carryover excess deductions for up to five years until the amount is exhausted.[103]

Suppose that Charles Collector has an adjusted gross income of $500,000. He has a Japanese print that he paid $75,000 for twenty years ago that is now worth $400,000. He donates the piece to the local museum to display as part of their collection. The gift qualifies as a related use, so he can deduct the current fair market value ($400,000). His deduction is limited in the current year to 30% of his adjusted gross income, which means he can reduce his taxable income by $150,000 in the year he made the gift (30% of $500,000). He can carry over the remaining $250,000 in excess deductions into the next year. Assuming his income remains at $500,000, he can deduct another $150,000 in year two and the remaining $100,000 in year three.

Loaning Works of Art to Museums and Other Charitable Institutions

Another philanthropically appealing method, if there are no cash flow issues and the collector has no interest in relinquishing control of the artwork, is to loan either the collection, or specific pieces in it, to museums or other charitable institutions. Loaning to a museum is an excellent option for the client interested in increasing the provenance of his or her collection while simultaneously enjoying the chance to share with the world those "Oh My God" pieces that may have gotten him or her interested in collecting in the first place.

Let's say the client decides to loan some of his or her collection to a museum. The museum can show a collection of pieces that it might not have been able to afford to buy, and the collector can enhance the provenance of his collection by having his collection shown in a museum. Since this is a loan and not a transfer of the property's ownership, the collector does not need to be concerned about any gift tax liability.[104] However, because the loan does not transfer any ownership, there is no charitable tax deduction available.[105] Furthermore, if the collector passes away, then the full fair market value of the loaned work is included in the collector's estate, and the loan becomes irrelevant.[106]

316

Charitable Remainder Trust

Another way to benefit a charity that is important to you is a Charitable Remainder Trust (CRT). This strategy is particularly useful if you have a highly appreciated piece that you are no longer emotionally attached to.

There are several advantages to this approach for both the collector and the institution:

1. The collector can take a charitable income tax deduction equal to the cost basis (acquisition cost) when the items are conveyed to the trust, since the trust is considered a non-related use.

2. The collector avoids estate taxes and probate by transferring the asset out of his or her estate.

3. The collector receives a regular income stream.

4. The collector and the institution can avoid capital gains taxes on the appreciated value of the items.

5. The institution receives a contribution at the time of the collector's death.

Here's how it works:

The first step in implementing this strategy is to create the trust. Generally, the collector will be named as the income beneficiary in the document, and a "qualified" charity will be named as the remainder beneficiary.[107] Next, the collector needs to convey the selected assets to the trust using an appropriate legal document. Title to the artwork transfers from the individual to the trust. Since the proceeds will be considered a non-related use, the donor is able to use only the cost basis for the income tax deduction, not the fair market value of the item, unless the item has declined in value from the time of purchase. If the item is worth less than the purchase price, the donor must use the current appraised value rather than the cost of acquisition to determine the income tax deduction.[108] For tax purposes, the donation is considered complete upon delivery of the art, either physical delivery of the piece or delivery of the deed, if physical delivery is too impractical or inconvenient.[109]

Because the trust is the official owner of the assets, the Trustee can sell the items privately through a dealer or at a well-planned auction sale. The proceeds of the sale, obviously, go into the trust. These proceeds should be invested and managed either by the Trustee or by an investment advisor.

Now that the items have been liquidated and the proceeds invested, the trust is required to make annual distributions to the income beneficiary. The IRS requires that "at least 5% (but not more than 50%)

of the initial fair market value of the trust [be] distributed annually to a beneficiary during the grantor's lifetime, with at least 10% of the remainder going to charity after the grantor's death." [110] There cannot be any retained life interests, nor future interests, and, generally, the income beneficiary cannot have any use of the collection.[111] Upon the collector's death, the remaining assets in the trust will be given to the charity, and, provided that the charity is a "qualified" charity, it will not have to pay income tax on the charitable gift.[112] This allows for a comfortable income stream for the original collector while providing future support for a favored charity.

Fractional Gifting

Collectors often have pieces in their collection to which they are very attached and that have experienced tremendous appreciation. It may be the "Oh My God" piece you bought years ago from an unknown artist whose reputation has grown over the years, triggering seven-figure appreciation. Or it could be the particularly fine piece your grandfather acquired, which the curator at the museum has been discussing with you for years. When a collector has been reluctant to give up these pieces, fractional gifting has historically been a useful tool, allowing the collector to donate a partial interest in a piece to a charitable organization, receive a charitable income tax deduction, and continue to enjoy the piece in his or her home. However, recent tax law changes in August 2006 (Section 1218 of the Pension Protection Act of 2006) have placed several important limitations on this type of gifting. These limitations make it a far less attractive planning tool, especially for artwork experiencing rapid appreciation or artwork owned by younger clients. If you are considering this approach, it may be time to rethink your strategy and look at other options.

Conceptually, fractional gifting is as easy to understand as its name. Simply put, it is a process where you donate, to a charitable institution, percentages of ownership in a specific piece of art over a multi-year timeframe. The percentage donated at a given point in time is the amount you are allowed to take as a charitable tax deduction. Under the prior tax law,[113] there were four key advantages to using fractional gifting as part of an overall art planning strategy:

1. **Estate Tax Reduction:** By removing highly appreciated or particularly valuable pieces of art from the estate, the collector can help reduce the amount of taxes that will need to be paid on the estate by the survivors following his or her death.

2. **Capital Gains Tax Reduction:** By donating a piece that has appreciated substantially to a charity rather than selling it, a collector can avoid a significant capital gains tax liability. Recall that capital gains on art and collectibles are taxed at 28%.

3. **Retain possession for a period of time:** By sharing ownership, the piece is held by the collector for a part of the year proportionally equal to the percentage ownership he or she has retained. Under the prior law, the museum or other institution had the right, but not the obligation, to take the donated work for its part of the year.[114]

4. **Potential Appreciation:** By being on display as part of a museum collection, the value of the piece may be enhanced. Previously, this could increase the value of later fractional gifts to the charitable institution. Under the old law, you could take charitable income tax deductions on fractional gifts

319

made in later years based on the increase in fair market value.

Consider the following example. Suppose a collector has a $10 million estate and one great painting that he paid $200,000 for 25 years ago—a study by one of the lesser-known Impressionist painters—that's now worth $1 million. The collector's family has no great interest in the art, and he is considering giving the painting to the museum as a bequest. If the collector gives a 25% share of a $1 million painting to a museum, he will reduce his adjusted gross income by $250,000 (up to 30% of the collector's adjusted gross income). The museum is entitled to use the work for 25% of the year (about 90 days), but under the old law did not have to actually take possession. The collector now has the benefit of both the tax deduction and of keeping and enjoying the art for three-quarters (and perhaps all) of the year. In addition, with the extra tax savings the collector will have more money to make additional charitable donations or simply to enjoy and then leave to his heirs. In this example, due to the nature of the piece, it is quite likely that the museum will exhibit it during the traditional summer Impressionist show where the piece will be seen by more people and potentially further increase its value. If in five years the painting appreciated in value to $2 million and the collector gifted another 25% share to the museum, under the old law his tax deduction would increase to $500,000 (25% of $2 million). Any ungifted portion is usually given to the museum on the collector's death.

Fractional gifting has also been useful to help manage liquidity and generate cash flow. For example, suppose a couple's assets are tied up in their home and in their art. By fractionally gifting a percentage of their artwork to a charity, they will have a charitable income tax deduction available to them. This frees up money that they would otherwise have to pay in taxes for other expenses while continuing to use and enjoy the work.

The Fractional Gifting Process

To implement a fractional gift, there are several issues that will need to be addressed:

- You need to identify the appropriate museum and make sure that it is willing to receive the gift—this will likely require the involvement of a qualified art advisor. You also need to find out if the museum will require a corresponding endowment to support the gift.

- You need to make sure the gift complies with the related use rule to optimize your tax deduction.[115]Once the fractional gift is made, the IRS will allow a deduction equal to the fair market value of the donation but only if the art is related to the charity's purpose, such as a museum or university. If the item donated is not related to the charity's purpose or function, then the deduction is equal only to the cost basis (what you paid for it, which is often much less than the current fair market value).

- You must prepare a deed of gift that describes the work of art and the terms of the gift; allocates responsibilities for insurance, storage, and shipping; and specifies the percentage to be donated over the next ten years, at which point the piece will be completely owned by the institution.

- You must obtain an appraisal from a qualified appraiser using one of the nationally recognized societies, as opposed to a dealer or a gallery. Appraisers have to be independent of the collector and the institution and should be chosen with care since the IRS has its own Art Advisory Panel to challenge the value of charitable deductions for gifts of art.[116]

The New Law— A Freeze on Fractional Gifting?

Even before the recent tax law changes, fractional gifts came with numerous issues to be dealt with, such as who will pay for transportation and insurance (the museum or the collector), how will the piece be displayed, and what happens if the piece is damaged? However, there are several major pitfalls found in the new tax law.

First, the new law requires you, the collector, to donate your entire interest in the piece to the charity within ten years of your initial gift or at death, whichever comes first.[117] For example, a collector that gifts 20% of a painting in 2006 must give the remaining 80% by 2016. Failure to do so will result in forfeiting your tax deductions and paying a 10% penalty (known as "recapture") to the IRS. Under prior law, there was no time limit to complete the gift. As a result, donors considering a fractional gift may want to postpone fractional gifts until later in life so that they do not have to give up ownership and the use and enjoyment of the art so soon.

Second, the museum or other charity must have "substantial physical possession of the property" within ten years of the initial contribution.[118] Under prior law, the museum had the right, but not the obligation, to take the work for the specified period of time (e.g., 20% of the year or about 72 days). Now, if the museum does not take possession of the piece for some part of the year (the law is ambiguous on the exact timeframe), the collector who made the fractional gift risks losing the tax deduction and incurring a 10% penalty. As a result, museums may be forced to take works even though they do not intend to exhibit them.

Finally, and most devastating to fractional gifts, is the "valuation freeze" required under the new law. In determining the value of subsequent fractional gifts of the art, the collector must use the lesser of the fair market value of the property at the time of the initial fractional contribution, or the value at the time of the additional contribution.[119] Art will often appreciate substantially. However, this "freeze" provision will limit future tax deductions for fractional gifts to the value at the date of the initial gift. For example, if a collector gives 20% of a painting in 2006 that is appraised for $1 million, his tax deduction would be $200,000. If he gives another 20% five years later in 2011 and the painting had appreciated to $2 million, his deduction would be limited to $200,000. Further, as a result of ambiguities in the new law, if the collector dies before he donates his entire interest to the museum, his estate could be taxed on the appreciation even if he passes his remaining interest to the museum in his will! This provision could be the death knell for fractional gifts unless Congress decides to amend it. Under prior law, the collector could have received a tax deduction based on the appreciated value in 2011 (20% of $2 million, or $400,000).

Therefore, in light of these new tax provisions, collectors would be wise to avoid fractional gifts and consider other planning options for the time being.

323

As you can see in the above example, from a tax benefit standpoint, the collector would be better off avoiding fractional giving completely and just passing the entire painting to the museum in his will. That way, at least his estate could deduct the (appreciated) fair market value at the time of his death. The IRS will likely have to clarify the new laws, making it extremely important for collectors to get qualified advice before considering this planning option.

12

Using Your Collection to Create Liquidity, Maximize Cash, and Generate Income

With Contributions From George Kasparian, Esq.

"I have enough money to last me the rest of my life, unless I buy something."

—Jackie Mason

"I'm living so far beyond my income that we may almost be said to be living apart."

—e e cummings

Some people just don't want to give their stuff away—even to charity—and, consequently, they will not include gifting as a component of their art succession plan. Others may need to explore alternative strategies because they have already used up the maximum charitable deduction allowed by the Internal Revenue Code, as we discussed in Chapter 11. More commonly, however, the collector is motivated by more practical reasons when he or she chooses to sell rather than give away all or specific pieces in the collection. The explanation is usually that the collector has found himself art rich and cash poor and wants to liquidate some of his art assets for any of several reasons:

- To raise money to live on.
- To raise money to pay taxes if the art is being given outright to the heirs.
- To leave a cash gift to the heirs who do not want the art.
- To buy more art.
- To fund other estate planning or business objectives.

Regardless of the reason, there are several ways to convert art into cash. Each option, of course, has various tradeoffs and consequences:

- Public Sale
- Private Sale
- Bargain Sale
- Borrowing Against Pieces in the Collection
- Sale within a Charitable Remainder Trust

When discussing these strategies with your advisors it is important that you are very clear on your objectives before making a decision to liquidate. You may want to meet with your financial advisor first to get clear on whether you need an infusion of cash or a steady stream of income, because you might choose different strategies based on the answer to this question. You will also need to think long and hard about which pieces in your collection you can part with and which pieces you simply cannot live without. It may be possible to borrow against a piece to raise the cash you need, allowing you to keep the item in your home, assuming you can make the payments.

327

The Expert's Perspective:
Alexandra Duch—
Public or Private Sale

Collectors and professional advisors are often inclined to believe that selling at auction is the easiest and most advantageous means to achieve the maximum return for a work of art. While auctions certainly provide a fluid and efficient avenue, they are by no means the only option available. As a rule of thumb, there are two primary avenues to consider, each with relative pros and cons, depending on the item in question: public sale or private sale. A public sale is best defined as a sale at auction. A private sale could involve selling through a private dealer (on commission or for a predetermined fee) or selling directly to another private collector or institution.

Selling at Auction

One of the most obvious benefits of selling at auction is timing and exposure. That is, an opportunity to sell a work of art will take place on a certain day at an appointed time in a fair and open market. While this in no way guarantees that an item will find a buyer, it does tend to provide a platform by which a work of art can be seen by a broad audience of interested collectors.

An example of the benefit provided by the exposure of an auction was the recent sale of a collection of designer handbags, shoes, and furs through a regional house. In this instance, one's first inclination might have been to try to place the pieces at a consignment shop or sell privately through an online source such as eBay®. In fact, the auction house was able to provide access not only to the same buyers on eBay® through a pre-existing arrangement, but also to their own clients who were not traditionally inclined to shop online. As a result of the double exposure, the collection achieved extremely strong prices across the board and, in several instances, matched current retail prices for the handbags.

Auctions also can help highlight standout items within a collection. For example, while working through an estate, an art consultant spotted a pair of small gilt bronze models of lions. The lions were initially included in the buy-out bids provided to the estate by a number of private dealers—with a high offer of $750. Although the majority of items belonging to the estate were not well suited to auction, the lions were excluded from the bids and presented to a major auction house for sale. The lions successfully sold for $13,000 because they were offered through an appropriate venue and to an interested and informed audience.

Selling through auction can also help in instances when a private collector possesses an exceptional but undocumented work of art. When an item is bought at auction, it is generally bought "as is" without any representations or warranties other than what is written in the auction catalog, as discussed in Chapter 6. Auction houses will, however, go to great lengths to determine the authenticity of a work of art, and this can be both a timely and costly endeavor. When seeking to authenticate a piece, the collector, working with the representatives at the auction house, needs to ensure that the authentication reflects international agreement among the leading scholars in the field regarding its origin.

As a case in point, an art consulting firm recently worked with the estate of a person who seemed an unlikely source of an undocumented portrait by the Italian Old Master Ludovico Carracci. The consultant discovered this work in the proverbial dark corridor, and immediately undertook the task of verifying its origin. The consultant began the process by completing her own due diligence and then approached both of the major auction houses. One dismissed the painting out of hand as a work by a minor artist with little value. The other auction house eagerly agreed to undertake the research necessary to verify the portrait's authenticity and to market its sale. As chance would have it, the world's leading Carracci scholar had recently passed away, and it was not possible for the work to be sold with a letter of authenticity. It was put forward as attributed to the artist with a pre-sale estimate in line with its description, $80,000 to $120,000. The painting sold for $1.6 million.

The benefit of auction sale in this instance was twofold. First, the auction house was able to lend its resources to conduct the extensive research necessary to bring the painting to market. Second, it placed the painting before an international audience who, given all the available evidence, were able to make up their own minds regarding its likely origin and its associated value. Again, international exposure allowed an unknown work to sell relatively quickly for a price that far exceeded the costs and additional time requirements of a private sale.

A final example of how an auction can help a collector realize the full value of a collection is the case of single owner and/or celebrity auctions. For example, in the past ten years the sale of the personal property belonging to Jackie Onassis, Marilyn Monroe, the Duke and Duchess of Windsor, and Barbara Streisand has resulted in tremendous sales totals. Aside from items that would have had a strong stand-alone value, such as the "Happy Birthday, Mr. President" dress worn by Monroe, even mundane household items have sold for multiples of their fair market value when sold at a well-promoted celebrity auction. When a sale is able to create widespread excitement, there can be an associated benefit to lesser items by virtue of association.

Selling Privately

While there are many benefits associated with selling through an auction, it is not always the best forum for the sale of valuable pieces of art or antiques. In fact, depending on the object or collecting category, clients can often receive stronger sales results by selling directly to private dealers, other collectors, or institutions.

For example, although the auction market for jewelry and coins is strong, one can often achieve higher prices by having private buyers make competitive, sealed bids on a collection. While this has broad applications, it is most clearly illustrated by the sale of estate jewelry. Generally speaking, while an estate may have any number of "auction worthy" pieces such as a fabulous diamond ring or a suite of jewelry from a saleable name such as Cartier or Boucheron, there are also likely to be a certain amount of residual, less marketable pieces such as an outdated bracelet or unimportant pin.

While the important pieces may find ready buyers at auction, the remainder goes unsold. In this instance, by allowing multiple, sealed, private bids on a jewelry collection, we have found that the sales process is not only expedited—upon agreement the collector receives a certified check for the lump sum—but also, the final totals garnered through competitive private bids often exceed the estimates put forward by the

331

auction houses. Although it is important to bear in mind that the transaction costs associated with private sales may be higher than at auction, the additional expenses are more than offset by the strength of the bids and enhanced sales proceeds realized by the collector.

Also, by their very nature, certain works of art are simply more difficult to sell at auction. For example, oversized paintings, outdoor sculpture, or works that have greater scholarly than commercial appeal tend to benefit from private rather than public sales. In the case of oversized works, although an auction has the ability to generate attention, a piece that requires larger than average exhibition space will by virtue of its attributes have fewer potential buyers simply because it is not easily displayed outside of a museum or a commercial venue. These works almost always benefit from a private sale because they require additional time to identify interested buyers with a suitable amount of space to accommodate the piece. Even the auction houses themselves will tend to negotiate private sales in these instances. For example, Sotheby's holds yearly private sales dedicated to outdoor sculpture—if they attempted this at a public auction, the sale would likely bomb.

Although size can often play a key role, works of a more scholarly nature share the benefits of private sales. Scholarly works tend to have a far more narrowly defined market—a dedicated collector or a museum looking to broaden its existing collection. A successful sale requires additional time not allowed in the framework of an auction to establish a list of potential buyers.

Alternatively, a work that is known to be a perfect fit for a museum collection may come up for sale. Again, a private sale may be a better means of both selling a work of art and allowing the institution enough time to raise and allocate the funds necessary to expand their collection to include the piece being offered. Finally, although the addition of a collector's or public personality's name to an item can generate interest at auction, private clients can be put off by the notoriety and gossip caused by a public sale and favor the anonymity of a private transaction.

Postmortem Liquidation

It is a common misunderstanding in the advisory community that when a collector dies, the only available option for art and antiques assets is an auction or public sale. It is important that advisors understand that other options exist for postmortem planning and that these other options generally result in solutions that create more value for the heirs. I estimate that up to 70% of the value of a collection is lost at an unplanned auction sale (more on this in Chapter 14). An art advisor can assist in postmortem situations at a minimum by simply managing the public or private sale—if this is the right solution. The advisor will make sure that the right pieces get to the right dealer or auction house. In an auction situation, the advisor will handle the negotiations and make sure the reserves are set properly. The advisor will make certain that the pieces are handled, restored, shipped, and displayed properly to optimize the sales price. The advisor will handle questions regarding provenance or title documentation issues. And finally, the advisor will manage the disposition of the pieces offered in the auction that do not sell, to avoid the taint of "damaged goods." It is also possible that the advisor might recommend that the heirs keep selected pieces, especially in a field of rising prices, making other arrangements to pay estate taxes, and then sell them in the future in order to maximize the investment value of the piece.

Some of the other strategies discussed below are also available in a postmortem fact pattern. I cannot emphasize enough, however, that lifetime planning offers far greater opportunities for creative approaches to meeting collectors' objectives—and greater opportunities for the professional advisor to be the hero or heroine by providing truly innovative planning solutions.

Bargain Sales

A bargain sale is kind of a "best of both worlds" planning strategy. Bargain selling is a method that allows a collector to structure a gift to a charitable institution in such a way that a piece is sold at a deeply discounted price to the receiving organization—allowing the collector to generate some cash, reduce capital gains, and take the remainder of the value of the piece as a charitable donation.

Take, for example, what happened to Allan Daniel, a renowned dealer and collector.[120] In the mid-1980s, Daniel went to a New England auction gallery looking for folk art. He discovered a Campeachy chair and felt attracted to its spare and functional design. However, its frame was walnut and he had never been attracted to "brown furniture" (see Photograph

334

9). Daniel bought what he came for and, on an impulse, returned to the sales room after paying his bill. At just that moment, the chair was on the block and the bidding had stalled. He put up his hand, and, to his surprise, the Campeachy chair was hammered down to him!

He gradually came to love the chair, despite it being "brown furniture," for its lines. His new wife, Kendra, even chose it from the warehouse as one of the included items when setting up their new home. Then, in July 1993, *Antiques* magazine devoted an entire issue to Thomas Jefferson's home, Monticello. Allan carefully studied the photographs in the magazine and, to his amazement, sitting in the living room at Monticello was an exact duplicate of the Daniel's chair. The excitement was unimaginable. Could their chair have been the missing mate to Jefferson's? Jefferson's chair was made by John Hemmings, a slave of Jefferson's and a cabinetmaker. In the late 1990s it was documented, with much fanfare, that Sally Hemmings, John Hemmings' sister, was Jefferson's mistress and the mother of several of his children. If Daniel's chair was the match to the one in the magazine spread, then it would be a chair with many important historical connections.

Allan and Kendra sent photos of the chair to Susan Stein, the curator of collections at Monticello. After seeing the photos she felt that it seemed to be the mate to the chair in their living room. So, in the spring of 2002, the Daniels drove the chair to Charlottesville, Virginia, where Susan and several members of her staff measured, photographed, and fondled it—and then proclaimed that it was indeed from the Monticello cabinet shop and made by the hand of John Hemmings! After Susan graciously toured the couple through the magnificent buildings and grounds, the Daniels promised that the chair would end up at Monticello.

In 2005, at the request of Allan and Kendra, the Campeachy chair was sold in a bargain sale transaction to Monticello, for an amount significantly less than its appraised value. This made it possible for the Jefferson Foundation to afford the chair, and the Daniels were able to claim the difference between the fair market value and sale price as a charitable deduction. It was the classic win-win situation.

How Does It Work, and Who Does It Help?

The bargain sale used by the Daniels is a method of gifting and selling that works exactly as the name implies: a piece or even an entire collection is sold at a bargain price—lower than its fair market value. At the end of the transaction, the purchasing organization acquires something it desires for its collection and the seller generates some liquidity. The seller also receives the additional benefit of being able to take a charitable deduction for the difference between the sale price and the property's value.[121]

The bargain sale method is beneficial to institutions and collectors alike. It is an excellent way to generate liquidity and create funds for wealth replacement for the collector or his or her heirs, who would like to see the property go to a charitable institution. It's also an important tool for the collector who has a piece or pieces in the collection that have appreciated since purchase, as it allows him or her to avoid the hefty capital gains tax on the appreciation during the sale.

As for the institutions, they are able to acquire pieces that they might not otherwise have been able to afford. For example, suppose a collector purchased a piece twenty years ago for $500,000 that is now worth $2 million. If he wishes to sell this $2 million piece to a museum, it is quite likely the museum will be unable afford the entire purchase price. By using the bargain sale method, the collector can sell property at a discounted price of $1 million, and treat the remaining $1 million as a gift to the museum. This way, the museum acquires the piece, and the collector is eligible to take a charitable income tax deduction on the $1 million gift, plus he reduces his total capital gains tax on the sale of the piece. Here is how the numbers would work in this case:

Cost Basis	$500,000
Fair Market Value (FMV)	$2 million
Discounted Sale Price	$1 million
Charitable Contribution	$1 million

However, the collector would still have a capital gain on the discounted sale. To estimate the amount of capital gain, you will first need to allocate a portion of the cost basis to the sale part of the transaction:

Basis allocated to sale =
Cost Basis / FMV x Discounted Sale Price
= $500,000 / $2 million x $1 million
= $250,000.

Then, you can estimate the capital gain:

Capital gain =
Discounted Sale Price - Allocated Basis =
$1 million - $250,000 = $750,000.

Before a collector decides to pursue this approach, there are four questions that he or she must answer affirmatively. If the collector can't answer yes to all four questions, then a bargain sale is probably not the way to go, and he or she should look at other methods of either liquidating or gifting the piece.

1. Is the collector willing to relinquish control of the property? In a bargain sale, the collector is selling the piece, totally relinquishing it. If he or she is not ready to do that, then it may be best to consider some other method to structure the gift.

2. Is the property being sold to a qualified donee organization? To take a charitable tax deduction, the receiving organization must be one approved by the IRS. (For information on how to determine the eligibility of an organization, see Chapter 11 for more on Types of Donee Organizations.)

3. Has the piece appreciated in value? When the collector has a highly appreciated piece, the bargain sale is often a great solution to a nasty capital gains issue. This makes it possible for the collector to take a charitable tax deduction; the deduction is the calculated difference between the sale price and the allocated basis, which is considered a long-term capital gain.[122]

4. Will the deduction amount be in excess of $5,000? If so, then a qualified appraisal will be needed before the sale.[123]

Loans Against the Collection

If philanthropy isn't the focus and the collector needs to generate liquidity or replace wealth, it may be advisable for a loan to be taken out against the collec-

338

tion. Such a cash injection can make it possible for the collector to do several things, including:

- Finance new purchases.

- Pay taxes.

- Monetize art for personal reasons in a confidential environment.

- Structure a cash flow annuity, i.e., a reverse mortgage.

- Establish a line of credit for short-term cash needs.

- Facilitate family wealth transfers.

- Purchase life insurance to pay estate taxes.

Borrowing against an art collection has additional benefits besides creating liquidity. By borrowing against the collection rather than selling outright, you:

- Keep possession and ownership of the art (and enjoy its future appreciation).

- Reduce estate taxes if a postmortem sale transpires, because the collection receives a stepped-up basis.

- Avoid the capital gains tax you would pay if you sold the art (as much as 30 to 40%).

- Reduce transaction costs—a sale generally involves 15 to 30% in transaction costs as compared to a loan which generally involves a 1% closing fee, plus the annual debt service.

Several companies, such as Fine Art Capital (founded by collector Andy Augenblick), Citigroup Art Advisory Service, Art Capital Group, and Rosenthal &

Rosenthal have entered the marketplace, offering loans using art and antiques as collateral. Generally they will lend up to 40 or 50% of the value of the object, with the term extending from six months to twenty years. Many private banks will also structure low interest arrangements for preferred clients or to finance intergenerational transfers within a family. One of the most commonly used approaches is to create a line of credit against the collection, which gives the collector particular flexibility so that he or she is in a position to acquire new works when an opportunity suddenly presents itself.

Some lenders take actual possession of all or part of the collection during the term of the loan, but increasingly lenders are becoming more comfortable with art as collateral and are willing to accept a security interest under the Uniform Commercial Code. In some cases the loans are only made to a very select group of clients who have other assets managed by the institution and have a longstanding relationship with the lender. In almost all cases, however, the lender will require a formal appraisal of the art.

A loan against the artwork also can be an important estate planning tool. If an executor borrows against the artwork to pay off estate taxes, the estate receives a step-up in cost basis, and it does not have to sell the art under adverse conditions. The executor can wait for a better time to sell off some of the artwork, so he or she does not have to deal with the consequences of a disadvantageous disposition of the artwork.

340

The Expert's Perspective:

Elizabeth Clement—Appraisals Made for Lending Secured by Art

An appraisal is also generally required for collateralized borrowing whether for a high-valued single item or an entire collection. The art is used as the security for the funds being lent, and the appraisal document is critical to the lending process. The borrower is responsible for paying the appraisal fee, much like the way the appraisal is handled in a real estate loan closing. Besides the credit-worthiness of the collector, the lender will look to the appraised value of the art for security, so the valuation must be accurate and arms length.

There are instances where the lender did not seek an appraisal on the art and was left, after the loan was in default, with property worth far, far less than the balance owed on the loan. After lengthy court battles and significant attorney's fees, the amount realized from the sale of the art, after marketing costs, sales commissions, transit costs, storage, and other associated costs of holding the property or repossessing it, can be considerably less than the original loan amount. If the lender had sought the services of a professional independent appraiser, the lender would have been aware of the true value of the collection upfront and perhaps would not have made the loan in the first place or would have agreed to loan a smaller amount.

341

Reverse Mortgage

Elderly collectors sometimes find themselves in a position of needing cash to live on but not wanting to part with their art. In this fact pattern, a reverse mortgage can be a very convenient approach. Let's look at a couple who gifted their home to a private college but continued to live in it with all of their possessions. At the time the gift was structured, there was no consideration of the artwork inside the home. The couple was straddled with very high property tax bills on the real estate and the art. The solution was to obtain a reverse mortgage using their art as collateral. In these situations the proceeds of the loan are paid to the collectors in monthly, quarterly, semi-annual, or annual installments. The interest that accrues on the dispersed amounts is added to the outstanding loan balance. The loan is to be paid off from money in the collectors' estate, and the art will go to the college as a bequest in their wills.

Charitable Remainder Trust

With some frequency, collectors find themselves in a position of needing to create income to live on because all of their net worth is tied up in the value of their collection. We collectors tend to overspend on art during our peak earning years, leaving ourselves without ready money for retirement. The first instinct is to sell a significant piece and raise a lot of cash. If the significant piece is a highly appreciated asset, an outright sale may not be a viable alternative because the capital gains tax will eat up much of the proceeds of the sale (recall the capital gains tax on items of personal property is 28%). In this situation, a Charitable Remainder Trust[124] allows you to structure a charitable donation in such a way that the collectors can receive an income stream during their lifetime as well as create philanthropic capital with the balance of the trust assets going to the charity upon the death of the collectors.

In the previous chapter we looked at this strategy as a way to structure a gift to an appropriate institution. In this section we are looking at the flip side and examining how this strategy can be used to create income for the collector. By transferring the art to a Charitable Remainder Trust, the trust can sell the pieces and invest the sales proceeds, thereby creating income for the collector during his or her lifetime. Since a requirement of a Charitable Remainder Trust is that it must distribute an annual income stream, the collector now has liquidity, and, at the end of the trust, will have made a sizeable charitable donation, again minimizing capital gains and estate taxes.

343

Take the example of collector Bill Pauly. His net worth is $20 million; however, most of his assets are in a collection of antique coins and rare books. He loves his pieces, but he can't live on them! It has become clear that he needs to liquidate some of his collection in order to raise some cash for living expenses. Beyond the collection, Pauly's only other significant asset is his home. In the past, he has made major donations to various institutions but doesn't feel that he can donate any more of his collection—not because he doesn't like charity but because he needs money to retire on. Instead of further gifting, he wants to sell the collection at auction or through a dealer.

While this sounds great at first, a competent advisory team will inform him that he will be hit with a large capital gains tax on the highly appreciated pieces in the collection. In addition, the unspent proceeds of the sale will become part of his estate, which will be taxable when he dies. The net result of this outright sale of the items is that much of the value of the collection is lost, because the proceeds of the sale are diminished by the tax obligations.

The advisors could recommend using a Charitable Remainder Trust. They tell Pauly that, by creating a Charitable Remainder Trust, the assets are no longer considered part of his estate, he avoids any capital gains tax, gets a charitable tax deduction, a stream of income to live on, and will be making a generous contribution to his favorite charity. *Wow!* What a fabulous solution!

344

You will not want to use this approach for items in the collection that you feel passionately about and want to keep in your possession. The whole idea here is that you are selling off the items that you are no longer emotionally attached to and creating a pool of funds that will be held in and managed by the trust until your death.

Sophisticated Planning Techniques— Doing More to Preserve the Value of Your Collection

With Contributions From George Kasparian, Esq.

Adam Kirwan, Esq. contributed to the 'Asset Protection' section of this chapter

"Objects are what matter. Only they carry the evidence that throughout the centuries something really happened among human beings. "

– Claude Leví-Strauss

The planning techniques discussed in this chapter generally require a higher level of expertise from your advisory team than those discussed in previous chapters, which are by and large within the scope of most estate planning attorneys practice. The techniques discussed in this chapter are most appropriate for collectors who either have a very large collection or significant value in a few very fine pieces and wish to integrate their art holdings into their multigenerational planning. These approaches also require a great deal of familiarity with the Internal Revenue Code especially in dealing with matters of tangible personal property and sophisticated drafting skills. The bottom line here is that collectors need to be very certain they have retained the services of a qualified attorney and tax planner, who understands the emotional, financial, and philanthropic needs of those who collect, before undertaking any of these planning tools.

Some states allow members of the bar to indicate specialization or areas of practice concentration. If you reside in one of these states you will want to seek out an attorney who specializes in estate or tax planning. You might also look for an attorney who is also a CPA (there is an organization[125] of attorney CPAs that can help you identify these practitioners in your area) because these practitioners often have particular familiarity with the tax code. I would also suggest asking fellow collectors, dealers, and other art experts you are presently working with to recommend attorneys in your area who have experience in this kind of planning who also understand the unique challenges of planning for art and antiques assets.

When to Consider These More Sophisticated Strategies

Some collectors with very important pieces (the "Oh My God" items) may not want to lose control of this part of their collection as would be the case if they simply gifted the pieces to a museum or other charity. The museum may not treat the collection the way the collector would envision (museums hold up to 95% of their collection in storage), and in all probability, would store the gift sometimes and even may sell some or all of it in the future. The strategies outlined in this chapter allow the collector to keep the collection in the control of the family while mitigating tax liability. Some of these approaches allow the family to create an art legacy which can take the form of creating art scholarships for needy students, bringing exhibits to venues which are not normally able to attract quality shows, and providing opportunities for family members to offer grants or other forms of financial support to worthy organizations. These strategies provide an opportunity for the family to express its values through philanthropic capital and offer individual members a way to participate in cause-driven activities which provide a sense of purpose to their lives.

Museum Without Walls

An innovative approach that we have developed, called a Museum Without Walls, utilizes a Private Operating Foundation (POF)[126] to manage the important historical and educational parts of the collection. The POF is founded in order to allow these items to become part of exhibitions that tour to various venues (hence the name Museum Without Walls).[127] Unlike the typical private foundation, which only writes checks to other charities, the Private Operating Foundation exists to actively manage a charitable program (in this case, the collection). Once the POF is created, the items in the collection that are most suited to exhibition are gifted to the foundation, and the collector receives an income tax deduction for the full fair market value of the gift.[128] The lesser items in the collection can then be gifted to the foundation and sold to create an endowment fund for the foundation to help manage the collection and hire a curator to create appropriate venues to exhibit the collection. The endowment funds the transportation, storage, display, opening night gala, and other expenses, allowing charities to use the exhibition as a pure fundraiser. For example, imagine if the Jackie O collection was coming to your town and all proceeds derived from the opening night party and ticket revenue was to help the local chapter of Ronald McDonald House. The Museum Without Walls allows the collector's children, grandchildren, and future generations of the family to run the foundation, creating family philanthropy for decades to come. Finally, the collector would enjoy a current income tax deduction but also would save on estate taxes since the donated items would not be included as part of the collector's taxable estate.

The Private Operating Foundation allows the collector to take advantage of charitable tax deductions as if he or she were gifting directly to a charitable institution. The collector can deduct the fair market value (FMV) of the art (up to 30% of Adjusted Gross Income) as long as the following requirements are met:

- The collector owned the piece for more than one year and did not receive it as a gift from the artist.

- The item satisfies the related use rule (use of the art is related to the foundation's purpose).

- There is an appraisal by a qualified appraiser.

- The item is gifted to the private operating foundation.[129]

The POF allows the collector and his family to maintain control of the collection by serving as president or as a member of the board of directors. However, the collector should avoid any "self-dealing" between himself and the foundation that would jeopardize the foundation's tax-exempt status. For example, the collector should avoid displaying the donated works at his home, as the IRS has determined this would not constitute tax-exempt activity.[130]

There are several requirements that must be met in order to qualify as a POF.[131] To qualify as a Private Operating Foundation, the Internal Revenue Code requires the foundation to meet the income test and either the asset test, endowment test, or the support test. These tests are designed to prevent abuses and ensure that the foundation is carrying out exempt purposes.

Income Test: The foundation must spend substantially all (at least 85%) of its income directly on exempt activities. For a Museum Without Walls, this would include amounts paid to maintain or acquire pieces as well as administrative expenses for insurance and storage.[132]

In addition the income test above, the POF must meet one of the following:

349

Assets Test: A POF will meet the asset test if 65% or more of its assets are devoted directly to the foundation's exempt activity. For a Museum Without Walls, this would include loaning the works to a museum, having them restored, or putting them in temporary storage.[133]

Endowment Test: A POF will meet the endowment test if it uses at least two-thirds of its minimum investment return (5%) for the conduct of its exempt activities. Foundations that satisfy the income test will usually satisfy the endowment test.

Support Test: The support test requires that 85% of the foundation's support comes from the general public and five or more unrelated exempt organizations. A collector would usually not rely on the support test since most of the Museum Without Walls funding is likely to come from the collector himself.

The POF is also useful when the collector wishes to donate to several organizations, but the donations fail to meet the related-use requirement for a charitable tax deduction. With a POF, the collector can have the charities select certain pieces that they want. Then, the collector can gift the remainder of the collection to a foundation and, since donation to the foundation complies with the related use requirement, receive the charitable tax deduction. At the time of the collector's death, the foundation may sell the pieces to create philanthropic capital. This way, the foundation can then benefit the various charities with money, scholarships, or any other type of donation without having to satisfy the related use requirement. However, to donate the pieces to a POF, the donation must meet an income test, and either the asset test, the endowment test, or the support test as outlined above.[134]

Private Foundations

A POF or Museum Without Walls may not be a collector's first choice if he or she does not want to manage and tour the collection. If instead the collector would like to sell the collection and manage the proceeds for charitable purposes, the traditional private foundation would be a good alternative. A private foundation is organized to make grants for scientific, educational, cultural, religious, or other charitable purposes. The private foundation receives its funding from only one source, which can be an individual, a family, or a corporation.[135]

The collector can gift the collection to a private foundation and receive a charitable income tax deduction. However, the charitable income tax deduction is limited to the collector's cost basis (what he or she paid for the collection) rather than the current FMV, which reduces the value of the deduction for highly appreciated assets (except for gifts of appreciated stock).[136]

For Collectors Only: The Foundation Refresher

For some collectors, the word "foundation" can be intimidating. It can sound very Bill and Melinda Gates-like—something good for the very wealthy to do but not necessarily appropriate for your art collection. Basically, a foundation is a nonprofit corporation or charitable trust organized to make grants to either unrelated organizations or to individuals for scientific, educational, cultural, religious, or other charitable purposes.[137] It doesn't have to be in the billions or even the millions. Rather, the focus is on creating a charitable organization.

351

The foundation could sell the assets to create philanthropic capital to benefit the charities and causes that the family values. In some cases, individual family members are allocated funds that they can distribute to the organizations they have researched and want to support. The foundation can use the proceeds to benefit other charities with grants, scholarships, or other types of donations. As president or by serving on the board, the collector and his or her family can decide which organizations should be the recipients of donations. It is important to note that foundations come with minimum distribution requirements, excise taxes, and numerous other regulations.

Family Limited Partnerships

Another more aggressive strategy that can help with a collector's estate planning is a Family Limited Partnership (FLP). An FLP is similar to a traditional limited partnership, consisting of general and limited partners. In an FLP, the general partner is usually the collector and/or his or her spouse (or, preferably, a corporation owned by the collector and/or his or her spouse) while the limited partners are beneficiaries and family members. The FLP is designed to gift limited partner shares to family members, while the general partner(s) manage the collection in the partnership. Limited partners have a closely held non-controlling interest over the assets in the partnership. [138]

The FLP may be advantageous to the collector who:

- May be unwilling to give up control of certain assets, such as artwork or collectibles.[139]

- May be facing significant income and estate tax issues when transferring the collection.

- May be concerned about other family members managing the collection or other assets competently.

- May be remarried, but have children from a first marriage, and wish to secure the children's inheritance (protecting it from the new spouse, should difficulties ensue).[140]

352

A key benefit of an FLP is called a valuation discount. Since the shares of limited partners are non-controlling and therefore not easily marketable, the collector can claim a discount on the value of the shares transferred. These discounts usually run between 10% and as much as 50%.[141] The valuation discount will help to reduce gift and/or estate taxes as demonstrated in the example below.

Suppose a collector creates an FLP and funds it with $8 million in assets. He allocates 1% to the general partner and 99% to the limited partner shares. On the collector's death, the limited partner's shares that pass to his family would be eligible for a discount since they are non-controlling and not easily marketable. So instead of having to pay estate taxes on the full $8 million (in 2007, 45% or $3.6 million in tax), his estate would only have to pay the estate tax on the discounted value. Assuming a 40% discount, the value subject to estate taxes would be $4.8 million, and the tax would be $2.2 million. Therefore, the collector's estate would save nearly $1.4 million in estate taxes.[142]

A Major Caveat

By allocating the FLP in this manner, the collector is able to remove valuable pieces of his or her collection from the estate, thereby effectively reducing the entire value of the estate for tax purposes, while retaining control over those pieces for the family. However, there is an important caveat that collectors should know about FLPs: the IRS has attacked FLPs and their valuation discounts in recent years.[143] The IRS has sought to include, under Section 2036(a) of the Internal Revenue Code, the entire value of assets transferred to FLPs for estate tax purpos-

353

The Advisor's FYI: Is the FLP Right for Your Client?

Although an FLP may seem like an ideal way to plan for your client's collectibles and artwork, it is not the appropriate tool for every estate plan. When discussing the possibility of an FLP there are several areas where the advisor needs to be particularly cautious, including:

• The significant costs and risks associated with an FLP

• The overall value of the collection—qualified assets should be worth at least $1 million or this might not be the most cost-effective way to manage the property

• What items within the collection are suitable to fund an FLP

Finally, because an FLP is such a complex vehicle, it should be set up only by an experienced attorney.

es, with no discount. In the past few years, the IRS has successfully made the argument in several court challenges that Section 2036(a) requires the full value of assets to be included in the donor's estate where the donor retained significant control over the transferred assets. In addition, an FLP needs to have some underlying business purpose (e.g., an art dealer) to pass muster with the IRS. For art, this could mean traveling exhibitions, but keeping the items in the collector's home would cause IRS scrutiny. In any case, an FLP would be a risky proposition for anyone who is not a dealer. It is extremely important to have a properly formed and managed FLP that does not commingle the partnership and personal funds. Therefore, collectors considering the FLP option need to work with an attorney with expertise in this area to avoid getting flagged by the IRS.

Irrevocable Life Insurance Trust

An Irrevocable Life Insurance Trust, or ILIT, is an estate planning tool that uses life insurance to fund broader objectives of the collector. An ILIT allows a collector to take the proceeds from a life insurance policy completely out of the collector's estate for estate tax purposes as well as to provide for their management and distribution.

Collectors should consider the possibility of establishing an Irrevocable Life Insurance Trust in situations such as the following:

- The collectors may wish to make a significant gift of art to their favorite museum while still leaving a meaningful amount to their family, so the collectors may use the ILIT for wealth replacement.

- The collectors may not want the collection broken apart, but at the same time they want to leave equal amounts to each of their children.

- The collectors may be in the somewhat unusual situation that their children actually want the art (perhaps the "Oh My God" pieces) rather than the cash, but they will need a source of funds to pay the estate tax liability after the collectors have passed on.

Example 1: Suppose Joe Collector has a home, securities, and a large collection of antique cars. His two sons would like to keep the collection in the family but are worried about being able to pay the estate taxes. Joe's advisors create an ILIT and fund it with a life insurance policy purchased on Joe's life. When Joe dies, the proceeds from the insurance policy in the ILIT pass tax-free to his sons and they are able to purchase the antique car collection from Joe's estate using this method.

Example 2: Mary wants to see her collection go to a museum but also is concerned about disinheriting her children, who will lose the value of the collection if she gives it away. Her advisors create a funded ILIT with the proceeds of the policy payable to her children. Upon her death, this money will replace the wealth that was given to the museum in the form of the art. The insurance proceeds make up for the loss in the value incurred because of Mary's charitable donation.

By definition, an ILIT is an unalterable ("irrevocable") trust funded with either an existing life insurance policy or a new policy purchased by the trust, naming the trust as the beneficiary of the policy. In either case, the policy is taken out on the life of the collector, and, upon his or her death, the proceeds generated by the policy can be used to pay estate taxes, pay off any loans against the collection, or distribute funds to family members.

When setting up an ILIT, the collector needs to name a third party trustee to manage it. Then, the collector has to choose between one of two ways to fund the trust—you can transfer an existing life insurance policy into the trust or have the trust purchase a new policy. If you choose to use the pre-existing policy, you need to be aware that a "three-year rule" allows for certain types of transferred property, including life insurance,[144] to be pulled back into your estate for estate tax purposes if you die within three years of the transfer.[145] Because of this, it is generally advisable to have the trust purchase the policy, making the three-year rule irrelevant.

There are several things that the collector needs to keep in mind when setting up an ILIT. First, an ILIT is, as its name indicates, irrevocable. It's the closest thing to "set-in-stone" that's done on paper. Second, when funding the ILIT, the collector must not possess any "incidents of ownership" in the insurance policy. If he or she does retain any incidents of ownership, then it may subject the life insurance policy to estate taxes,[146] defeating the purpose of the ILIT. Third, it is advisable for the collector to pay the premiums on the insurance policy by transferring funds to the ILIT using the annual gift tax exclusion ($12,000 in 2007). This way, the ILIT will have liquidity to pay the premiums, but the collector will not have to pay gift taxes on the transfer, nor will he or she have to use any of his or her lifetime gift tax exemption when transferring funds into the ILIT. The annual gift tax exclusion applies on a per beneficiary basis, so the more beneficiaries there are in the trust, the more the collector can benefit from the annual exclusion. For example, if the collector has named four children and six grandchildren as beneficiaries of the ILIT, he can transfer up to $120,000 annually into the ILIT tax-free (10 beneficiaries x $12,000 gift tax exclusion). If the collector is married, he can use his spouse's annual gift tax exclusion for an additional $120,000 in tax-free transfers. Any amounts transferred beyond the annual exclusion amounts will require filing a gift tax return.

Note: For such payments to qualify for the annual gift tax exclusion,[147] a *Crummey* power (named for a party in the court case that established this rule) should be used. Please consult a tax attorney to make sure that premium payments are structured correctly for gift tax purposes.[148]

The Advisor's FYI: Incidents of Ownership

You must make sure that the collector does not retain any "incidents of ownership" in the insurance policy so that it will not be subject to estate taxes.[149] Examples of "incidents of ownership" that could trigger estate taxes include the following:

- The power to surrender or cancel the policy, to assign the policy, to revoke an assignment, to pledge the policy for a loan, or to borrow against the surrender value of the policy.[150]

- The power to change the beneficiaries.[151]

- Retention of a reversionary interest in either the policy or its proceeds that exceeds 5% of the value of the policy.[152]

357

Generation-Skipping Transfer Trusts

Another way an ILIT can be used is to fund a Generation-Skipping Transfer (GST) Trust.[153] This technique is useful when grandparents want to transfer major pieces in their collection—which they believe will significantly increase in value over the next 20 to 30 years—to their grandchildren.

As its name indicates, the premise behind a GST is that the assets will skip one generation and go to the next. In other words, the beneficiaries of the GST are more than one generation removed from the collector. It is advisable for the collector and advisor to explore the possibility of a GST when, for example, the collector wants to include grandchildren as beneficiaries of the estate. In a situation like this, the collector would set up an ILIT in the recommended fashion by funding it with an insurance policy and naming the trust as the policy's beneficiary. The collector would then name his or her grandchildren as the beneficiaries of the trust.

The inner workings of a GST are very intricate and complex. There are various rules dictating how a GST can work and who can receive funds, in addition to how a GST trust and its funds are taxed. The rules for a GST are found beginning with §2601 of the IRC and with §26.2601 of the Treasury Regulations.[154] It is essential that, when setting up a GST, the collector and advisor consult not only an attorney but also an insurance agent and a tax professional about GST issues.

Section 1031 Exchanges

Another way for a collector to dispose of some assets while deferring capital gains taxes is through a Section 1031 "like-kind" exchange. Recall that in the typical sales of art, you have to pay a capital gains tax on any profit from the sale beyond what the item cost when you bought it. In 2007, the capital gains tax rate is 28% at the federal level for art and collectibles. However, with a Section 1031 exchange, the capital gains tax is deferred to sometime in the future when the new item is sold. In essence, one item is "exchanged" for another similar item without triggering an immediate tax liability. Section 1031 states that "like-kind" exchanges can be made income tax-free if:

1. There is an exchange of property that qualifies under Section 1031(a);

2. The two properties being exchanged are of like-kind to each other; and

3. Both properties are held for productive use in a trade or business or for investment.[155]

While this may be an effective tax planning tool, there are hurdles that collectors may face when trying to qualify for a Section 1031 exchange. One problem is proving that you collect the artwork for an investment and not as a hobby.[156] Generally speaking, there is no specific definition for an "investment." Various Internal Revenue Code sections indicate that, to be an investor, one must hold the property (in this case, the artwork) primarily for profit. The burden of proof falls to the collector to prove he or she invests in art to generate income.[157] In this instance, it might be logical to assume that if you have spent

359

millions of dollars on a piece of art, it is most likely for investment, but this assumption cannot be guaranteed.[158] A collector who buys and sells with regularity would probably be considered an "investor" for Section 1031 purposes. The test to determine whether property is held for investment is applied at the time of the exchange, regardless of the collector's intentions before the exchange[159] (and, if the exchange does qualify, you must file IRS Form 8824).[160]

An additional problem that you may face pertains to the definition of "like-kind" property. The term "like-kind" refers to the nature or character of the property and not to its grade or quality; thus, one kind or class of property may not be exchanged for property of a different kind or class.[161] The definition of "like-kind" is narrow for personal property such as art, antiques, and collectibles.

Example 1: A collector who purchased U.S. gold coins as an investment could not avoid paying capital gains tax as a "like-kind" exchange when he traded the coins for gold bullion. The coins had numismatic value but the bullion's value is determined solely by its gold content.[162]

Example 2: Suppose Tom Ford invests in antique cars. If he purchased a 1966 Corvette for $40,000 ten years ago that is now worth $80,000 and he decided to exchange it for a 1971 Mercedes valued at $80,000, his $40,000 gain could be deferred as a "like-kind" exchange. If he instead exchanged the Corvette for an $80,000 sculpture, his $40,000 would be subject to tax since the assets are not of "like-kind."[163]

Beware of the "boot": A collector must pay tax on gains from "boot" (non-like-kind property or money) that is part of the "like-kind" transaction.[164] Boot is often a part of the transaction since the exchanged items are usually not of equal value. In Example 2 above, suppose Tom Ford traded his 1971 Mercedes valued at $80,000 (for which he paid $40,000) for a 1973 Mustang valued at $70,000 plus $10,000 cash. The $10,000 in cash would be subject to immediate capital gains tax while the remaining $30,000 in gain would be deferred as a "like-kind" exchange.

Finally, "like-kind" exchanges can be applied to multi-party transactions.[165] For example, let's say that Jerry has a Paul Trouillebert that he wishes to exchange for Elaine's Corot, but Elaine does not want the Trouillebert; instead, she wants cash. Jerry can seek out an agent who will act as an intermediary and facilitate the exchange. This transaction, known as a *Starkey* transaction,[166] would look something like this:

• Jerry transfers title of the Trouillebert to the agent.

• Agent sells the Trouillebert.

• Agent uses proceeds from the sale of the Trouillebert to purchase the Corot from Elaine.

• Elaine receives the cash.

• Agent delivers the Corot to Jerry.[167]

• Jerry has completed a multi-party like-kind exchange and needs to file IRS Form 8824.

Section 1031 exchanges are a useful tool for collectors to defer capital gains taxes while building their collections. However, it is essential to get qualified tax advice in order to ensure that the transaction is structured in a way that will comply with all of the relevant regulations.

Asset Protection – Placing Your Collection Beyond the Reach of Creditors

Some of you may be asking why is asset protection discussed in a book about planning for the disposition of art and other personal property assets? The answer is this—smart collectors who recognize the importance of lifetime planning for the disposition of their art assets are frequently high net worth individuals who are more vulnerable than others to the claims of creditors. Creditor's claims can arise as a result of a professional liability or negligence lawsuit, a business failure, a messy divorce, a disgruntled employee, an irresponsible child, or any unanticipated, uninsured disaster. If your art and antiques assets represent a significant percentage of your net worth, it is important to understand that they will be subject to seizure for satisfaction of a judgment just like all of your other assets. If you do not take the same kind of protective action with these assets that you do for the other things you own, they can be seized and/or liquidated just as your investment property, your savings account, and your vacation home can be.

This section of the book is intended to raise your consciousness to the fact that certain people are more exposed to the claims of creditors than others and, if you understand that you are in that class of persons, there are things you can do proactively to protect the wealth that you have accumulated during your lifetime. Certain professions have more exposure than others—doctors (because of malpractice lawsuits), real estate developers (because of cash flow volatility), entrepreneurs (because you never know if the business model is viable or not)—and if you are in one of these or other high risk professions you may want to ask your advisory team to consider asset protection strategies in parallel to the estate and financial planning that is crucial to the disposition of your collection.

Asset protection planning is a process of using legal methods to organize your assets, affairs, and business structures at a time when there are no legal actions pending, threatened, or expected. A key concept in your thinking about asset protection is that you need to act before something bad happens. The whole idea of asset protection is that you are harboring your assets—whether it is your real estate, your art, your furniture collection, or your stocks—in a way that they are beyond the reach of creditors when and if something bad does happen in the future.

363

Beyond the reach of creditors can mean many different things. Beyond the reach can mean the assets are titled in a way that your creditors cannot get to them. They may be sheltered in a trust or offshore vehicle that puts them outside the jurisdiction of the legal proceeding. Or it can mean that you have liquidated the equity in the asset such that it is no longer attractive for satisfaction of the judgment. Regardless of the mechanism which puts them outside the grasp of your creditors, some collectors need to consider these issues more than others.

It is important to understand as a preliminary factor that protecting yourself and your assets is a perfectly legitimate exercise supported by the legal infrastructure in the US. Individuals have every right to protect the wealth they have accumulated using the legal structures that have been put in place to protect assets. Most of these tools, however, are defined by state law and consequently there is a great deal of variation from state to state as to which vehicles are appropriate in what situations. In some cases a strategy that is available in one state is not an option in another. The operative concept here is that as a collector you need to be very aware of the laws in the jurisdiction of your residency. Some states are known for favoring debtors, other states laws are more sympathetic to creditors. As a savvy art collector what you need to know is that you must be aware of the rules of the game in the state of your residency and you need to consult with your advisory team to be sure you have protected your collection. It is absolutely imperative, if you feel asset protection is an important part of the planning that you should be doing, that you consult with a qualified specialist in the state of your residence.

It is also important to understand that transferring assets after something bad happens with the intent of hindering, delaying, or defrauding a creditor is considered a fraudulent transfer and can be voided, meaning the transfer can be set aside enabling the creditor to reach the asset. The bottom line is if you want to protect your art and antiques assets you need to act NOW, in advance of a problematic situation and certainly in advance of the filing of a lawsuit.

Move to Florida

Many of you may be doing some asset protection planning without knowing it. Moving to Florida, believe it or not, is one of the best asset protection strategies you can implement. And you thought it was just the weather. Florida is known as "The Debtors Haven" because the statutory framework there pro-

364

vides for certain exemptions that benefit the debtor. Called the Homestead Exemption, this Florida provision protects your house (in most cases), assuming you have established Florida residency, but does not protect what is inside it. So if a creditor is seeking to reach your collection in your Florida home, it is vulnerable in the absence of additional planning.

Special Strategies for Married People

The legal and tax system includes many provisions that offer special benefits to people who are conventionally married. The laws of many states allow married people to jointly own property in a form of ownership called Tenants By the Entireties. Some states allow only real estate to be owned in this manner, but many states will allow your art and other personal property assets to be held in this form of ownership.

365

The advantage to titling your art in this manner is that rather than viewing the joint ownership as an arrangement of half-and-half ownership, this form provides that either spouse can be viewed as owning the entire property to the exclusion of the other. The effect of this is that if a creditor is coming after only one spouse, assets titled as Tenants by the Entireties are beyond the reach, because they can be viewed as belonging completely to the other spouse.

It is important that you make your intention of owning property as Tenants by the Entireties very clear. The best way to do this is to work with your legal advisor who will create appropriate legal documents and explain the other consequences (beyond asset protection) of owning property with your spouse in this manner.

Another strategy that can be effective in an appropriate fact pattern is for the high risk spouse to place the collection in the name of the low risk spouse. For example, if the wife is a celebrity OB-GYN and her husband makes $40,000/year as a tennis pro, it may make sense to place the art and antiques collection in his name. This strategy also requires documentation, detailed discussions with your legal advisor and careful implementation depending on the state of your residence, but in some circumstances it can be effective.

Gifting

In the example above the OB-GYN gifted the art collection to her husband, the tennis pro. Gifts between spouses can be made in any amount without gift tax consequences. But gifting can also be a viable asset protection strategy outside the marriage relationship. The gift could be made to your children, your sibling, your aunt or a friend. The hitch here is the gift tax. People can give gifts of up to $12,000 each year to as many recipients as they like, without triggering a gift tax obligation. So hypothetically, you could give a painting worth $7,500 to your daughter and two prints worth $4,000 each to your son without gift tax consequences which would put these assets beyond the reach of your creditors. However, you have now lost control over the art. It is out of your house and into theirs. If this result is acceptable to you (you intended to give them the pieces anyway) then gifting might be a viable asset protection strategy for you. Generally, however, it makes more sense to give the gift in a trust or through a Family Limited Partnership (see below).

If you leave the art hanging in your own house or your real intention is to have your kids give you the art back once the lawsuit has blown over—this will put you in hot water and the transfer is likely to be viewed as a fraudulent conveyance. If this is proven the creditor can reach the art and it will be lost in satisfaction of the judgment. So if you are are going to transfer items in your collection to others, you need to do it with integrity and a full understanding that it will not come back to you.

Conveying the Art to a Trust in the US

367

In some situations trusts can be a useful way to place your collection beyond the reach of both your creditors and your child's creditors. Putting your collection in a revocable trust you create under which you are also a beneficiary often has estate planning utility but this approach offers you no protection from creditors. Similarly, if you create an irrevocable trust and name yourself as one of the beneficiaries most states will not allow you to place your assets beyond the reach of your creditors, even when you use the special provisions described below.

A few states allow something called a Domestic Asset Protection Trust or DAPT. These states permit a person to create a trust, name himself as a beneficiary, and protect the assets of the trust from the claims of creditors. DAPT's are sophisticated (and expensive) planning tools with many complex permutations, but very useful in some circumstances. Consult with your advisory team to determine if this is an appropriate approach for you.

There is a situation where a trust strategy can be useful, assuming the state law allows for this approach. Establishing an irrevocable trust naming your child as the beneficiary can be useful in a situation where your goal is to keep the art in the family —you intend to give it to your children—but you fear that your child may not behave responsibly or is in a high risk profession and your goal is to protect the art from his creditors. A properly drafted trust offers two techniques that protect the collection—the first is a spendthrift clause, effective only where state law supports this approach, and the second is discretionary distribution provisions.

368

A spendthrift clause restricts the beneficiary's (your child's) ability to transfer, sell, or otherwise give away any of his rights in the trust. So, if you established a trust for the benefit of your child and conveyed your collection, or particular items in it, to the trust, these items (absent other countervailing circumstances) cannot be reached by the child's creditors and would not be exposed if the child attempted to assign or otherwise use the trust assets as collateral for a debt.

The second important language that should be included in the trust document is a provision that says the Trustee has discretion over whether or not to make distributions of money to the beneficiary. Once distributions are made to the child, obviously the creditor can reach those assets. As long as the assets are still held in the trust the creditor cannot reach them. In this situation, the selection of the Trustee is important because this person will need to have the judgment and the wisdom to know when discretionary distributions are not an appropriate alternative.

Conveying the Art to an Offshore Entity

There are additional options available to collectors using offshore entities that remove assets from the jurisdiction of the US legal system. The trade off here is that for these offshore approaches to truly provide meaningful protection from creditors, it is best to also remove the assets—the art—to the foreign jurisdiction. So in order to optimize an offshore strategy you need to take the relevant items in your collection to the offshore destination. For most collectors this is not a reasonable option—we want to live with our art. But for the collector who finds this trade off palatable, foreign entities can provide another level of protection.

369

Equity Stripping

Stripping the equity out of the collection and using the proceeds to purchase life insurance or an annuity is another useful asset protection strategy for art. It involves taking an asset that is difficult to protect (e.g., art) and removing (stripping) the asset's equity by borrowing against it. The art is pledged as collateral for the loan. If a $1 million painting has been pledged as collateral for a $1 million bank loan, the painting has no value to a creditor. The asset is less attractive to creditors because a security interest is placed against the art at the time of the loan which must be satisfied prior to the creditor's claim. The loan proceeds can be used to purchase life insurance or annuities that are held in a way that is beyond reach.

14

Putting Your Plan in Place Using PowerGifting™ and Other Approaches to Accomplish Your Intentions

With Contributions From
George Kasparian, Esq.
and Steven Friedricks

"Art is our chief means of breaking bread with the dead."

—W.H. Auden

At this point, your collection has been inventoried and appraised, you have documented the provenance, certified the authenticity, determined you have good title, and have it insured. So now you are ready to think about what you want to happen to the collection when all is said and done.

I have made a strong case in this book for the importance of bringing in a professional art succession planner when you start thinking about what is to become of your collection. I am increasingly aware that people are not familiar with this term or the services provided by these fee-based professionals. I preface this summation chapter with a description of what these advisors do because I believe the strategies discussed in the scenarios below require the participation of an art succession planner in order to fully realize the value of the collection and the intentions of the collector.

The Role of the Art Succession Planner

Art succession planners become a member of the collector's advisory team—which is generally comprised of the attorney, the CPA, the investment advisor/financial planner, the insurance person, and the appraiser or dealer. Ideally, the art succession planner is brought in during the estate planning process when the team is planning for the disposition of all of the rest of the collector's assets (real estate, stocks, insurance, retirement assets, business interests, boats, planes, etc.). If the planning is done at this phase there are all kinds of options available for the disposition of the art depending on what the collectors want to do with it. Do they want to give it to a museum, to their college, to the hospital, or to their kids? Do they need to sell some stuff off to raise some cash to live on? Do they need to create a stream of income for the surviving spouse? Do they want to exhibit the collection and have it tour the world? Do they have huge capital gains that need to be addressed? Using the PowerGifting™ strategies discussed in this book, the collector working with an informed advisory team can usually reduce the tax liability, create philanthropic capital, and transfer more wealth to the kids.

Attorneys and other professional advisors are not accustomed to thinking about art as a financial asset that can be used to create income, nor are they accustomed to using it to fund a trust or as an asset that is part of the estate planning process. Even when the art is worth millions of dollars, many attorneys just don't think to plan for it—they sometimes don't even figure out that it is worth millions or that it represents a significant percentage of the client's net worth.

373

The art succession planner works with the collector's advisory team to implement the client's objectives. Sometimes the succession planner is negotiating with the museum or the planned giving person at the hospital or college. Sometimes the succession planner is finding the right dealer or the right auction house in order to liquidate some pieces. Sometimes he or she is setting reserves and negotiating consignment agreements at the auction house. Sometimes the succession planner is locating conservation or restoration experts or dealing with authentication problems or chain of title issues. Most of the time the succession planner is answering the questions of the rest of the advisory team because they don't know which way to turn. They don't know what they are dealing with. They understand stock, real estate, and partnership interests. But they don't know a Rothko from a Degas from a paint-by-number. They know nothing about porcelain or textiles or 35mm film or medieval manuscripts or Arts and Crafts furniture and have no clue what to do with it. The art succession planner makes sure that the value of these assets is not only preserved but transferred to the collector's beneficiaries in keeping with the collector's intentions.

If the collector dies without having planned for the disposition of the collection, the art succession planner is brought in to do damage control. In the post-mortem situation, the options are not as extensive as when the advisory team is planning during the collector's lifetime, so, as a general rule, there will be some loss of value. The succession planner's post-mortem role is to minimize the loss of value given the less than perfect circumstances of the situation.

The following case studies illustrate the various planning strategies discussed individually in prior chapters. In this material we are looking at how these strategies are used in hypothetical fact patterns and how they can be used in combination and sometimes in layers or phases so that the advisors are fully accomplishing the intentions of the collector.

Case Study #1

The first sample scenario involves Cole and Annette Frank, both age 70, who have $25 million in total assets of which about $5 million is an eclectic collection consisting of 19th century paintings, American furniture, and important folk art sculptures. Their cost of acquiring the art was about $500,000. They have three children (Max, Ben, and William) and six grandchildren. The scenarios below discuss several possible outcomes for the Frank family beginning with a postmortem trip to the auction house.

Scenario #1: The Postmortem Auction Sale When the Kids Don't Want the Art

A common misconception of collectors is "I love my stuff and so will my kids." So they don't do any specific planning for their art assets, allowing them to be distributed by the terms of their will, along with all of their other assets, often falling into the residuary clause. This approach inevitably results in the kids being unsure what to do with the collection, which they never really cared for in the first place. In this case study, we will suppose the Franks failed to do any lifetime planning for the collection, and it went to the kids on the death of the second spouse. The kids were not interested in the collection, and told their advisors they wanted to cash out. The probate attorney, who is now the involuntary curator of the art, followed conventional wisdom and recommended auctioning off the collection and dispersing the proceeds among the heirs. The auction house set the pre-sale estimates between $4.5 million and $5.5 million. This decision could cost the children over $3 million in taxes and fees! Here's why:

Industry averages say that 20 to 30% of the $5 million collection ($750,000) will not sell because bidding fails to meet the reserve (minimum acceptable bid) or no one bids on the items at all. Within the industry these are called buy-ins. These items may be sold later at a discount—usually the seller will receive only about one-third of the estimated market value if forced into this approach. (In a postmortem fact pattern the attorney is always in a rush

375

The Advisor's FYI:

Often the probate attorney cannot complete an auction sale within the 9-month period allowed before the federal estate taxes are due. In this circumstance the attorney can get a qualified appraisal (for around $4 million) and file a final tax return based on this value. A year or two later, when the auction takes place, the collection might sell for $2.2 million. The heirs paid taxes on $4 million, but only realized $2.2 million—again not a very good result. Question: Should the attorney reopen the estate?

to dispose of the left over pieces because the estate tax return needs to be filed within nine months of the date of death.)

So best case, this auction sale will generate about $4.25 million for the heirs, after subtracting out the buy-ins. From this amount, the auction house will deduct its commission and expenses—seller's fees, and the costs associated with the property's insurance, photography, storage, cataloging, and any other costs they incurred in marketing the collection. This generally amounts to another 15%, leaving the heirs with $3.5 million. Then, estate taxes kick in. The federal estate tax is calculated on the $3.5 million proceeds added to the $750,000 in unsold items, or about 47% of $4.25 million, equaling about $2 million. (There are also sometimes additional amounts due the state.) The net then, after all these deductions, from the auction sale is about $1.5 million. Assume over time the kids can sell the pieces they had to buy back (the $750,000 in unsold items), for about $250,000. They would be left with a total of $1.75 million—about 35% of the original estimate of the value of the collection (see Figure 1). It is apparent that failing to plan is the most expensive art succession plan.

Figure 1 – Selling at an Unplanned Auction Sale

Art sold at auction by executor at the date of death of the second spouse:

$4.25 million proceeds from auction of the
    collection (value less 15% buy-ins*)
-$750,000 transaction costs—auction fees,
    commissions, etc.

 $3.5 million (net proceeds from the auction).

$4.25 million is subject to estate tax, however (add back the 15% unsold items).

Estimated estate tax due (47% of $4.25 million) – $2 million.

 $3.5 million (net proceeds from the auction)
-$2.0 million (estimated estate tax)
+$250,000 (amount realized eventually for items
    unsold at auction)

 $1.75 million (amount to heirs).

Of the $5 million collection only 35% goes to the heirs, **65%** is lost to taxes and fees.

* Industry average-20 to 30% of collection at auction does not sell because items fail to meet the reserve (minimum acceptable bid). Within the industry this is called buy-in. These items may be sold later at a deep discount—usually the seller will receive only about one-third of the estimated value.

The Expert's Perspective:
David Frohman—
The State of the Art Market

In 2006 the global art market came within striking distance of 1990 highs, up 25% in the course of the year. In the United States, however, prices are up 32% from the peak of 1990. The global fine art market generated total revenue of $6.4 billion, an increase of 52% over 2005. New York continues to be the center of the global art market, commanding 46% of sales, with Sotheby's and Christie's dominating auction sales. In 2006, 407 works sold for over $1 million at the US auction houses, primarily at the Impressionist and Modern Art sales where most of the 7-figure action has taken place post-9/11. Post-War and Contemporary Art also held its own in sales over a million. Buying at this level has been fueled by new wealth, much of it from m[b]illionaires outside the US—China, Russia, India, Brazil, Mexico, and the Arab emirates. Within the US, the market has been dominated by hedge fund wealth, dot com IPO affluence, and old family money spent at breath-taking levels which has resulted in the unprecedented growth in the market.

The recent economic slowdown triggered by corrections relating to sub-prime lending issues could portent an adjustment in the art market. But currency-exchange advantages and the fact that the super wealthy do not change their purchasing habits easily may cause the fall auctions to surpass even last year's numbers. The fact that the art market is twenty times as large as it was in 1990 and that most high net worth individuals have bought into the idea of art as an asset diversification strategy suggest that if the market does suffer a near-term correction it will be short lived and not of the depth of the events of 1990.

The Mei-Moses Fine Art Index shows a 14.5% return in the art market in 2005 and in certain categories—specifically contemporary art–indicates art has actually exceeded the S&P 500 in investment results. Since 2004, as art prices have shown enormous appreciation, several art hedge funds have emerged. A few have survived, the only one with a multi-year track record is Phillip Hoffman's Fine Art Fund out of London. The Fine Art Fund invests in Old Masters, Impressionist, Modern, and Contemporary Art, buying works of art in the range of $10,000-$5,000,000, with an average value of $600,000 per work.

In 2004, Fernwood Art Investments made a big splash entering the market in Boston. The fund failed, however, and the manager is being sued for embezzlement of $8 million. A new entrant into the field appeared recently in the form of the Art Trading Fund (also out of London) which buys and sells pieces directly using a private network of resources, targeting a 3- to 12-month turn around. This fund hedges by taking short positions in stocks that are closely related to the art market —things like luxury goods and Sotheby's itself.

Auctions houses have historically been viewed as the only option for the liquidation of art antiques and collectibles. The advisory community is particularly guilty of failing to explore other options that frequently will result in a greater yield to the selling collector. A postmortem fact pattern where the probate attorney is rushing to dispose of the art assets within the 9-month filing period for the estate tax return frequently results in the loss of a significant percentage of the value of the collection. Between the low hammer prices that are the product of a poorly planned consignment, estate taxes, transaction fees, charges by the auction house (Christie's just raised its buyer's premium to 25% of the first $20,000), and the 30% (on average) of the collection that does not sell; auction sales can result in a loss of 70% of the collection's value.

Scenario #2: A Bequest of the Art to the Kids – The Plan That Is Really No Plan

Collectors will sometimes, with the best of intentions, give specific pieces to specific beneficiaries not thinking through or planning for the tax consequences of these gifts. This situation is a half-baked effort to plan during the collector's lifetime. But because the plan is not well conceived, the attempt to leave a generous gift to a loved one is thwarted and can turn into a nightmare. Let's examine specific bequests of three very fine pieces, each worth $1.2 million, to each of the three Frank boys. Cole and Annette made these bequests with visions of the pieces hanging in the homes of each of their sons. The unfortunate reality is that unless there is a large source of cash accompanying these bequests to pay the estate tax liability, the boys will be forced to sell their beautiful pieces to pay the IRS. If the probate attorney once again recommends a hasty auction sale, the result in this fact pattern will be very similar to the result in Scenario #1.

Scenario #3: An Outright Gift of the Art to a Museum

The simplest and most overlooked lifetime planning technique is to create a charitable gifting strategy using the "Ohs" of the collection. The Franks can donate artwork directly to their favorite museum and take a charitable income tax deduction. To do this they should obtain 1) a qualified appraisal and 2) acknowledgement from the receiving charity that it has a related use. The deduction will be in the amount of the current fair market value of the piece (as stated in the appraisal). If Cole and Annette choose $100,000 of appraised artwork to gift outright, and they are in the maximum tax bracket (40%), this "gift" would be the same as putting $40,000 in their pockets. This money can be used for additional cash flow, the purchase of more art, gifting to members of the family, or to fund other estate planning objectives.

Scenario #4: Charitable Remainder Trust

In this scenario let's assume the Franks knew their kids were not interested in the collection, so they decided to liquidate it and invest the proceeds to generate some income for their retirement years. If they sold the collection outright for the appraised value, they would be looking at a $1.575 million capital gains tax ($5 million sale - $500,000 cost basis = $4.5 million gain x 35% combined Federal and State cap gains rate = $1.575 million). Assuming a 5% annual return, the capital gains tax would result in about $78,750 in lost income every year.

If instead of the outright sale, the Franks gift the same pieces to a Charitable Remainder Trust (CRT) naming their favorite art museum as the remainder beneficiary they will be in a significantly better position. The Franks would receive a charitable income tax deduction equal to the acquisition cost of the collection ($500,000) for the non-related use. They can deduct up to 30% of AGI with a 5-year carryover. More importantly, they avoid the large capital gains tax ($1.575 million). When the pieces in the CRT are sold, the art is converted to $5 million in income-producing assets. Assuming 5% annual payments from the CRT generated by the $5 million in trust, the Franks would have $250,000/year in income for the rest of their lives. Of the $250,000 in annual income from the CRT, $78,750 is earned by avoiding the capital gains tax on the sale of the collection. Over a 15-year life expectancy, total income would equal $3.75 million (see Figure 2).

Figure 2 – The Value of the Charitable Remainder Trust

Charitable Deduction = $500,000 (Franks can deduct up to 30% of AGI and, the deduction can be carried forward for up to five years until it is used up.)

Value of the deduction (tax savings) assuming the Franks are in the combined 40% federal and state tax bracket: $500,000 X 40% = $200,000

Capital Gains Tax = 0 (would have owed $1.575 million without CRT)

Estate Tax = 0 (would have owed about $2.3 million without CRT)

Assume 5% annual payments from CRT based on $5 million in trust = $250,000/year in income for the life of the donor. Over a 15-year life expectancy, total income = $3.75 million. This allows donor to use the amount he would have paid in capital gains taxes ($1.575 million) for investment. Of the $250,000 annual return, $78,750 is earned by avoiding the capital gains tax. For income tax purposes, income payments from a CRT are considered a combination of ordinary income, capital gains, tax exempt, and return on capital.

Scenario #5: A Bargain Sale Allows the Collectors to Be Charitable and Create Cash

Another alternative for the Franks, which allows them to benefit their favorite museum and generate some cash for them to live on, is a bargain sale. A big benefit from this type of transaction for art and collectibles is that it eliminates auction pitfalls such as buy-ins, sales fees, and poor results. This strategy involves selling the collection to a museum for a price less than the current fair market value and taking a charitable deduction for the difference between the sale price and the FMV. The Franks and their advisory team negotiate an arrangement with the museum so that they are receiving 50% of the value of the collection in cash – $2.5 million. The Franks are then entitled to an income tax deduction equal to the difference between the sale price ($2.5 million) and current fair market value ($5 million). They take a charitable income tax deduction of $2.5 million. This approach gives the Franks immediate liquidity and significantly lowers their capital gains tax liability by removing the remainder of the collection from their estate (see Figure 3).

Figure 3 – Benefits of a Bargain Sale

FMV of collection = $5 million.
Cost basis of collection = $500,000.
Bargain Sale Price = $2.5 million.

Charitable Contribution = $5 million (FMV) - $2.5 million (Sale price)= $2.5 million.

Value of the charitable deduction (tax savings) assuming the Franks are in the combined 40% federal and state tax bracket:

$2.5 million X 40% = $1 million.

Capital Gains Tax will have to be paid on the non-contributed portion of the collection and is calculated as followed:

$2.5 million = Bargain Sale Price = Amount realized on non-contributed portion= 50% of FMV of collection

Adjusted basis = $500,000 x 50% (percent realized from bargain sale) = $250,000.

$2.5 million (Bargain Sale Price)
-$250,000 (adjusted basis)

$2.25 million (amount of gain)
x 28% (Federal cap gains rate)

$630,000 (Capital Gains Tax)

Total Proceeds from Bargain Sale
$2.5 million (Bargain Sale Price)
+$1 million (Value of charitable income tax deduction)
-$630,000 (Capital gains tax)

$2.87 million

Scenario #6: Borrowing Against the Art to Purchase Life Insurance for an ILIT

In this fact pattern, let's suppose the kids are still teenagers and are not really ready to decide whether they would like to keep the art or liquidate for cash. The approach illustrated in this scenario allows the Franks to obtain the benefits of lifetime planning without locking the kids into one option or the other. The Franks decide to create an estate tax-free fund to allow each child to later decide if he or she would like to purchase some of the art or receive a cash distribution. This objective is achieved by borrowing $1 million against the total value of the collection and using the collection as collateral. It may be possible, depending upon the length of the loan, which could be for up to 20 years, to have the interest fold back into the principal of the loan.

The $1 million loan proceeds are gifted to an Irrevocable Life Insurance Trust (ILIT). Though there is a potential gift tax liability on this transfer, Cole and Annette each have a $1 million lifetime gift tax exclusion that they can use to avoid the tax. The ILIT then uses the $1 million to purchase a 2nd-to-die life insurance policy (single premium) in the amount of $6.5 million. At the death of the second parent, the life insurance proceeds ($6.5 million) will pass to the children without incurring any estate or income tax liability. The children can at that point decide whether to use the proceeds to keep all or part of the collection or simply to take the money.

This approach provides tremendous flexibility in planning for the art assets because it allows the collectors to enjoy the art during their lifetime, eliminates the transaction fees and taxes associated with selling the art, and provides wealth replacement for the kids.

Scenario #7: Leveraging for Your Favorite Charity

Suppose the Franks would like to set up a fund for the local hospital to build a pediatric wing. They could use a similar approach to Scenario #6. First, they can borrow $1 million against the total value of the collection, using the collection as collateral. Then they can gift the $1 million loan proceeds to the hospital. The Franks will receive a $1 million charitable income tax deduction (up to 50% Adjusted Gross Income with 5-year carryover) for the gift. Assuming they are in the 40% tax bracket, the deduction would be worth $400,000. The hospital could use the $1 million gift to purchase a 2nd-to-die life insurance policy in the amount of $6.5 million on the Franks and name itself as the beneficiary. That way, the initial $1 million gift will ultimately be worth $6.5 million to the charity. The loan will be paid off using other assets during the collectors' lifetimes or at their death as part of the estate settlement. This approach will allow the Franks to enjoy the collection during their lifetimes, provide the insurance proceeds for the hospital, and keep control of the collection in the family by using other planning strategies.

Scenario #8: Reverse Mortgage Collateralized by the Art

Suppose the Franks have spent most of their money on art and now they need income to live on, but they cannot bear to part with their collection. By us-

387

ing the collection as collateral, they can take out a reverse mortgage (Cash Flow Annuity) which would generate a tax-free monthly stream of income. For example, the Franks could receive $12,000/month tax-free with a reverse mortgage on their collection. The interest can be added to the outstanding balance, and the Franks get to keep the collection while enjoying future appreciation. The total loan amount on $12,000/month ($144,000/year) over a 10-year period would be about $1.8 million with compound interest, which is still less than half of the value of the collection. The loan will be repaid when the collection is sold either during their lifetime or when they die and the children receive the balance. Since the loan amount against the collection is deductible for estate tax purposes, the federal government is actually helping to pay off nearly 50% of it.

Now let's change the facts a little and look at a couple of cases where we layer and phase strategies in order to accomplish the objectives of two collectors who have the foresight to include their art and antiques assets in the estate planning process.

Case Study #2: PowerGifting™ the Collection to the Alma Mater, Retirement Income for the Collector, and Wealth Replacement for the Kids

Fact Pattern: The collector is a retired college professor at a prestigious West Coast state university. He and his wife have four children and six grandchildren. Their major asset is a $15 million important and well-documented rare book collection. Their current income is generated from a state pension plan, social security, and a small investment account.

388

His goals:

- To keep the finest parts of the collection together and gift it to his alma mater, which has expressed tremendous interest, to be studied, respected, and displayed.

- To create additional current cash flow for living expenses.

- To keep part of the collection in his home for the remainder of his lifetime.

- To create wealth replacement strategies so that he has an inheritance to leave to his children and grandchildren.

- To create an endowment and curatorial fund to accompany the gift to the university to properly care for and maintain the collection.

The PowerGifting™ plan:

The initial step in a situation like this is to analyze the collection and divide it into the "Ohs," the "Oh Mys," and the "Oh My Gods." This approach will allow us to use the lesser pieces to generate liquidity, the mid-tier ("Oh Mys") for wealth replacement, while preserving the best pieces ("Oh My Gods") in the collection to create philanthropic capital. For purposes of this case study, we will assume that each of the three tiers is valued at about $5 million. Using a multi-level PowerGifting™ approach, we pursue the following art succession planning strategy:

First, we setup a Charitable Remainder Trust (CRT) and gift the "Ohs" (because of the caliber of this collection, his "Ohs" would have been anyone else's "Oh My Gods"), naming the university as the remainder beneficiary. The pieces gifted to the CRT are then sold, creating $5 million in income-producing assets in the CRT. Assuming 5% annual payments from the CRT, the professor would have $250,000/year in income for life. He receives a charitable income tax deduction equal to the acquisition cost of the pieces. And he has funded the endowment in the form of the corpus of the trust which will go to the university at the professor's death.

Second, as a wealth replacement strategy for his children and grandchildren, he borrows $1 million against the "Oh Mys," using this portion of the collection as collateral. Then, utilizing an Irrevocable Life Insurance Trust (ILIT), the professor gifts the $1 million loan proceeds to the ILIT, which purchases a $6 million 2nd-to-die life insurance policy on the professor and his wife. The insurance proceeds in the ILIT will pass to his children and grandchildren free of estate taxes on his death. The kids can then decide whether to use the proceeds to preserve this share of the collection or keep the cash.

Third, the professor enters into a bargain sale agreement (selling for less than fair market value) with the university for a group of the "Oh My Gods" of the collection. The sales proceeds paid as part of the bargain sale transaction will generate additional cash flow. The professor takes a charitable deduction equal to the difference between the FMV and bargain sale price, saves on capital gains taxes, and removes this portion of the collection from his estate. When negotiating with the university, he can discuss naming opportunities, permanent display, and other conditions in order to keep this part of the collection intact.

Fourth, he develops an annual gifting strategy to keep the very finest pieces in the family without incurring estate or gift tax liabilities. Under the current tax code, an individual can transfer up to $12,000/year (for a married couple, $24,000/year) per person to as many people as he or she chooses, completely tax-free. This amount is known as the gift tax annual exclusion. Therefore, the professor and his wife can transfer up to $336,000 per year tax-free ($24,000 annual gift tax exclusion for married couple x 4 children, 4 spouses, and 6 grandchildren = $24,000 x 14 = $336,000). The annual exclusion strategy is used to gift these best pieces to the children and grandchildren tax-free over a period of years. The children enter into an agreement with the institution making a long-term loan and later promise gifts of this part of the collection to the university.

391

One of the things we have accomplished in this scenario is we have moved tax deductions, which can never be used up in the collector's lifetime, to future generations of their family. It is also possible to achieve additional tax benefits by funneling part of the proceeds into 529 College Savings Plans for the benefit of the grandchildren. A 529 plan (from Section 529 of the Internal Revenue Code) is designed to help families set aside funds for future college costs. Contributions to 529 plans can grow tax-free (similar to an IRA) as long as the money is ultimately used to pay for higher education.

The result of this multi-layered PowerGifting™ strategy—the professor and his wife increase their retirement income, the children get an inheritance, and the university gets the best parts of the collection as well as a supporting endowment.

Case Study #3: Creating Philanthropic Capital and an Art Legacy for Multigenerational Collectors

Fact Pattern:

Grandpa and Grandma—the first generation—both aged 75, are the matriarch and patriarch of a prominent family with a net worth of $100 million. They have four children and six grandchildren. They have been acquiring very fine pieces for 40 years—some of them with a very modest cost basis because Grandma was very good at spotting the next great genius ahead of the crowd—and have assembled an internationally renowned collection valued at $25 million. They are major donors to their local museum, giving personal funds to help the museum with its building and acquisitions campaigns as well as holding an annual fundraiser in their home using their art as the star attraction. They also have loaned many of their pieces to museums throughout the world for exhibitions.

Mom, Dad, and various other members of the second generation collect photographs, contemporary art, Asian art, art books, and other things that appeal to their personal interests. Some of the grandchildren in the third generation also have the collecting gene and have begun acquiring vintage electric guitars, Grateful Dead memorabilia, LPs and turntables, VW Beetles, and unusual hashish pipes.

The first generation in consultation with their estate planning attorney decides to gift their collection to several different museums. The attorney suggests a "grab bag approach," having the curators select items from the collection that they want, and informs

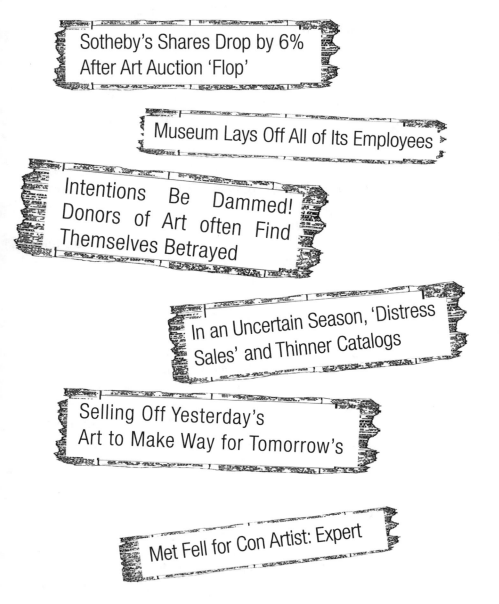

Sotheby's Shares Drop by 6%
After Art Auction 'Flop'

Museum Lays Off All of Its Employees

Intentions Be Dammed!
Donors of Art often Find
Themselves Betrayed

In an Uncertain Season, 'Distress
Sales' and Thinner Catalogs

Selling Off Yesterday's
Art to Make Way for Tomorrow's

Met Fell for Con Artist: Expert

the family office art consultant that he intends to structure the gift in this manner. The art consultant becomes distressed at this approach because she is aware that many gifted pieces never or rarely get exhibited and she is outraged at the current wave of deaccessions. Museums have been selling off pieces in their permanent collection in order to raise funds for general operating expenses, to fund a building campaign, or to acquire other works of art.

The children and grandchildren call a meeting, at the request of their family office art consultant, to address the family's growing concern over the manner in which museums all across the United States are treating gifted artworks. Grandma and Grandpa are thrilled that their children and grandchildren are taking an interest in the legacy of the family's collection. At this meeting Mom suggests bringing in an art succession planner that she heard speak at the museum where she sits on the board.

The succession planner introduced the family to an innovative approach called a Museum Without Walls, which utilizes a private operating foundation (POF), so the family can manage and preserve the collection while avoiding huge estate tax liabilities (more about how these work in Chapter 13).

First, the best pieces in the collection (the "Oh My Gods") are gifted to the POF, and Grandma and Grandpa will receive an income tax deduction for the current fair market value of the gift (up to 30% of Adjusted Gross Income). Gifting to the POF will eliminate estate tax and/or capital gains taxes on the "Oh My God" pieces in the collection, allow the family to manage the collection, and make it available to tour internationally, raising money for charitable causes.

Second, some of the other lesser pieces in the collection (the "Ohs" and "Oh Mys") are gifted to the foundation and sold to create an endowment fund to pay for storage, insurance, conservation, and other expenses related to the preservation of the collection. This endowment fund will also absorb all of the costs associated with running the family's Museum Without Walls such as hiring a curator, developing exhibition venues, transportation, installation, and sponsorship of the fundraising gala. It will enable charities that are favored by the family to use all of the proceeds from the exhibition for their purposes.

The foundation will also produce a book and a curatorial video providing a way for Grandma and Grandpa to share their mesmerizing stories of how they put the collection together and all the fascinating artists Grandma knew when she lived in Greenwich Village and hung out with the Beat Poets. This creates an art legacy that will allow the grandchildren a few years from now to host a party to raise funds for a local Habitat for Humanity project with their grandparents' art and have the accompanying video and book as the star attractions.

The Museum Without Walls will allow the collectors, their family, and future generations to maintain control of the collection by serving as president or as members of the board of directors. They could also receive stipends for their work on the POF. In addition to exhibiting the collection, the collectors' children and grandchildren who have an interest in charitable giving can become philanthropists themselves, using the foundation resources to award grants to their favorite art and non-art related charities and create scholarships for art students. In addition to exhibiting the collection, this plan provides a philanthropic venue for multigenerations long into the future.

A Final Word from Michael:

I hope these scenarios illustrate the importance of lifetime art succession planning. As you can see, the first step is to understand your goals and objectives for your collection. Then discuss the appropriate planning options with your advisory team. Why not have the collection end up the way you want—benefiting your family and favorite charities rather than having half the value go to the IRS and all the players in the art marketplace?

The greatest joy is always the collecting and the indescribable feeling of walking into your home after a tough day and seeing the beautiful items you have on the walls, the pedestals, and the shelves. Somehow the cares of the day just evaporate, and you are overtaken by the wonderful good energy that passes through you when you look at your collection. You have many choices enabling you to share these wonderful objects with the public and with the future generations of your family. Lifetime planning puts you in control of those choices.

Gael and I want to give something back to the world which has blessed us in so many ways. Part of that giving back takes the form of gifting some of our finest pieces to various museums that are a good fit. And oh, the euphoria of the opening night party—there is nothing more fun than being the toast of the art world for your one special night. But we have reserved our finest pieces for our grandchildren. Our finest pieces are quite literally an extension of who Gael and I are as human beings. They are a big piece of our legacy on this earth. What greater way to share something of ourselves with our grandchildren.

396

At holiday dinners around our table, we'll be telling the "Will the Thrill" story for many years. We'll watch Will become a young man and learn to value, respect, and love the treasures we have in our home. My greatest hope is that Will and my other grandchildren will acquire the collecting gene so that they can appreciate and carry on the collection that Gael and I have started. I can think of no greater tribute than to have your children and grandchildren continue to build and grow the collection you have begun. So if I could look into a crystal ball, I would love to see 25 years into the future … and there's Will, but now embroiled in the thrill of the hunt!

397

Endnotes

1. Daniel Biebuyck and Nelly van den Abbeele, *The Power of Headdresses, A Cross Cultural Study of Forms and Functions* (Brussels: Tendi S.A., 1984).

2. William N. Goetzmann, "How Costly is the Fall from Fashion? Survivorship Bias in the Painting Market" (Working Paper Series F #42, Yale School of Management, August 1994).

3. Herbert Muschamp, "New York's Bizarre Museum Moment," *The New York Times*, July 11, 2004.

4. See UCC Article 9, §501.

5. Thomas Danziger and Charles Danziger, "The Perils of Consigning: Protecting your stake in an artwork may not be as simple as it seems, especially when you consign it to a gallery," *Art + Auction Investment Annual 2006*, 51.

6. Carter B. Horsley, "Auction Angst: The Anti-Trust Investigations Are Looking At Fee-Fixing, But What About Reserves, Estimates, Guarantees and Post-Auction Sales?" *The City Review*, September 20, 2000 (updated February 24, 2003), http://www.thecityreview.com/auctions.html.

7. "Strong Museum and Eldred's Settle Lawsuit over $1.55 Million Chinese Vase," *Maine Antique Digest*, January 2004.

8. Scott Sutherland, "An Editor's Fashion Legacy Ends on a Quiet and Distant Runway," *The New York Times*, May 11, 2003.

9. Alan Bamberger, "Auction Estimates, Reserves, Opening Bids: A Primer," http://www.artbusiness.com/highres.html.

10. Ibid.

11. Lita Solis-Cohen, "Indian Weathervane Sells For Record $5,840,000," *Maine Antique Digest*, November 2006.

12. Ibid.

13. "Egan Collection Bullish for Bourgeault," *Antiques and Arts Weekly*, August 2006, 43.

14. Judy Tully, "Playing The Odds: Guarantees Are A Big Gamble For Auction Houses, But In Today's Booming Market, The Strategy Is Paying Off Big-Time," *Art + Auction Investment Annual* 2006, 25-27.

15. Ibid.

16. Ibid.

17. Hollis Taggart Gallery Art Market Report Fall/Winter 2006; used with permission from Hollis Taggart.

18. "Manhattan Art Gallery Owner Sentenced to 41 Months," *Maine Antique Digest*, August 2005.

19. "Collector wins £1.9m urns case," BBC News, May 19, 2004, http://news.bbc.co.uk/1/hi/england/norfolk/3727623.stm.

20. "Auction house wins vases appeal," BBC News, May 12, 2005, http://news.bbc.co.uk/1/hi/england/norfolk/4539707.stm.

21. Dan Berry, "A Collector Was Someone Else, And Art Was Someone Else's," *The New York Times*, October 25, 2006.

22. *Associated Press*, "Sotheby's Climbs on Upgrade," Yahoo! Finance, January 22, 2007, http://biz.yahoo.com/ap/070122/sotheby_s_mover.html.

23. David Hewett, "$1 Million Painting Sold at Shannon's Was Stolen; Arrest Made," *Maine Antique Digest*, December 2006.

24. Should the auction house be required to send their auction catalog to the leading stolen art databases such as the Art Loss Register in London (artloss.com) or IFAR (International Foundation for Art Research, IFAR.org), who run stolen art/artifacts databases? Other databases for stolen art are Interpol (Interpol.int), FBI Art Theft Division (fbi.gov/hq/cid/arttheft), and in London, Swift-Find (www.swift-find.com).

25. Lita Solis-Cohen, "Consignor Sued Over Returned Banner," *Maine Antique Digest*, October 2006.

26. Carol Vogel, "A Solid Sale of $128 Million Opens Fine Art Auctions," *The New York Times*, November 4, 2004.

27. Linda Sandler, "Sotheby's Narrows Gap With Christie's in First-Half Auctions," *Bloomberg*, July 18, 2006, http://www.bloomberg.com/apps/news?pid=20601088&sid=ahFSS0J1zbzl&refer=culture.

28. "Stock Pick: Manager suggests Sotheby's, Cabela's," *MSN Money*, August 23, 2006, http://articles.moneycentral.msn.com/Investing/CNBC/StockPicks/StockPick-SothebysCabelas.aspx.

29. Carol Vogel, "Big Prices, Big Risks At Fall Auctions," *The New York Times*, November 2, 2006.

30. USPAP 7-2(e(III))

31. USPAP 7-3(B)

32. USPAP 7-3(a – b)

33. Lawrence Lo, "Linear B," Ancient Scripts, http://www.an-

cientscripts.com/linearb.html (accessed October 2006).

34. The Chicago Conservation Center, "CCC Disaster Prepared-ness Tips," http://www.chicagoconservation.com/pages/tips_di-saster.htm (accessed November 2006).

35. Collectify LLC 514.932.8990 / 800.932.5811, www.collectify.com; for a review of this product, see Carol Kino, "Digital Tool for the Organized Collector," *Art + Auction*, May 2003. Available at http://www.collectify.com/mystuff/reviews/index.php?key=14.

36. Art, Antiques Organizer Deluxe by PrimaSoft 604.951.1085 / http://www.primasoft.com/deluxeprg/artfdlx.htm

Artbase/ Collector
212.675.6399 / orders@artbaseinc.com
orders@artbaseinc.com

Artsystems/ Collections
773.348.6106 / Keith@artsystems.com
www.artsystems.com

Gallery Systems/ EmbARK Collections Manager
646.733.2239 / info@gallerysystems.com
www.gallerysystems.com

37. Barton Bjorneberg, seminar at Bernacki and Associates, May 2004; personal telephone interview, November 8, 2006.

38. Ibid.

39. Ibid.

40. The Chicago Conservation Center, "CCC Long Term Care for your Collection," http://www.chicagoconservation.com/pages/tips_longterm.htm (accessed November 2006).

41. Nick Paumgarten, "Doh! Dept.: The $40-Million Elbow," *The New Yorker*, October 10, 2006.

42. Jane C. H. Jacob, "How to Keep it Out of Your Collection: Part 1," *Chub Collectors*, September 3, 2002.

43. The Chicago Conservation Center, "CCC Disaster Preparedness Tips," http://www.chicagoconservation.com/pages/tips_disaster.htm (accessed November 15, 2006).

44. Mary Louise Schumacher, "Martinifest leaves art museum shaken and stirred," *Milwaukee Journal Sentinel*, February 27, 2006, http://www.jsonline.com/story/index.aspx?id=404718 (accessed October 30, 2006).

45. Mary Louise Schumacher, "Major party did minor damage to sculptures," *Milwaukee Journal Sentinel*, March 10, 2006, http://www.jsonline.com/story/?id=407151 (accessed October 30, 2006).

46. The Pensions Protection Act of 2006, H.R., §6695A(c)(E)(ii).

47. The Appraisal Foundation, *Uniform Standards of Professional Appraisal Practice*, July 1, 2006. Available at http://commerce.appraisalfoundation.org/html/2006%20USPAP/toc.htm (accessed August 14, 2006).

48. American Society of Appraisers
555 Herndon Parkway, Suite 125
Herndon, VA 20170
Phone: 703.478.2228
http://www.appraisers.org

Appraisers Association of America
386 Park Avenue South Suite 2000
New York, NY 10016
Phone: 212.889.5404
http://www.appraiserassoc.org/

International Society of Appraisers
1131 SW 7th Street Suite 105
Renton, WA 98057-1215
Phone: 206.241.0359
http://www.isa-appraisers.org

49. The Appraisal Foundation, *Uniform Standards of Professional Appraisal Practice*, July 1, 2006. Available at http://commerce.appraisalfoundation.org/html/2006%20USPAP/toc.htm (accessed August 14, 2006).

50. Patricia C. Soucy and Janella N. Smyth, *The Appraisal of Personal Property: Principles, Theories and Practice Methods for the Professional Appraiser* (Washington, D.C.: American Society of Appraisers, 1994), 229.

51. Ibid. 56.

52. Internal Revenue Service, "Noncash Charitable Contributions: Instructions for Form 8283," rev. December 2005. Available at http://www.irs.gov/pub/irs-pdf/i8283.pdf (accessed June 12, 2006).

53. Ibid.

54. Karen E. Carolan, *The Art Advisory Panel of the Commissioner of Internal Review Annual Summary Report for 2005* (Closed Meeting Activity), Internal Revenue Service. Available at http://www.irs.gov/pub/irs-pdf/annrep05.pdf (accessed October 31, 2006).

55. See Treas. Reg. §20.2031-6.

56. John J. Havens and Paul G. Schervish, "Millionaires and the Millennium: New Estimates of the Forthcoming Wealth Transfer and the Prospects for a Golden Age of Philanthropy," Boston College Social Welfare Institute, October 19, 1999, http://www.

404

bc.edu/research/swri/meta-elements/pdf/m&m.pdf#search=%2
2Social%20Welfare%20Institute%20at%20Boston%202052%
22

57. Louis Uchitelle, "Gilded Paychecks—Very Rich Are Leaving the Merely Rich Behind," *The New York Times*, November 27, 2006.

58. Michael Moses and Jianping Mei, "Art As an Investment and the Underperformance of Masterpieces" (NYU Finance Working Paper No. 01-012, February 2002), http://papers.ssrn.com/sol3/papers.cfm?abstract_id=311701 (accessed May 20, 2006).

59. Jori Finkel, "Uncrunching the Numbers," *Art + Auction Investment Annual* 2006.

405

60. Both the names and circumstances of the Morton family are a composite of many people and situations I have encountered over the years.

61. Alan Bamberger, "Art Provenance: What It Is and How to Verify It," http://www.artbusiness.com/provwarn.html.

62. Kelly Crow, "Eastman Family Hits Court in Feud Over Mother-well," *The Wall Street Journal*, February 24, 2006.

63. Serge Kovaleski, "Astor Painting Becomes Focus of Courtroom Battle," *The New York Times*, September 1, 2006.

64. Serge Kovaleski, "Major Error Is Reported in Tax Paid by Mrs. Astor on Sale of Painting," *The New York Times*, September 24, 2006.

65. Joseph P. Warner, Hanson S. Reynolds, et al., *Massachusetts Probate Manual* (Boston: Massachusetts Continuing Legal Education, 1996), Ch. 2 and 5.

66. Ibid.

67. Ibid.

68. Ibid.

69. Ibid. Ch. 4.

70. Ibid. Ch. 9.

71. Harold Weinstock, *Planning an Estate*, 3rd ed. (Colorado Springs: Shepard's/McGraw-Hill, 1988).

72. See IRC §2001(c).

73. See IRC §2505.

74. See IRC §2503.

75. See IRC §2523.

76. See IRC §2035.

77. See IRC §2033-2046.

78. See IRC §2053-2056.

79. See IRC §2010(c).

80. See IRC §2001(c).

81. See IRC §1 (h) (5) (A) ; see also Treas. Reg. §1.1 (i)-1T.

82. See IRC §1015.

83. See IRC §1014.

84. "He Is Not Only Smart, But Very Careful, Too," *The New York Times*, July 2, 2006.

85. IRC §170 has limits depending on the type of charitable donation.

86. IRC §170(b)(1).

87. Ibid.

88. Treas. Reg. §1-501(c)(3)(b)(1)(i) states that the articles of organization must "limit the purposes of such organization to one or more exempt purposes; and [not] expressly empower the organization to engage, otherwise than as an insubstantial part of its activities, in activities which in themselves are not in furtherance of one or more exempt purpose."

89. Treas. Reg. §1-501(c)(3)-1(d)(1)(ii) states that an exempt organization is one where "no substantial part of the activities of which is carrying on propaganda, or otherwise attempting, to influence legislation (except as otherwise provided in subsection (h)), and which does not participate in, or intervene in (including the publishing or distributing of statements), any political campaign on behalf of (or in opposition to) any candidate for public office."

90. Treas. Reg. §1-501(c)(3)-1(d)(1)(i)(a)-(g).

91. Internal Revenue Service, "Noncash Charitable Contributions: Instructions for Form 8283," rev. December 2005, p. 4, sec. B. Available at http://www.irs.gov/pub/irs-pdf/i8283.pdf.

92. Treas. Reg. §1.170A-13(c)(3)(i).

93. Maria Puente, "Antiquities scandal: An ill wind blows," *USAToday*, October 17, 2005, http://www.usatoday.com/life/2005-10-17-getty-scandal_x.htm.

407

94. See IRC §2055(e)(4).

95. See IRC §2522(c) and §2055(e), which discuss treating a work of art and the copyright on the work as separate properties for gift or estate tax charitable valuation purposes.

96. Serge Kovaleski, "New York Library officials pay? Shh...," *The New York Times*, November 19, 2006.

97. Daniel Green, "Met Withdraws Sculpture," *Maine Antique Digest*, March 2006.

98. Ibid.

99. "Gates to Lend Da Vinci's Codex Hammer to Italian Underbidder," Computer Business Review 2547 (November 18, 1994).

100. IRC §170e.

101. IRC §170e(1)(B)(i); Treas. Reg. §1.170A-4(b)(3)(i).

102. IRC §1221(a)(3)(A); Treas. Reg. §1.1221-1(c)(1).

103. Association of Art Museum Directors, "Report and Recommendation of the Association of Art Museum Directors," http://www. aamd.org/advocacy/ tax_rec.php.

104. IRC §170(e)(1).

105. Ibid.; see also IRC §170, Treas. Reg. §1-170A-10.

106. IRC §2503(g).

107. See IRS Pub. 526, "Charitable Contributions."

108. IRC §2033.

109. Qualified charities can be found in IRC §170(c) and 501(c).

110. IRC §170(e)(1)(B); see also *Withers v. Commissioner*, 69 T.C. 900 (1978).

111. Ralph E. Lerner and Judith Bresler, Art Law: *The Guide for Collectors*, Investors, Dealers, & Artists, 3rd. ed. (New York: Practising Law Institute, 2005), 1597.

112. IRC 26 USC §664(d).

113. See Treas. Reg. §1.170A-1, 1.170A-13 (c)(2-3).

114. See *Winokur v. Commissioner*, 90 T.C. 733 (1988).

115. See IRC §170(e)(1).

116. See Treas. Reg. §1.170A-13(c); see also "Valuing Art," Trusts & Estates, February 2005.

117. IRC §170(o)(3).

118. Ibid.

119. IRC §170(o)(2).

120. A special thank you to Allan Daniel for sharing the details of this transaction with the author.

121. See IRC §170(e)(2) for rules on bargain sales.

122. Treas. Reg. §1.1011-2(a)(1).

123. Treas. Reg. §1.170A-13(c).

124. See IRC §664 for requirements for classification as a Chari-

409

table Remainder Trust.

125. http://www.attorney-cpa.com.

126. An alternative to a traditional foundation is a Supporting Organization. It is best to consult a tax advisor to compare the benefits of a Supporting Organization versus a foundation. See "Choose Supporting Organizations," *Trusts & Estates*, January 2003.

127. See IRS Pub. 578, "Tax Information for Private Foundations and Foundation Managers."

128. See IRS Pub. 526, "Charitable Contributions."

129. Ralph E. Lerner and Judith Bresler, *Art Law: The Guide for Collectors, Investors, Dealers, & Artists*, 3rd. ed. (New York: Practising Law Institute, 2005), 1598.; see also IRC §170(b)(1)(a)(vi) and 170(b)(1)(E)(i).

130. See IRS Revenue Ruling 74-600.

131. For a detailed explanation of the four tests, see IRC §4942(j)(3)(A), 4942(j)(3)(B)(i), and 4942(j)(3)(B)(ii).

132. See IRS Reg. §53.4942(b).

133. See IRS Revenue Ruling 74-498.

134. See IRC §4942(j)(3)(A), 4942(j)(3)(B)(i), and 4942(j)(3)(B)(ii).

135. IRC §501(c)(3).

136. See IRC §170(b)(1).

137. See IRC §501(c)(3).

138. B. Dane Dudley, Steven M. Fast, and Darren M. Wallace, "Get Real or Get Out," *Trusts & Estates*, July 2003.

139. Larry Ribstein and Robert Keatinge, *Limited Liability Companies*, vol. 2 (St. Paul, MN: Thomson/West, 2004), Ch. 18, sec. 3 and 4.

140. Ibid.

141. Owen G. Fiore and John W. Prokey, "The 2036 Threat to Valuation Discounts," *Trusts & Estates*, March 2003.

142. Larry Ribstein and Robert Keatinge, *Limited Liability Companies*, vol. 2 (St. Paul, MN: Thomson/West, 2004), Ch. 18, sec. 7 and 8.

143. B. Dane Dudley, Steven M. Fast, and Darren M. Wallace, "Get Real or Get Out," *Trusts & Estates*, July 2003.

144. 26 USC §2042.

145. 26 USC §2035.

146. 26 CFR §20-2042-1(c)(3). See this section for further requirements regarding a reversionary interest.

147. *Crummey v. Commissioner*, 397 F.2d 82 (9th Cir. 1968).

148. This section is to alert insurance agents to the existence of Crummey powers. There are additional ways in which Crummey powers may be used, including granting powers to contingent beneficiaries, granting limited powers of appointment, and including "hanging powers." The description of these may be beyond the scope of this chapter.

149. 26 CFR §20.2042-1(c)(2).

150. Ibid.

151. 26 CFR §20.2042-1(c)(4).

152. See IRS Revenue Ruling 79-143.

153. 26 USC §2611.

154. See 26 USC §2601 et seq. and 26 CFR §26.2601 et seq.

155. IRC §1031.

156. Ralph E. Lerner and Judith Bresler, Art Law: *The Guide for Collectors, Investors, Dealers, & Artists*, 3rd. ed. (New York: Practising Law Institute, 2005), 1450.

157. Ibid. See also §§162, 165, 182, and 212.

158. Ibid.; see also Treas. Reg. §1.1031(a)-1(b), which refers to unproductive real estate. It is undetermined as to whether this philosophy applies to collectibles as well.

159. Ibid.

160. Ibid., 1453.

161. Treas. Reg. §1.1031(a)-1(b).

162. This ruling is in Private Letter Ruling 81-27-089, which pertains to IRC §1033.

163. *Standard Federal Tax Reports,* vol. 12 (Chicago: Commerce Clearing House, 2006), §29,608.033.

164. See IRC §1031(b).

165. *See Standard Federal Tax Reports,* vol. 12 (Chicago: Commerce Clearing House, 2006), §29,621 for more information about multi-party like-kind exchanges.

166. This scenario is named for the court case from which it was derived, *Starkey v. United States*, 602 F.2d 1341 (9th Cir. 1979).

167. Ralph E. Lerner and Judith Bresler, *Art Law: The Guide for Collectors, Investors, Dealers, & Artists*, 3rd. ed. (New York: Practising Law Institute, 2005), 1451.

168. David Ebony, "Ganz sale dominates fall auctions—the Christie's sale of modern and contemporary art owned by Victor and Sally Ganz," *Art in America*, January 1998. Available at http://www.findarticles.com/p/articles/mi_m1248/is_n1_v86/ai_20148110.

169. Ibid.

413

Recommended Reading List

- Ackerman, Martin S. *Smart Money and Art: Investing in Fine Art.* Station Hill Press (1986).

- Arnold, Ken. *Cabinets For The Curious: Looking Back At Early English Museums.* Ashgate Publishing (2006).

- Bamberger, Alan. *The Art of Buying Art.* Gordon's Art Reference Inc. (2002).

- Blom, Philipp. *To Have and to Hold–An Intimate History of Collectors and Collecting*. Overlook Press (2002).

- Davis, Ron. *Art Dealer's Field Guide: How to Profit in Art, Buying and Selling Valuable Paintings.* Capital Letters Press (2005).

- Falk, Peter Hastings. *Art Price Index International.* Sound View Press (1994).

- Falk, Peter Hastings. *Who Was Who in American Art.* Sound View Press (1999).

- Freund, Thatcher. *Objects of Desire: The Lives of Antiques and Those Who Pursue Them.* Penguin Books (1995).

- Heilbrun, James, and Charles M. Gray. *The Economics of Art and Culture.* Cambridge University Press (2001).

- Hildesley, C. Hugh. *The Complete Guide to Buying and Selling at Auction*. W W Norton & Co. Inc. (1997).

- Klevit, Alan. *Art Collecting 101: Buying Art for Profit And Pleasure.* Booklocker.com (2005).

- Krishna, Vijay. *Auction Theory.* Academic Press (2002).

- Lacey, Robert. ***Sotheby's: Bidding for Class.*** Warner Books (2002).

- Lerner, Ralph E., and Judith Bresler. ***Art Law: The Guide for Collectors, Artists, Investors, Dealers, and Artists,*** Third Edition. Practising Law Institute (2005).

- Mason, Christopher. ***The Art of the Steal: Inside the Sotheby's-Christie's Auction House Scandal.*** G.P. Putnam's Sons (2004).

- Ridlehuber, Ted. ***Affluent for Life.*** Charter Financial Pub Network (2006).

- Roberston, Jack S. ***Twentieth-Century Artists on Art: An Index to Writings, Statements, and Interviews by Artists, Architects, and Designers***. MacMillan Publishing Company (1996).

- Starchild, Adam. ***Charitable Giving.*** Books for Business (2005).

- Towner, Wesley. ***The Elegant Auctioneers***. Hill & Want (1970).

- Vartian, Armen. ***Legal Guide to Buying and Selling Art and Collectibles***. Bonus Books (1997).

- Wright, Christopher. ***The Art of the Forger.*** Dodd, Mead & Co. (1984).

416

About the Author

Michael Mendelsohn is Founder and President of Briddge Art Strategies Ltd., the premier art succession planning firm in the country. He is an art collector, philanthropist, lecturer, and writer on inheritance planning and preservation of assets. Michael's innovative inheritance planning strategies for art and antiques assets have been featured in T*rusts and Estates*, *Registered Rep*, and *Wealth Management Business* magazines. Michael has been quoted in articles in *The Wall Street Journal, The Financial Times, BusinessWeek, The NY Post, Forbes,* and *Worth* magazine. He is a frequent contining education presenter on lifetime and postmortem planning strategies with a background in accounting, taxation, and philanthropic studies.

As philanthropists, Michael and his wife Gael have gifted select pieces to the Museum of American Folk Art, the Philadelphia Museum of Art, the Milwaukee Museum, the Smithsonian Institution, and the High Museum of Art. Michael is a highly regarded speaker on the artistic, tax-planning, and philanthropic needs of collectors and has given presentations at the Smithsonian American Art Museum, Philadelphia Museum of Fine Art, Bank of America, U.S. Trust, Museum Trustee Association, Estate Planning Council of Philadelphia, New York State Society of CPAs, the AAA-CPA, and various family office symposiums.

419

Michael formed Briddge Art Strategies Ltd. to create innovative family philanthropic opportunities, help fellow collectors become aware of their ability to keep collections intact, and advocate with collectors and their advisors to develop more tax efficient art distributions to heirs and art-related institutions. The successful application of this strategy to their own private collection is a key reason why Michael and Gael were recognized by *Art & Antiques* as among America's Top 100 Collectors. Their collection is chronicled in *The Intuitive Eye*, a book prepared in conjunction with the 2000 New York exhibition *Masterpieces from the Mendelsohn Collection*.

Contributors

Paige Stover Hague, Esq.

Paige is an attorney who has practiced in both Florida and Massachusetts focusing on a client base in the financial services industry. She has also worked in legal publishing, having held senior management positions on both the product development and sales and marketing sides of the business. She developed and marketed print and electronic products for the legal, tax, accounting, and financial services markets for Butterworth Legal Publishers, Shepherds/McGraw-Hill, Aspen Publishers, and Lawyers Co-op, among others.

Paige is a frequent speaker on the topics of product development, marketing, and public relations and also presents continuing education programs for lawyers, accountants and financial advisors on art succession planning. With Michael Mendelsohn, she has published articles, in *Antiques & Fine Art, National Underwriter, Wealth Management Business, Arts & Antiques,* and *Insurance News Net.* She was the host of the radio talk show "Financially Speaking" in Boston for 4 years which broadcast legal, political and financial commentary, news, and celebrity interviews. She is a contributor to *49 Marketing Secrets (that work) to Grow Sales* (Morgan James Publishing, 2007). Paige is a graduate of Duke University and Nova Southeastern University Law School.

Paige is also a collector concentrating in the Arts & Crafts movement. She collects furniture, art, pottery, books, and ephemera of the period. Her collection resides in her period bungalow, which she is renovating in the craftsman style.

421

Elizabeth Clement, AM

Elizabeth Clement, Director of Elizabeth Clement & Associates, LLC, is a full-time accredited appraiser and consultant on art and antiques for Insurance/Damage Loss, IRS Charitable Contribution/ Estate, Market Value, Divorce, and Liquidation purposes. She is an Accredited member of the American Society of Appraisers (ASA) and is current on the Uniform Standards of Professional Appraisal Practice (USPAP). Ms. Clement is presently serving as both the 1st Vice President of the ASA's Boston Chapter and, for the past three years, as the Personal Property Chair.

Ms. Clement has lectured extensively to various insurance companies, brokers and agents, museums and galleries, art collectors, associations, and private collectors on fine and decorative art appraising, collections management, conservation, and fine arts insurance in this country, Europe, and South America. She is qualified as an expert witness in New York and Massachusetts and has worked with the United States Secret Service as an expert witness in cases of art fraud.

422

Kendra Cliver Daniel

With a career stretching through stints as a portrait painter, muralist, picture frame designer, gallery owner, and interior designer, currently Kendra can best be described as an art dealer and collector. Formerly the co-owner of Whistler Gallery and a dealer in American paintings, Kendra switched her art emphasis and pioneered the interest in original vintage art by illustrators for children.

Under her professional name Kendra Krienke, her NYC Gallery was the first to be devoted solely to this type of art and led to her participation in museum exhibitions both as a lender and curator in America and in Europe. She has been featured with her art in books and periodicals and has contributed articles to professional magazines and catalogs. Kendra has also worked as an appraiser for museums including the Metropolitan Museum of Art and several Japanese institutions.

As a collector with her husband, Allan Daniel, she has amassed a major collection of children's art which will be on solo exhibition in two museums. She is also known for a stunning collection of couture jewelry by Yves Saint Laurent which gained the attention of *Vogue* magazine and has been exhibited in museums. Kendra is listed in *Who's Who in American Art* and is a member of the *Society of Illustrators*.

An advocate of animal rights, she aids in the rescue and adoption of dogs and horses. Kendra lives with her husband and two rescued senior dogs, Jazzpup and Dolly, dividing her time between New Jersey and their farm in Massachusetts.

Alexandra Duch

Alexandra Duch works in the Business Development Department at Gurr Johns Masterson, Inc. in New York. Prior to joining Gurr Johns, she worked for Christie's European Porcelain and Glass Department in New York; she completed her MBA at Oxford University and her master's in Art History at The Courtauld Institute in London.

Peter Hastings Falk

Peter Hastings Falk is an author, art advisor, appraiser, and speaker. He is the author of the biographical dictionary, *Who Was Who in American Art,* as well as numerous auction indices tracking art in the market, including *The Photographic Art Market, Print Price Index*, and *Art Price Index International.*

For 30 years, Falk has provided advisory services for serious collectors, corporations, and artist estates. His feature articles on various aspects of art as investment and the art market have appeared in *Art + Auction* magazine. Well-known as an appraiser, Falk has served on a number of important trial cases as an expert witness, including the 1994 "Warhol War" and other high-profile litigation cases involving the paintings of Monet, Picasso, Malevich, and other masters.

Falk is listed in *Who's Who in America* and has lectured throughout the United States and Europe, including the Family Office Symposium. He has served as the Editor-in-Chief of the three major online art information companies, and founded his own imprint, the Falk Art Reference, where he continues to publish a series of important reference books on American art. He earned his bachelor's in Art History from Brown University and completed his graduate work in Architecture at the Rhode Island School of Design.

Steven M. Friedricks

Steven Friedricks is the founder of the Stevensohn Group in Purchase, NY. For over 25 years he has been a leader and innovator in his industry, providing comprehensive insurance-based solutions for his clientele of high net worth individuals. He specializes in developing personalized estate planning strategies for the art community and collectors as well as in the funding of museum endowments in order to secure their future. Clients include The Walt Disney Company, Miramax Films, and J.C. Penney Company, Inc., among others. Mr. Friedricks has been a guest speaker at numerous tax and wealth replacement seminars on the subject of financial, philanthropic, and endowment planning.

David Frohman

David Frohman is a financial advisor who has specialized in asset protection and estate and wealth succession plans for the last 20 years. David is someone with the rare ability to listen to and instinctively understand the clients' needs and wishes. His knowledge and diligence as a planner have created numerous client-centered strategies for the private business owner and affluent families.

David serves as a liaison between the art world and the financial planning realm for Briddge Art Strategies. He was a noted photojournalist and fundraiser for a small but significant non-governmental organization of the U.N. and spent years working with diverse cultures developing rural food and energy technology products. The prints from his work have become valuable pieces in his own extensive photography collection.

Fred Giampietro

After more than two decades, Fred Giampietro has emerged as a leading expert in the field of American folk art. He has been instrumental in the formation of many major private collections. Hundreds of exceptional items he has discovered or handled are published in many of the seminal books on American folk art.

A native of Connecticut, Fred Giampietro is a trained classical musician. He holds a Master's degree in Music Performance from Yale University. A double bassist, he has performed with the Miami Philharmonic, Palm Beach Symphony, and New Haven Symphony.

425

Over twenty-five years ago, he opened his first shop, bringing his discipline and skills in the musical arts to his antiques business. This early exposure to a broad range of American antiques has nurtured an inherent ability to analyze antiques and art from both the standpoint of originality and form.

Many years of handling 18th and 19th century material that includes furniture, pottery, textiles, and metals have augmented his expertise in the field of American folk art.

Fred Giampietro has been an exhibitor in major antiques venues including the prestigious Winter Antiques Show in New York City. He maintained a gallery in New York from 1994 to 1999.

In addition to serving clients for acquisition and as a broker at auction, he is in demand for appraisal services and dispersal of collections and estates. He has set a twenty-five-year tradition in the business with a gallery open by appointment in New Haven, Connecticut, where he resides with his wife, Kathryn, and son, Claude.

Fred Giampietro subscribes to a clear but demanding set of standards in his business, scrutinizing items with an educated and intuitive approach. It is his philosophy that an object is only as strong as its weakest element.

Fred Giampietro is a leading source for the best in American folk art.

Joseph Jacobs

Joseph Jacobs is executive director of The Renee & Chaim Gross Foundation and an independent art historian, curator, and critic living in New York City. He was curator of American art at The Newark Museum in Newark, New Jersey (1991 to 2003); director of the Oklahoma City Art Museum (1989 to 1991); curator of modern art at the John and Mable Ringling Museum of Art in Sarasota, Florida (1986 to 1989); and director of the museum at Bucknell University, Lewisburg, Pennsylvania (1982 to 1986). His numerous publications include *Since the Harlem Renaissance: 50 Years of African-American Art; This Is Not a Photograph: 20 Years of Large-Scale Photography;* and *A World of Their Own: Twentieth-Century American Folk Art.* He has just completed *"Section Four: The Modern World, 1750-2005"* for the 7th edition of H.W. Janson's *History of Art* (2006), which, as the most popular textbook on art history, is probably the single most prestigious art book in the world. The new edition sold out immediately. He is now beginning a new book, *Art Since 1945*, to be published by Vendome Press. He has written for numerous art magazines, including *Art in America, ARTnews,* and *Art & Antiques*, and has contributed numerous essays to major publications, including the award-winning *Off Limits: Avant-Garde Art at Rutgers University, 1957-1963.* Mr. Jacobs is an expert on the art market and has advised collectors and museums for over 25 years.

George Kasparian, Esq.

George Kasparian is a graduate of Tufts University and Boston College Law School and is a member of the Massachusetts bar. He spent several years practicing law in the Boston area concentrating in estate planning, probate, and taxation. Leveraging his background in computer science, he has worked for several high-tech start ups developing software and web-based applications for the legal, tax, and financial services sectors. He has served as an adjunct professor at Tufts teaching American Politics and contributed to several academic research projects which were formally presented and published in academic circles. He was co-host and political commentator for the radio show "Financially Speaking" and is a frequent contributor to law and tax publications.

George is currently Vice-President and Chief Technology Officer of The Ictus Initiative, a Boston-based marketing and product development firm. He is a member of the American Bar Association's Real Property, Probate, and Trust Law Section.

427

Adam Kirwan, Esq.

Adam O. Kirwan, J.D., LL.M., is a leading expert in asset protection and the architect of Integrated Wealth Planning, a comprehensive asset protection and wealth planning system. The Kirwan Law Firm specializes in asset protection, trust and estate planning, family business succession planning, and complex business and tax planning. The emphasis of this personalized planning is to help individuals and businesses safeguard their wealth, minimize taxes, create an intelligent legacy for the family and/or business, and meet numerous other personal and business objectives.

Mr. Kirwan is the author of *The Asset Protection Guide for Florida Physicians*, which is now in its third edition. It is the only book written exclusively for physicians and that specifically addresses Florida law. It provides a roadmap for Florida physicians looking for comprehensive asset protection by giving an unbiased explanation of the numerous asset protection tools available together with their upsides, downsides, and traps for the unwary. He has also authored a number of articles for the *Florida Medical Association Quarterly Journal* and the Florida Physicians Association.

Mr. Kirwan lectures frequently on the topic of asset protection planning at the national, state, and local levels. He has appeared on several television and radio talk shows to discuss his integrated wealth planning model and the topic of asset protection.

Adam Kirwan is a member of the Florida Bar, the American Bar Association, Central Florida Estate Planning Counsel, and the Planned Giving Council of Central Florida.

428 Mr. Kirwan's firm is based in Orlando, Fla. He received his J.D. at University of Nebraska School of Law, where he was awarded the Robert Lloyd Jeffery Scholarship for Excellence in Tax Law. He also received his Master of Law degree (an LL.M.) in taxation at the University of Miami School of Law.

Charles Rosoff, ASA

Charles Rosoff, ASA, is a generalist appraiser of 19th and 20th century Western European and American fine art, antiques, and decorative arts. His practice focuses on providing forensic valuations for dispute resolution and litigation. Active as an appraiser for over twenty years, Mr. Rosoff was the Legal Issues columnist for the *American Society of Appraisers Personal Property Journal*, taught Appraisal Research Methods at NYU, and is currently teaching the ASA PP204 Legal Issues course at Northwestern University, the University of Georgia, and Pratt Institute. Mr. Rosoff has a bachelor's in History of Art from the University of Michigan, attended the one year Works of Art Course at Sotheby's London, completed the certificate program in appraisal studies at NYU and all the ASA's courses, attended graduate courses in decorative arts at the Cooper Hewitt, has worked for Christie's, and is an Accredited Senior Appraiser designated by the American Society of Appraisers.

Bill Roth and Norma Roth

William Roth and his wife, Norma Canelas Roth, reside in Winter Haven, Florida. They have been avid art collectors in their 31 years of marriage and have actively supported numerous museums with gifts and loans. *Art & Antiques* magazine has named them repeatedly as Top 100 Collectors in America. William is a graduate of Stetson University, College of Law and is a member of the Florida Bar.

Franklin Silverstone

Franklin Silverstone is the co-founder and Chairman of Collectify, an art collecting software tool that fulfills the needs for recording, tracking, and managing information about art, antiques, and collectible assets. He has been an art consultant, appraiser, and auction house expert for over 35 years.

Mr. Silverstone has worked at Phillips Son & Neale, the third largest auction house in the world, where he was a partner, as well as the director of the company's Fine Art department. He headed Phillip's expansion into North America and established salesrooms in Montreal, Toronto, and New York City. After Phillips, he went on to form Franklin Silverstone Fine Arts, through which he is a private dealer, buying and selling paintings, drawings, and sculpture for clients. He also works as an appraiser and consultant, specializing in 18th and 19th century paintings. The company continues to consult for The Royal Trust Company, Canada's leading trust company, as well as smaller concerns and individual clients in North America.

Mr. Silverstone served as the curator for Charles Bronfman, which led to an appointment as curator for the Claridge Collection of Canadian Arts and Crafts, a position he still holds. He is a member of the Appraisers Association of America. He lives in New York City with his wife Holly Hotchner, Director of the Museum of Arts and Design formerly the American Craft Museum.

Daniel Waintrup, MBA

Dan Waintrup entered the financial services industry following a career as a tennis pro at several of the top country clubs in New England. He worked in a business development capacity with a top investment management company prior to affiliating with Briddge. Dan works with many charitable organizations in the Boston area and has played leadership and fundraising roles in several of these.

Dan is the author of *It's Not My Fault or Can a Rabbi's Son Find Happiness as a Tennis Pro?* (Acanthus Publishing 2005) and contributed two articles to *49 Marketing Secrets (that work) to Grow Sales* (Morgan James Publishing, 2007). Dan was a nationally ranked tennis player during his undergraduate years at Temple University, a ranked New England Men's Singles player in the 80's and 90's and the 2005, 2006 and 2007 Men's Singles Champion at the Palm Beach Country Club. He has an MBA from Babson College and frequently appears on radio as a humorous commentator on the topics of tennis, business, and the art of winning.

Rebecca Korach Woan, MBA

Rebecca Korach Woan, with a bachelor's degree from the University of Pennsylvania and a MBA from the University of Chicago, is the principal and founder of Chartwell Insurance Services in Chicago. Rebecca regularly comments on insurance matters for national and local publications. She currently serves on the Governing Committee of the Illinois Fair Plan and is a board member of the Professional Independent Insurance Agents of Illinois (PIIAI).